THE JUSTICE OF CONTRADICTIONS

RICHARD L. HASEN

The Justice of Contradictions

ANTONIN SCALIA AND THE
POLITICS OF DISRUPTION

Yale
UNIVERSITY PRESS

NEW HAVEN & LONDON

Published with assistance from the Ralph S. Brown Memorial
Publication Fund, and from the Mary Cady Tew Memorial Fund.

Yale University Press books may be purchased in quantity for
educational, business, or promotional use. For information, please e-mail
sales.press@yale.edu (U.S. office) or sales@yaleup.co.uk (U.K. office).

Set in Scala and Scala Sans type by Integrated Publishing Solutions,
Grand Rapids, Michigan.
Printed in the United States of America.

ISBN 978-0-300-22864-9 (hardcover : alk. paper)
Library of Congress Control Number: 2017952553
A catalogue record for this book is available from the British Library.

This paper meets the requirements of ANSI/NISO Z39.48-1992
(Permanence of Paper).

10 9 8 7 6 5 4 3 2 1

For Lori,
who continues to amaze, support, and inspire

CONTENTS

PREFACE

JUSTICE ANTONIN SCALIA WAS A POLARIZING figure in polarized times, a disruptor of the challenged political order who arrived on the scene decades before the election of Donald Trump as president. To many on the right, he was a hero, a rare principled Supreme Court justice who established and applied neutral principles to the most difficult cases, even when doing so meant going against his own conservative preferences. His supporters believe he fearlessly spoke up for those who otherwise had no voice among the Ivy League elites dominating law and government. To many on the left he was an unscrupulous foe, a justice who let his political, religious, and social conservatism drive him to result-oriented decisions and who needlessly hurled vicious insults at fellow justices and others.

Neither caricature is fair, nor does it capture the full picture of one of the most important figures in the American legal scene in the last century. More than anything, Justice Scalia was full of contradictions, and not just in his written opinions.

He wrote that his ideas could increase the legitimacy of judicial decisionmaking, yet his attacks on his opponents may have undermined it. He offered jurisprudential theories to guide all cases, yet these doctrines were flexible enough to allow him, in most of the cases most important to him, to deliver opinions consistent with his ideology. He was an "originalist" who believed constitutional provisions should be interpreted in line with their public meaning at the time of enactment, except when he wasn't. He sometimes followed what he considered to be errant precedent because the law was "settled," and at other times he simply ignored originalist analysis altogether.

He saw judges as having a limited role in ensuring compliance with the rule of law, articulating a faith in popular sovereignty, freedom, and majority rule that did not always guide his actions. For example, in *United States v. Windsor*, a decision from 2013 striking down part of the federal Defense of Marriage Act aimed at limiting the rights of same-sex couples, he protested that the Court had "no power under the Constitution to invalidate this democratically adopted legislation." This statement came a day after he unselfconsciously joined the majority opinion in *Shelby County v. Holder*, striking down a key part of the federal Voting Rights Act, a law Congress had enacted in 1965 and which large bipartisan congressional majorities had repeatedly reenacted and expanded.[1]

His writings and interactions with others revealed more contradictions. He was a Harvard Law School graduate who peppered his sophisticated writing with folksy terms like "jiggery pokery." He called himself a language "snoot" but railed against Ivy League elites determining the path of American law. He was a relentless critic of the ideas and writing of others, but he sometimes bristled at criticism directed at him, and in many instances he simply ignored serious good-faith critiques of his ideas and theories.[2]

He was a disruptor of the established order, seeking to undermine common approaches to American jurisprudence with new and revamped theories of interpretation. But he was not willing to disrupt too much, often rejecting his fellow originalist Clarence Thomas's efforts to follow originalism to its logical conclusion and upset settled precedent. Scalia often was bolder in his pronouncements than in his judicial votes, leading supporters and detractors alike to criticize him for not remaining true to the theories he espoused.

Scalia was a bombastic, larger-than-life figure who engendered strong feelings across the political spectrum with his words and actions both on and off the bench, and he did not hold back in expressing his views. He was an exceptionally effective writer. His tone was nimble, direct, and conversational, yet he did not dumb things down for his audience. He got attention for his ideas, especially among law students and lawyers, through the clarity, forcefulness, and more than occasionally the nastiness of his words.

He was an American patriot who believed he was offering ideas to improve the American legal system and democracy. He changed the way judges think and talk about statutes. He gave key conservative acolytes tools, which he represented as politically neutral, to advance an ideological agenda. And he opened the door for others to delegitimize ideological opponents, rather than simply disagreeing with them.

In the end, the contradictions of his approach appear likely to limit his longer-term influence, whether the Supreme Court ends up being populated with many more originalists and textualists such as the newly appointed Justice Neil Gorsuch or not. He helped make the Court a more political institution, a legacy that could well affect American law and American politics for decades. He proved no more able to escape his contradictions than to create a purely neutral approach to judging cases on the Supreme Court.

$$⚖$$

This book is not a biography. Many fine ones are out there, including Joan Biskupic's excellent book from 2009, *American Original: The Life and Constitution of Supreme Court Justice Antonin Scalia.* If you want to understand what made Justice Scalia tick—his upbringing, his religious convictions, and his family life—Biskupic's book is an excellent place to start. You might also consult some of the many tributes to Justice Scalia written by his supporters. Kannon Shanmugam, a former clerk for Scalia and one of the nation's top Supreme Court litigators, described what he called Scalia's "extraordinary personal qualities," writing that "Justice Scalia was devoted above all to his family and to his faith. He was also an utterly charming person who lived life to the fullest. Spending time with Justice Scalia was like being in the presence of a one-man party."[3]

Neither is this book meant to be a comprehensive examination of all of Scalia's opinions and ideas. Such a catalogue would easily be five times longer, much denser, and (I hope) less enjoyable to read.

Instead, I explore Scalia's fundamental contradictions through an examination of his jurisprudential theories of textualism and originalism, his inimitable and often caustic tone in dealing with his adversaries on and off the Court, and his jurisprudence in key areas of modern American law: cases in the culture wars, including abortion, same-sex marriage, guns, affirmative action, and religion; cases bearing on democracy, including campaign finance and the First Amendment, gerrymandering, voting rights, federalism, and separation of powers; and cases in criminal law, including his views on the death penalty, the constitutional right of criminal defendants to confront their accusers, and the war on terror. The resulting book is holistic rather than chronological, and thematic rather than comprehensive. It gives a view from this point in time of his likely legacy, recognizing that things may look different fifty or a hundred years from now.

Scalia purported to advocate a completely neutral approach that would lift the Court above the realm of politics, but his inconsistency in applying it and his intense partisanship inside and outside the Court tended to drag the institution into the muck. He hoped to persuade justices and judges to focus strictly on "the law" and to put aside outside influences, but his often intemperate writings deflected attention from a strict focus on legal principles and his jurisprudential approach obscured the fundamental indeterminacy of many difficult legal questions.

He was full of charm and yet full of venom, an exemplar of personal collegiality among justices, but he made collegiality more difficult with the attacks embedded in his opinions. He said he opposed polarization on the Court, but his dissenting opinions promoted exactly that, as did his role as a public intellectual in appearances around the country.

He likely will not be universally admired as one of the great justices of the Court: instead, the people who agreed with him ideologically will deify him, and those who disagreed with him will continue to vilify him until he fades from current memory. What likely will remain of his legacy in the longer term is his clever and acerbic writing style, his reorientation of courts to focus on nuances of language in ordinary cases, and the tools he offered for delegitimizing opponents.

Scalia was a hugely influential figure while he was on the Court, but not by the most common measures: he did not write as many majority opinions as some of his contemporaries or serve as the swing justice moving the Court from one side to the other of a 5–4 divide. Few of his majority opinions outside the area of criminal procedure are considered major decisions. He achieved influence instead through his intellect and the sheer force of his writing. The contradictions in his approach prevented him from having even greater influence, ultimately undermining the main goal he said he was trying to accomplish: upsetting the existing legal order and starting justices down the path toward using neutral tools to rein in judges and legitimate the judicial enterprise.

ACKNOWLEDGMENTS

BECAUSE THIS BOOK SPANS A BROAD range of legal subjects that made up the docket of cases considered by Justice Antonin Scalia of the Supreme Court, I benefitted greatly from the expertise and wisdom of generous readers across multiple disciplines. I thank the following people who read all or parts of the manuscript: Ellen Aprill, Howard Bashman, Bob Bauer, Joan Biskupic, Ross Davies, David Ettinger, Barry Friedman, Howard Gillman, Amanda Hollis-Brusky, Judge Robert Katzmann, Steve Kay, Hal Krent, Leah Litman, Joshua Matz, Richard McAdams, Sasha Natapoff, Doug NeJaime, Richard Re, Ian Samuel, Eric Segall, Gil Seinfeld, Ann Southworth, Chris Walker, Michael Waterstone, Adam Winkler, and the anonymous readers for Yale University Press. Thanks also to Jonathan Adler, Ron Collins, Linda Greenhouse, Sarah Lawsky, Dahlia Lithwick, and Calvin TerBeek for useful comments and suggestions. The book is much improved thanks to their input. All remaining errors are mine alone.

I owe a special thanks to Erwin Chemerinsky. Erwin supported this project as dean of the University of California, Irvine, School of Law and as a friend. He provided detailed and extremely helpful comments on multiple iterations of this work. He also served as a sounding board and reality check each time I needed him, always with enthusiasm and a critical eye.

Thanks to Bill Frucht of Yale University Press, who pushed me to find my voice and strengthen the manuscript into the project he and I both hoped it would be, and to my agent, John Wright, who made sure the book had a good home and careful attention along the way. Phillip King improved and clarified my prose, saving me from more than one poor turn of phrase.

Nassim Alisobhani, Anika Kahn, and Christopher Valentino provided excellent research assistance, with Chris bearing the heaviest load and doing an outstanding job. Stacy Tran provided professional and helpful administrative assistance and Lisa Junghahn, Jessica Pierucci, Dianna Sahhar, and Christina Tsou provided first-rate library support.

Most of all, I thank my wife, Lori Klein, for her unwavering support, sage advice, love, and patience. Her support makes everything possible.

Some of the material in this book appeared in altered form in some earlier writing of mine. I gratefully acknowledge permission to reprint parts of these works:

Celebrity Justice: Supreme Court Edition, 19 Green Bag 2d 157 (2016)
The Most Sarcastic Justice, 18 Green Bag 2d 215 (2015)
After Scalia: The Future of United States Election Law, America-ho (Biannual journal of Japanese American Society for Legal Studies) (2017) (in Japanese)
The Democracy Canon, 62 Stan. L. Rev. 69 (2009)
Why the Most Urgent Civil Rights Cause of Our Time is the Supreme Court Itself, TPM Café, Sept. 28, 2015, http://talkingpointsmemo.com/cafe/supreme-court-greatest-civil-rights-cause.

When I quote Justice Scalia or others in this book, I leave out most internal citations and footnotes, and I occasionally change capitalization, punctuation, and other formalities for ease of reading. For cases and other works I cite extensively over a few paragraphs, I generally provide a single citation rather than individual pin cites indicating where to find each quote within the case. Readers should consult the original cited source materials for the full and unaltered quotations.

THE JUSTICE OF CONTRADICTIONS

1

The Disruptor

WHEN ANTONIN SCALIA HAD A BAD couple of days, he was not shy about sharing his feelings. The end of the Supreme Court's 2014–2015 term brought a pair of especially bad days, thanks to two decisions that seemed to undermine the transformative work he had tried to do on the Court since he joined it in 1986.

The ends of Court terms are often filled with blockbuster decisions. Within days after oral argument in each of the roughly eighty cases argued each term (out of seven thousand to eight thousand petitions submitted), the nine justices meet to take a tentative vote on the case's outcome. The chief justice, or the most senior justice in the majority if the chief is in dissent, assigns one of the justices to draft a majority opinion. That justice writes a draft and circulates it to the other justices, who express their disagreements on reasoning, results, or both, sometimes writing new drafts that become concurring opinions. The dissenters, meanwhile, do the same for their side. It is a formal and courteous process, with drafts carried by hand to each chamber.[1]

Sometimes justices change their votes, and authors gain or lose majorities. Exchanges of drafts continue for each case until all the justices are done writing and responding, but with the expectation that the cases argued that term beginning in October normally will get resolved by the end of June. Harder, more controversial cases often involve multiple drafts being shuffled back and forth among the justices' chambers, which is one of the reasons why the biggest, most dramatic cases often are not announced until the last few days of the term.[2]

The term that began on the first Monday of October, 2014, and ended in June 2015 was especially dramatic. The fate of President Obama's health care law and the constitutionality of same-sex marriage both hung in the balance. For Justice Scalia, at the end of what turned out to be his last full term as an associate justice on the Court, both decisions brought stinging defeats.

In the first case, *King v. Burwell,* which challenged a key provision of President Obama's controversial health care law, the Court rejected Scalia's views of how to properly read a statute, a theory known as textualism. In the same-sex marriage case, *Obergefell v. Hodges,* the majority rejected Scalia's views of how to properly interpret the Constitution, a theory known as originalism. These theories posit that courts should read statutes and con- stitutional provisions in line with their accepted original meanings at the time of enactment, though Justice Scalia's originalism looked more broadly to find original meaning. Because he believed neither *King* nor *Obergefell* adhered to his preferred interpretation, he thought they represented imper- missible judicial overreaching.[3]

In *King v. Burwell,* the Supreme Court rejected, for the second time in three years, a major challenge to the Patient Protection and Affordable Care Act of 2010, the 2,700-page health care law commonly known as Obama- care. Back in 2012, Chief Justice Roberts had joined the four liberal justices in upholding the constitutionality of the act's requirement that individuals without insurance either purchase it or pay a penalty. Opponents had ar- gued that Congress lacked the power to impose this mandate. Roberts con- cluded that Congress could do so under its power to tax. The liberal justices also had a different theory, justifying the law based on the Constitution's Commerce Clause. Chief Justice Roberts and the four dissenters, including Justice Scalia, rejected the Commerce Clause argument, but with Roberts and the liberals' vote for the tax argument, the law survived.[4]

The *King* case decided in 2015 concerned a key provision in the Afforda- ble Care Act related to the requirement that each state establish a health care marketplace, or "exchange," from which individuals could buy insur- ance. The federal government could not force states to establish these ex- changes, and for the thirty-four (Republican, anti-Obamacare) states that did not do so, the federal government created an exchange from which individuals could buy insurance. To make the insurance affordable, the law provided tax credits for individuals who bought insurance on an exchange "established by the state." At issue was whether individuals from those thirty-four states using the federal exchange could get tax credits. Without those tax credits, the exchanges would likely collapse because the insurance market, losing too many healthy people, would not be economically viable.

Chief Justice Roberts wrote a majority opinion for himself, the liberal justices, and the perennial swing justice Anthony Kennedy, holding that for purposes of the law, the tax credit available to those participating on an exchange "established by the state" were available as well to those who buy insurance through an exchange established by the federal government.

Roberts explained that his interpretation of the phrase "established by the state" to include exchanges established by the federal government in those states that refused to set up their own exchanges was in line with Congress's intent for the statute as a whole, and it reflected a proper textualist reading of the clause in context. Accepting the position of the law's challengers—that those low-income citizens participating on federal exchanges were not entitled to tax credits—would send the health care law into a "death spiral," Roberts wrote, because the exchanges would lack enough healthy people to make them economically viable. Congress, when it passed the massive law, did not intend that suicidal result.[5]

Justice Scalia read a summary of his dissent aloud from the bench, a step justices take when they want to emphasize strong disagreement with a Court majority. Caustically suggesting that we "should start calling this law SCOTUSCare," a line that drew laughter from the audience, he ended by challenging not only the majority's reasoning but its good faith: "This Court's two decisions on the Act will surely be remembered through the years. The somersaults of statutory interpretation they have performed ('penalty' means tax . . . 'established by the State' means not established by the State) will be cited by litigants endlessly, to the confusion of honest jurisprudence. And the cases will publish forever the discouraging truth that the Supreme Court of the United States favors some laws over others, and is prepared to do whatever it takes to uphold and assist its favorites. I dissent."[6]

Just a day later, in *Obergefell v. Hodges,* the Court recognized a constitutional right of same-sex couples to marry. Justice Kennedy, writing for himself and the four more liberal Supreme Court justices, held that a state ban on same-sex couples' marriages violated the Fourteenth Amendment's Due Process Clause and Equal Protection Clause under theories of constitutional interpretation that Justice Scalia had long rejected. The Court embraced the notion of a living Constitution, one whose meaning shifts over time: "The nature of injustice is that we may not always see it in our own times. The generations that wrote and ratified the Bill of Rights and the Fourteenth Amendment did not presume to know the extent of freedom in all of its dimensions, and so they entrusted to future generations a charter protecting the right of all persons to enjoy liberty as we learn its meaning." The Court held that the right of same-sex couples to marry was within that liberty.[7]

Scalia issued one of the most scathing dissents he had ever written, excoriating Justice Kennedy's opinion and the theory of a living Constitution. Although Roberts and Alito also dissented from the majority's decision, they declined to join in Scalia's opinion; only Justice Thomas did. One of Scalia's footnotes was especially harsh:

> If, even as the price to be paid for a fifth vote, I ever joined an opinion for the Court that began: "The Constitution promises liberty to all within its reach, a liberty that includes certain specific rights that allow persons, within a lawful realm, to define and express their identity," I would hide my head in a bag. The Supreme Court of the United States has descended from the disciplined legal reasoning of John Marshall and Joseph Story to the mystical aphorisms of the fortune cookie.[8]

He described the majority opinion as "couched in a style that is as pretentious as its content is egotistic."[9]

Those who do not regularly read Supreme Court opinions may not appreciate how rare such intemperate language is. Most judicial insults, such as they are, are indirect. The justices are together for years, sometimes decades, and they tend to show each other a great deal of formal respect even in the face of strong substantive disagreements. Consider this line from a dissent by Justice John Paul Stevens in the deeply divisive case of *Bush v.*

Gore, which ended a recount of ballots in Florida and effectively handed the presidential election of 2000 to the Republican George W. Bush over the Democrat Al Gore. Stevens wrote: "One thing, however, is certain. Although we may never know with complete certainty the identity of the winner of this year's Presidential election, the identity of the loser is perfectly clear. It is the Nation's confidence in the judge as an impartial guardian of the rule of law." That was about as nasty as Stevens ever got—a strong statement, no doubt, but nowhere approaching Scalia's ferocity. It is hard to think of another line as caustic as "hide my head in a bag" in the modern history of Supreme Court written opinions.[10]

Scalia was just as controversial off the bench. At public forums and in televised interviews, he strongly defended his jurisprudential views and his mostly conservative decisions. To those who disagreed with the *Bush v. Gore* decision, he had a simple message: "Get over it."[11]

⚖

Justice Scalia challenged the established legal order, disrupting the Supreme Court like Speaker of the House Newt Gingrich disrupted the House of Representatives in 1994 and Donald Trump disrupted the presidency in 2016. Scalia claimed he alone had discovered the legitimate tools for constitutional and statutory interpretation. He upset the eclectic and ecumenical approach to interpretation most American judges and Supreme Court justices had used for two hundred years and he did so loudly, both on and off the bench, calling out what he saw as those not just on the wrong side of a principled divide, but whose alternative theories of interpretation lacked legitimacy, undermined the rule of law, and promoted unwarranted judicial supremacy.

He envisioned judges using neutral, language-based tools of interpretation so as not to usurp popular sovereignty and impose their personal value choices on society by judicial fiat. He saw judicial imposition in both *Obergefell* and *King,* and his concern about lack of judicial restraint animated his most vociferous dissents on the Court.

For constitutional review, he believed that courts should interpret a constitutional provision as its words were understood at the time it was adopted. Following this theory of public meaning originalism, he believed that same-sex couples have no constitutional right to marry because no one around when the Fourteenth Amendment was ratified after the Civil War would have believed its provisions to apply to protect same-sex relationships. For statutes, he believed courts should follow the ordinary meaning at the time that the legislative body passed the statute. Because the Affordable Care Act was worded as it was, he believed that individuals on federal health exchanges were not entitled to tax subsidies, even if that would make the law go into a death spiral. It was not the Court's job to save Congress from its mistakes.

Scalia considered his theories of interpretation to be neutral, required by the Constitution's limited grant of power to judges, and essential for the rule of law. He rejected other methods of interpretation as illegitimate. Interpreting statutes in light of what members of Congress said the statute meant as a bill was debated, or in light of an otherwise apparent congressional purpose, or reading statutes and constitutional provisions so that they worked in rational ways to help a modern society function, or using contemporary values to define the meaning of constitutional phrases like "equal protection" and "due process," were all outside the Court's purview, and deprived the people, acting through their elected representatives, of popular sovereignty.

And forget reliance on foreign law, as though there was something to learn from the way the judiciaries in other countries handled similar issues. Foreign laws "can never, never be relevant to the meaning of the U.S. Constitution," he told an audience in May 2015 at the George Mason School of Law (which changed its name, controversially, to the Antonin Scalia Law School after his death). "Who cares? We have our laws, they have theirs."[12]

He sold his jurisprudence as providing tools restraining judges from going too far, and he believed in other pre-commitment methods for self-restraint. He wanted judges to tie themselves to the mast by stating clear rules which could be applied in future cases as precedent. In a 1989 law review article, "The Rule of Law as a Law of Rules," he wrote that "when, in writing for the majority of the Court, I adopt a general rule, and say, 'This is the basis of our decision,' I not only constrain lower courts, I constrain myself as well."[13]

He also saw the Constitution as a democratically enacted pre-commitment mechanism, protecting essential elements of freedom, as when parts of the Bill of Rights protected criminal defendants' rights against vengeful judges or juries, structural parts of the Constitution protected the states against the massive federal government, and the First Amendment protected unpopular speech against government censorship and regulation.

His jurisprudence and judicial philosophy embraced a type of populist, nationalist, conservative libertarianism, a vision of individual freedom from overreach built into the Constitution itself: freedom of citizens and businesses from intrusive and unconstitutional government regulation and overreach, freedom of the states from federal government overreach, and, most importantly, freedom of the people, ordinarily acting through laws passed by their legislative bodies, from judicial overreach. When Scalia dissented in a case involving what he saw as an encroachment on these freedoms, watch out.[14]

⚖️

Scalia's words were his most potent weapon in his struggle to get the Court to rethink first principles and apply his views of freedom. Few could turn a phrase as he could or so thoroughly point out the logical flaws in the other side's arguments. People were drawn to read his opinions. He was sharp, funny, and incisive. But his words were also his greatest weakness, used to hurl insults and in some cases to demean the positions of his fellow justices and others in ways that alienated would-be allies. For someone who cared so much about the legitimacy of the Court, much of what he said about the work of other justices seemed aimed at delegitimizing them as judges.

He was bombastic and brilliant, a larger-than-life persona appearing to crave controversy and upset the accepted order up to the point when he passed away unexpectedly in February 2016, of an apparent heart attack while spending the weekend at a Texas ranch owned by John B. Poindexter, a wealthy businessman and investor whose company had a case turned down by the Supreme Court a year earlier. Even after his death, people raised questions about who paid for the trip and whether the gathering was connected to a secret society of elite hunters dating back to the 1600s called the International Society of St. Hubertus. From 2004 until the time of his death, he had taken more than 250 privately funded trips.[15]

The circumstances of his death called to mind Scalia's duck-hunting trip in 2004 with Vice President Dick Cheney, who later was sued in a case that reached the Supreme Court. Environmental activists were seeking an order to force Cheney's office to release internal documents from an energy task force Cheney headed, because they wanted to look for unreported contacts between task force members and energy industry lobbyists. Despite widespread condemnation from the left for staying on the case, Justice Scalia had declined to recuse himself, writing: "The people must have confidence in the integrity of the Justices, and that cannot exist in a system that assumes them to be corruptible by the slightest friendship or favor, and in an atmosphere where the press will be eager to find foot-faults."[16]

Whatever motivated him to challenge elites, stick up for the white working class, and upset the existing order, he went from a middle-class upbringing to traveling in elite circles before joining the Court. Antonin Gregory Scalia was born in New Jersey on March 11, 1936, an only child of his father Salvadore, a Sicilian immigrant and romance languages professor, and his mother Catherine, an elementary school teacher and homemaker. "Nino" was raised as a devout Catholic. He and his wife, Maureen, had nine children, thanks to what Scalia called "Vatican roulette." He graduated first in his class at Georgetown and magna cum laude from Harvard Law School, then worked in private practice, government, and as a law professor at the University of Virginia and the University of Chicago. He served as general counsel for the Office of Telecommunications Policy and then as head of the Administrative Conference of the United States in the Nixon administration. He worked in the Office of Legal Counsel for President Ford. President Reagan considered him for the position of solicitor general but declined to nominate him, a decision that Scalia later told the journalist Joan Biskupic "bitterly disappointed" him. But Reagan later nominated him for the prestigious United States Court of Appeals for the District of Columbia Circuit, a court widely seen as second in importance only to the Supreme Court and a stepping-stone for a seat on that Court.[17]

After serving on the D.C. Circuit from 1982 to 1986, Scalia was nominated by President Reagan to serve as an Associate Justice of the Supreme Court, a position he held until his death in February 2016.

By some measures Scalia was the most influential justice of the past two generations. A study by Professor Frank B. Cross of a ten-year set of opinions from the Rehnquist Court showed that those written by Scalia— majority opinions, concurrences, and dissents—were more than twice as likely to be cited by lower court judges in the decade after they were issued than the opinions of other justices who served with him during that period. Cross found that Scalia's opinions had high citation rates both positively and negatively. For a judge who believed courts often should defer to the political branches, Scalia wrote many "maximalist" opinions setting out broad statements of law, according to Cross: "It appears that the relatively maximalist nature of Justice Scalia's writing translates into considerable precedential influence for lower courts." Cross found that the "typical Scalia opinion gets over one hundred more citations than average at both the circuit and district court levels."[18]

Scalia's opinions and ideas also appeared more frequently in legal casebooks used to teach law students, thanks in part to his punchy writing style. In a leading constitutional law casebook, Justice Scalia's opinions were third most excerpted, after Rehnquist and Stevens, compared with his contemporaries on the Court. In a leading textbook on legislation, focusing a great deal on statutory interpretation, Scalia's name appeared almost twice as often as the next closest justice, Justice Stevens, and more than four times the average of all the justices with whom he served.[19]

He told an interviewer in 2013 that he wrote his dissents for law students, presumably to maximize his influence on future generations: "they will read dissents that are breezy and have some thrust to them. That's who I write for."[20]

He also was part of a five-justice conservative majority that, over nearly three decades, transformed much American law in a conservative direction on issues such as state power, gun rights, and racial discrimination. The law never reached fully where Justice Scalia wanted it to go, but it moved considerably in his preferred direction on many key issues. For the entire time that he served on the Court, first under the leadership of Chief Justice William Rehnquist and then under Chief Justice Roberts, it had a majority of justices generally viewed as conservative, with some more conservative than others. According to the most widely accepted measure, the "Martin-Quinn" scores, Scalia was among the most conservative justices on the Court, for much of the time ranking second in conservatism only to Clarence Thomas, who applied his own originalist methodology.[21]

Scalia voted with the majority in 75 percent of the cases argued before the Court from the 1986 through 2014 terms. In the non-unanimous cases, he was in the majority more than half the time in all terms except the 2014 term, which included the *King* and *Obergefell* cases. He wrote 270 majority opinions in argued cases, and nearly as many dissents, 256. He also wrote 324 concurrences—agreeing with a majority result but disagreeing at least partially with its reasoning. By contrast, Justice Stevens, who served from 1975 to 2009 and was one of the Court's moderate liberals for much of Scalia's tenure, wrote 375 majority opinions, 679 dissents, and 395 concurrences.[22]

Scalia's reach extended beyond the number of his majority opinions. His focus on language changed the way justices, judges, law professors, and lawyers structure their legal analyses of statutes and constitutional provisions. As Justice Elena Kagan, one of the leading liberals on the Court, remarked in a "Scalia lecture" at Harvard Law School in 2015, "We are all textualists now." In the less contentious cases, and in the lower courts, Scalia's linguistic focus appears to have had a lasting impact on legal argumentation.[23]

Still, it seems far less likely that Scalia's linguistic focus affected how justices and judges decide how to vote in difficult cases. They may be more apt to describe their results using Scalia's methodologies—think of how the Chief Justice (and the liberal justices including Justice Kagan) in *King v. Burwell* went out of their way to make a textualist argument for how health care exchanges "established by the state" can include the federal exchanges—but the substance of their decisions often still divides along ideological lines. And Scalia's tone and style may have had a coarsening influence on the legal profession in general.

Scalia's vision of the proper role of American courts was never fully realized. Aside from his *District of Columbia v. Heller* decision on guns and some criminal procedure opinions, he wrote few groundbreaking majority opinions. Although Scalia was with the majority more often than not, he was not the justice most often in the middle, the one breaking the 4–4 ties. That role of median justice was held by others while Scalia was on the Court, first by Lewis Powell, then by Byron White, David Souter, Sandra Day O'Connor, and Anthony Kennedy. By this measure, Scalia was never as influential as those justices.[24]

It was perennial swing voter Kennedy who was in the majority in both *King v. Burwell* and *Obergefell v. Hodges,* the decision Scalia derided as "pretentious" and "egotistical." After Scalia died, leaving a 4–4 conservative/liberal split on the Supreme Court at the end of the October 2015 term, it was Justice Kennedy who sided with the liberals to support the University of Texas's affirmative action plan in *Fisher v. University of Texas* (leaving a 4–3 tally, with Justice Kagan recused presumably because she had worked on the case before joining the Court) and with the pro-choice side in the *Whole Woman's Health* case challenging Texas's strict abortion restrictions (a 5–3 vote, which almost certainly would have been 5–4 had Scalia survived to vote on it).[25]

The rejection of Scalia's ideas in *King v. Burwell* and *Obergefell v. Hodges* shows the limits of his influence even among fellow conservative justices. Not only was he rarely the swing justice, but he left the Court with only one other originalist on it, Justice Thomas, who often differed with Scalia on proper originalist methodology in key cases. Georgetown law scholar David Cole, in a bit of exaggeration, described Scalia as "the most influential justice without influence in the Court's history."[26]

⚖

The rest of the book aims to prove the claims I have made here, looking at Justice Scalia's theories of interpretation, his tone and rhetoric, and three key areas of his judicial opinions: the culture wars, including abortion, same-sex marriage, guns, and religion; democratic politics, including campaign money, gerrymandering, and separation of powers; and crime and punishment, from search and seizure to the war on terror.

The examination of the justice's jurisprudence across a range of subjects and cases in key areas of American law reveals someone who by all accounts believed in the theories he espoused and in their potential to improve the judicial role in a well-functioning democracy, and one who appeared oblivious to the sometimes counterproductive nature of his strident approaches.

He made the other Supreme Court justices work harder to clarify their reasoning, but the principles he articulated had little predictive power. On the Supreme Court as a whole, whether a justice used originalism or textualism turns out to be a terrible predictor of his or her voting pattern. Instead, the ideological views of the justice, which increasingly line up with the party of the president who made the appointment, are a very accurate predictor of votes in the most contentious cases.

He believed there were determinate answers to some of the most difficult legal questions facing the country, and he sometimes reached results at odds with his personal conservatism, especially in some cases involving constitutional protections for criminal defendants. But his ostensibly neutral principles and commitment to the rule of law usually failed to cabin the considerable discretion afforded Supreme Court justices. It was not that Scalia was less principled or more result-oriented than the other justices, but that he held himself up to a higher standard that neither he nor the other justices could meet.

If the neutrality Justice Scalia strived for proved elusive, one reason is that he was not a consistent originalist or even textualist. Indeed, he did not always follow his arguments to their logical conclusion, often either demurring to the force of precedent or to some amorphous view of "tradition," ignoring contrary data and refusing to engage originalist evidence. It appeared he sometimes could not accept the implications of the theories he urged on others.

He convinced a generation of ardent followers that his way was the only legitimate means of interpretation, and that only his ideological opponents played politics with the Constitution. If anything, his followers later criticized Scalia for not being sufficiently true to his own principles.

Perhaps more than anything, Scalia will be remembered for his searing rhetoric and challenge to the existing order. In a deeply polarized time, his disruption of established legal norms moved the nation toward coarser legal rhetoric and greater polarization. In the end, he could neither elevate himself above his own ideology nor free himself sufficiently from the language of disdain and mockery to build more judicial coalitions. Instead, during his time on the Court, disdain and mockery became more pronounced in American politics, as political parties became more ideologically uniform and polarized and as the Court became less immune to charges of partisanship.

Most importantly and ironically, Scalia used his ostensibly neutral jurisprudential theories—which he argued were necessary to legitimize judicial decisionmaking, even though he did not consistently follow them—to politicize the Court and delegitimize his opponents, leaving us with a weakened Supreme Court.

2
Word Games

PAUL GREEN WORKED FOR SIX DAYS AT the Lemoyne Minit Car Wash near Harrisburg, Pennsylvania, on a prison work release program. He was nineteen years old and serving time for several felonies, including burglary. On June 23, 1984, Green stuck his right hand into a towel dryer, trying to stop the heavy rotating drum from spinning, and the machine ripped his entire arm off at the shoulder. He sued the manufacturer, Bock Laundry Machine Company, for damages in federal court, claiming the company failed to adequately warn of the dangers of putting one's arm into the moving machine. The jury in the products liability tort suit sided with Bock Laundry Machine, and the United States Court of Appeals for the Third Circuit rejected Green's appeal without issuing an opinion.[1]

On the surface, the case seemed too small to interest the Supreme Court. But the Court nonetheless took the case to resolve a dispute that had divided the lower courts: the meaning of Rule 609 of the Federal Rules of Evidence. The trial court, following an earlier Third Circuit interpretation of Rule 609, held that it had no choice but to allow the company to introduce Green's felony convictions into evidence as a way of impeaching his credibility. Rule 609 was premised on the controversial idea that criminals are more likely to be liars even if the crime they committed was not a crime involving dishonesty.

The text of Rule 609 is dense, but it is worth taking a moment to focus on it because the dispute in *Green v. Bock Laundry Machine Company* nicely illustrates the type of case that the Supreme Court decides without getting front-page headlines in the *New York Times*. More important for our purposes, it shows the limits of Justice Scalia's textualist approach to deciding the meaning of statutes, and how he viewed disputes over the scope of statutory rights more like word puzzles to be solved than questions about human conflict and potential loss. And it shows how the justice's vote in the *Burwell* Obamacare case was not mandated by his own methods of interpretation.

At the time of *Green*, Rule 609 read in part:

> For the purpose of attacking the credibility of a witness, evidence that the witness has been convicted of a crime shall be admitted if elicited from the witness or established by public record during cross-examination but only if the crime (1) was punishable by death or imprisonment in excess of one year under the law under which the witness was convicted, and the court determines that the probative value of admitting this evidence outweighs its prejudicial effect to the defendant, or (2) involved dishonesty or false statement, regardless of the punishment.

Just to unpack this a bit, the rule says that at a trial—civil or criminal—a party can attack a witness's credibility by introducing into evidence either that the witness committed a crime involving dishonesty, or that the witness committed a felony. The trial court *must* allow this evidence when the witness's crime involved dishonesty or false statement, like forgery. For other felonies, however, Rule 609 appears to give the trial court some discretion. The court may allow introduction of impeachment evidence of a witness only if "the probative value of admitting this evidence outweighs its prejudicial effect to the defendant."

A rule requiring weighing makes some sense. On one hand, it could well be that felons are more likely than other witnesses to lie on the stand. On the other hand, hearing that a witness was guilty of a felony such as burglary may make a jury less likely to side with that witness, wholly apart from the honesty of that witness's testimony. People generally don't like felons, and they could punish the party offering a felon as a witness, including the felon himself.

But note the oddly one-sided language of Rule 609. In cases involving felonies (aside from those dealing with dishonesty), the rule does not require the court to weigh the probative value of a felony conviction against its prejudicial effect to any *party;* it requires a weighing of probative value against prejudicial effect "to the *defendant.*" The rule appears to give the benefit of weighting only to defendants.

In a criminal case, this one-sided rule seems acceptable. Criminal defendants get all sorts of advantages at trial. We require the prosecution to prove its case beyond a reasonable doubt, we give the defendant the right not to testify to avoid self-incrimination, and we provide the defendant with a lawyer if he cannot afford one. As written, Rule 609 allows a criminal defendant to automatically admit evidence that a witness testifying against him was a convicted felon, since such evidence would never unduly prejudice the jury against the defendant. But if the prosecution seeks to admit similar evidence about a witness (including about the defendant himself), the court would have to weigh the value of the jury's hearing about that felony against the chance that such knowledge would prejudice the jury.

Whether or not this is a sensible rule in criminal trials, it makes no sense in a civil proceeding like Paul Green's product liability case against the Bock Laundry Machine Company. In this case, Green is the plaintiff (the party suing in civil court) while Bock is the defendant (the party being sued). Read literally, Rule 609 would allow the jury to hear all evidence that a witness had committed a felony to impeach that witness's credibility, unless the prejudicial value of the testimony *to Bock Laundry Machine,* the defendant, outweighed its probative value. But it was Green, the plaintiff, whose credibility could be harmed by admission of his felony convictions. There is no good reason to have a one-sided rule that helps only civil defendants and not civil plaintiffs. It might even be unconstitutional, a violation of the Fourteenth Amendment's Due Process Clause or Equal Protection Clause, to give such an advantage to one side in a civil case.

In the *Green* case, the trial court ruled that it had no choice but to let in Bock Laundry's evidence of Green's felony convictions, and it was not permitted to consider whether admission of this evidence unduly prejudiced Green's testimony. (If it were permitted to weigh the question, the court said, it would have let the evidence in anyway.) Green worried, perhaps justifiably, that the jury decided against him in his tort suit because jurors did not want to side with a convicted felon. After he lost, he argued on appeal that the trial court had to balance the evidentiary value of the information that he was a felon against the prejudice to him, and that the balance favored excluding evidence of his felonies.

The United States Court of Appeals for the Third Circuit denied the appeal without even issuing an opinion. This was not surprising. Earlier the same year, in a case called *Diggs v. Lyons,* it had held that trial courts had discretion in applying Rule 609 only in criminal cases, and that in civil cases evidence of a prior felony conviction must be admitted against any witness. The majority adopted this reading even while conceding that Rule 609 made little sense: "We recognize that the mandatory admission of all felony convictions on the issue of credibility may in some cases produce unjust and even bizarre results. Evidence that a witness has in the past been convicted of manslaughter by automobile, for example, can have but little relevance to his credibility as a witness in a totally different matter." The court continued: "If the rule is to be amended to eliminate these possibilities of injustice, it must be done by those who have the authority to amend the rules, the Supreme Court and the Congress. We, therefore, leave the problem to them. It is not for us as enforcers of the rule to amend it under the guise of construing it."

The judge who dissented noted that other circuit courts had reached a different conclusion, holding that courts should engage in balancing for both plaintiffs and defendants in civil cases, which he said lined up with Congress's intent to carve out a special one-sided rule just for criminal cases. "In this circuit, on the other hand, concededly bizarre results will be mandated by our rigid application of Rule 609(a) in civil cases which were not of real concern to Congress."[2]

Green brought the issue to the Supreme Court.

⚖

John Paul Stevens, Justice Scalia's frequent sparring partner on the Court, wrote the majority opinion agreeing with the Third Circuit and holding that only criminal defendants get the benefit of balancing in the case of felon witnesses. For civil plaintiffs and civil defendants, evidence of a witness's prior felony convictions must be admitted.[3]

Stevens began his opinion by noting that although criticism of the rule was widespread, the Court's task was "not to fashion the rule we deem desirable but to identify the rule Congress fashioned." In other words, the courts were not to rewrite a statute passed by Congress but should strive to "identify" its meaning. For Stevens, this was a complex task, and his analysis takes up many pages in the *United States Reports*. He acknowledged that the "Rule's plain language commands weighing of prejudice to a defendant in a civil trial as well as in a criminal trial. But that literal reading would compel an odd result in a case like this."

The rest of Stevens's opinion explained why it was appropriate to ignore that literal reading. Despite claiming not to "fashion the rule we deem desirable," he noted that a rule which would help civil defendants over civil plaintiffs could violate the Constitution's Due Process Clause. Such a rule also seemed nonsensical. Quoting another lower court, Stevens said the rule "can't mean what it says." Here, Justice Stevens followed in a large tradition of statutory interpretation that sought to construe the words of statutes, often ambiguous, in a way that furthers the drafters' overall or specific purpose.

The opinion then followed the very many twists and turns of Rule 609's evolution, from a legal treatise in 1940 to a meeting of the American Law Institute in 1942, to a meeting of the American Bar Association in 1953 to litigation over earlier rules on this topic, to a court case in 1965 interpreting an earlier version of the rule, to an Advisory Committee set up in 1969 to propose a revised set of evidence rules for Congress, including what became Rule 609. Stevens described every nuance in the deliberations over the rule, first in the Advisory Committee and then in Congress as those interested in the question fought over its language. The House of Representatives passed one version of the larger set of evidence rules with its own take on Rule 609's language, while the Senate passed another. The two chambers appointed a conference committee to hash out differences, and the committee produced a version of Rule 609 that differed from both the House and Senate versions. This is what became the official rule when Congress passed a larger law containing Rule 609.

Justice Stevens said that the report accompanying the conference committee version "makes it perfectly clear" that the rule was not intended to allow balancing for all nonparty witnesses who are felons. The report referenced "convictions" and "the accused," suggesting that conferees (or whoever wrote the committee report) were thinking about criminal cases.

Citing more bits and pieces of statements from legislators as Congress considered the rule, Justice Stevens concluded that Rule 609 allowed only criminal defendants to benefit from balancing. For all civil defendants and civil plaintiffs, courts must admit evidence of witnesses' prior felonies for impeachment purposes, without balancing.

⚖

Students of the jurisprudence of Antonin Scalia will not be surprised to learn that he disagreed vehemently with Justice Stevens's reliance on the legislative history of Rule 609. But they might be surprised to learn that Scalia too was willing to ignore the apparently plain meaning of the statute and agree with Stevens that under Rule 609, only criminal defendants get the benefit of balancing on the credibility question when a witness has committed a felony.

Scalia's attack on legislative history as a means of discerning the meaning of a statute is perhaps the most notable aspect of his jurisprudence. His approach, dubbed "the New Textualism" by William Eskridge of Yale Law School, states an aim to apply a fair reading of a statute as its meaning would have been understood by common speakers of English at the time it was drafted. As he described this method in his book *A Matter of Interpretation,* based on his Tanner Lectures of 1995 at Princeton University: "A text should not be construed strictly, and it should not be construed leniently; it should be construed reasonably, to contain all that it fairly means. . . . While a good textualist is not a literalist, neither is he a nihilist. Words do have a limited range of meaning, and no interpretation that goes beyond that range is permissible."[4]

Scalia was far from the first judge or lawyer to focus on the plain meaning of statutory language. But he elevated the use of technical textual methods for reading statutes into a major interpretative tool in American courts.

Under Scalia's theory, deciding a statute's meaning is more akin to solving a word puzzle than to delving into the minds of the legislators who passed it, or figuring out the best policy answer or the fairest result given current circumstances. To solve these word puzzles, Scalia often would rely upon rules of thumb (or "canons of construction") for parsing meaning. *Reading Law,* the book on statutory interpretation that he wrote with the attorney and language expert Bryan Garner, offers more than five hundred pages of rules, canons, explanations, and appendices for solving these puzzles.

Consider, for example, the *ejusdem generis* canon: "When the general words follow the enumeration of two or more things, they generally apply only to persons or things of the same general kind or class specifically mentioned." As an example of this canon's use, Scalia and Garner offer the interpretation of a will bequeathing to some person "my furniture, clothes, cooking utensils, housewares, motor vehicles, and all other property." "In the absence of any other indication . . . almost any court will construe the last phrase to include only [personal property] and not real estate."[5]

In the course of his judicial opinions and writings on understanding the meaning of statutes, Scalia offered three interrelated reasons for relying primarily on the text of the statute and these canons of construction rather than legislative history.

First, legislative history may be unreliable. Scalia quoted U.S. Court of Appeals Judge Harold Levanthal, who described judicial use of legislative history as "the equivalent of entering a crowded cocktail party and looking over the heads of the guests for one's friends." It is too easy for a judge to pick out the parts of the legislative history supporting a desired result, rather than make a fair assessment of the history as a whole.[6]

Second, he argued that legislative history does not necessarily represent the views of even a majority of legislators. As Professor Kenneth Shepsle has put it, "Congress is a they, not an it." Legislative history may represent nothing more than the views of one legislator, or perhaps those of a staffer or lobbyist.[7]

To illustrate this problem, Scalia offered an exchange over a tax bill between Robert Dole (then the chairman of the Senate Finance Committee) and William Armstrong on the floor of the U.S. Senate:[8]

> MR. ARMSTRONG. . . . My question, which may take [the chairman] by surprise, is this: Is it the intention of the chairman that the Internal Revenue Service and the Tax Court and other courts take guidance as to the intention of Congress from the committee report which accompanies this bill?

Mr. Dole. I would certainly hope so. . . .

Mr. Armstrong. Mr. President, will the Senator tell me whether or not he wrote the committee report?

Mr. Dole. Did I write the committee report?

Mr. Armstrong. Yes.

Mr. Dole. No; the Senator from Kansas did not write the committee report.

Mr. Armstrong. Did any Senator write the committee report?

Mr. Dole. I have to check.

Mr. Armstrong. Does the Senator know of any Senator who wrote the committee report?

Mr. Dole. I might be able to identify one, but I would have to search. I was here all during the time it was written, I might say, and worked carefully with the staff as they worked. . . .

Mr. Armstrong. Mr. President, has the Senator from Kansas, the chairman of the Finance Committee, read the committee report in its entirety?

Mr. Dole. I am working on it. It is not a bestseller, but I am working on it.

Mr. Armstrong. Mr. President, did members of the Finance Committee vote on the committee report?

Mr. Dole. No.

Mr. Armstrong. Mr. President, the reason I raise the issue is not perhaps apparent on the surface, and let me just state it: . . . The report itself is not considered by the Committee on Finance. It was not subject to amendment by the Committee on Finance. It is not subject to amendment now by the Senate. . . . If there were matter within this report which was disagreed to by the Senator from Colorado or even by a majority of all Senators, there would be no way for us to change the report. I could not offer an amendment tonight to amend the committee report. . . . For any jurist, administrator, bureaucrat, tax practitioner, or others who might chance upon the written record of this proceeding, let me just make the point that this is not the law, it was not voted on, it is not subject to amendment, and we should discipline ourselves to the task of expressing congressional intent in the statute.

Scalia's third point was that he believed reliance on legislative history went beyond the judicial power. The only "law" that Congress passes in a statute is contained in the words of the statute. Congress did not consider or vote upon the legislative history, which is therefore not part of the "law." Thus the "greatest defect of legislative history is its illegitimacy. We are governed by laws, not the intention of legislators."[9]

This textualist approach to understanding statutes explains Scalia's rabid reaction in *King v. Burwell,* the health care dispute discussed in the previous chapter. He was incensed that a majority of justices could read the phrase "established by the state" to include health-insurance exchanges established not by any state but by the federal government. To Scalia, the text was clear and that was that, whether or not his interpretation of the statute would send Obamacare into a death spiral.

But he took a different approach in the *Green* case.

⚖

Scalia's opinion in *Green* was considerably shorter than Stevens's. Not surprisingly, he rejected the majority's reliance on the legislative history, although he said it would be appropriate to look at the history to make sure that Congress did not actually intend what he termed "an absurd, and perhaps unconstitutional" reading of the law that would allow civil defendants but not civil plaintiffs the benefit of balancing. He wrote, however, that the majority's opinion went beyond this, devoting "four-fifths of its substantive analysis" to "determining what, precisely, the Rule does mean."[10]

He saw "no reason to believe that any more than a handful of the Members of Congress who enacted Rule 609 were aware of its interesting evolution from the 1942 Model Code; or that any more than a handful of them (if any) voted, with respect to their understanding of the word 'defendant' and the relationship between Rule 609 and Rule 403, on the basis of the referenced statements in the Subcommittee, Committee, or Conference Committee Reports, or floor debates—statements so marginally relevant, to such minute details, in such relatively inconsequential legislation." He wrote that the statute's meaning should not be determined by what a "larger handful" of members of Congress thought but instead on the "basis of which meaning is (1) most in accord with context and ordinary usage, and thus most likely to have been understood by the *whole* Congress which voted on the words of the statute (not to mention the citizens subject to it), and (2) most compatible with the surrounding body of law into which the provision must be integrated—a compatibility which, by a benign fiction, we assume Congress always has in mind." He would have not allowed legislative history to lead him to a different result.

So far, so good, in terms of Scalia's general textualist philosophy. But then his opinion took a surprising turn. He could have said simply that the statute means what it says, that it treats civil defendants better than civil plaintiffs, and found it unconstitutional. The result would have been a victory for Green. With the rule thrown out, Green would have had a chance to argue that under a general balancing test contained in the evidence rules, the evidence of his prior felony convictions should not have been admitted.

But Scalia refused to apply the clear and plain meaning of the statute. Like Stevens, he said the word "defendant" could not rationally (and probably not constitutionally) mean "civil defendants" but not "civil plaintiffs."

> The available alternatives are to interpret "defendant" to mean (a) "civil plaintiff, civil defendant, prosecutor, and criminal defendant," (b) "civil plaintiff and defendant and criminal defendant," or (c) "criminal defendant." Quite obviously, the last does least violence to the text. It adds a qualification that the word "defendant" does not contain but, unlike the others, does not give the word a meaning ("plaintiff" or "prosecutor") it simply will not bear. The qualification it adds, moreover, is one that could understandably have been omitted by inadvertence—and sometimes is omitted in normal conversation ("I believe strongly in defendants' rights"). Finally, this last interpretation is consistent with the policy of the law in general and the Rules of Evidence in particular of providing special protection to defendants in criminal cases.

It is important to be explicit about what Scalia did here. Faced with what he considered an absurd literal interpretation of a statute, he rewrote the statute. He redefined the word "defendant" to mean only "criminal defendant," justifying this choice as "quite obviously" the interpretation that does the "least damage" to the statute's text.

One should beware whenever a judge or lawyer says something is "obvious." It usually masks great uncertainty just beneath the surface. In this case, Scalia's *Green* opinion demonstrates what Professor Eskridge calls the "plasticity of textualism"—by which the professor meant that "Scalia left the statute more chaotic than it was originally." In a civil case, "Scalia's version would have told the judge to follow a very strange rule: allow plaintiff Green to be impeached by his prior felony convictions, but only if the probative value outweighs prejudice 'to the *criminal* defendant.' Which criminal defendant? Should the judge pretend that the civil defendant is a criminal one? Or should she import one from another case?" Eskridge concluded that "under the pretense of doing the 'least violence' to the statutory text, Scalia's rewrite deprived the judge of an intelligible rule."[11]

Arguably, Eskridge wrote, it was Justice Harry Blackmun's dissent in *Green,* reading the word "defendant" to mean "party," that did the "least violence" to the text of Rule 609. An even better reading, Eskridge suggested, would have been to insert the phrase "in a criminal case" into the statute to clarify that it applied only to criminal defendants.[12]

Blackmun's dissent did indeed argue that Rule 609 should be interpreted to give both civil plaintiffs and civil defendants the benefit of balancing. He found the legislative history uncertain and noted that neither his nor the majority's interpretation of Rule 609 was consistent with the rule's plain language. But he defended his interpretation over the majority's on different grounds.

Blackmun saw his rule as fairer to litigants, and consistent with the general approach of the Federal Rules of Evidence to spare litigants unnecessary hardship. "This case should have been decided on the basis of whether the Bock Laundry Machine Company designed and sold a dangerously defective machine without providing adequate warnings. The fact that Paul Green was a convicted felon, in a work-release program at a county prison, has little, if anything, to do with these issues. We cannot know precisely why the jury refused to compensate him for the sad and excruciating loss of his arm, but there is a very real possibility that it was influenced improperly by his criminal record. I believe that this is not a result Congress conceivably could have intended, and it is not a result this Court should endorse."[13]

Edward Lazarus, who was a clerk for Blackmun at the time and worked on the *Green* case, explained that Blackmun's approach to statutory interpretation was neither a search for legislative purpose or intent, like Stevens's, nor an exercise in linguistics, like Scalia's. Instead, Blackmun was driven by empathy. "In Justice Blackmun's view, the judicial rewriting of Rule 609(a)(1) was not to be accomplished on the basis of an exhaustive search for recondite snippets of legislative history to determine what Congress might have intended with its ambiguous and perhaps even inadvertent use of the word 'defendant' in the Rule. A man had lost an arm. And that man had been denied compensation almost certainly in part because

a jury had heard irrelevant and inflammatory evidence about his criminal past." Lazarus noted that after the case the federal advisory committee which drafts the evidence rules rewrote them consistent with Justice
Blackmun's approach (although the rewrite was even more consistent with
Eskridge's suggested reading).[14]

⚖

One might defend Justice Scalia's opinion in *Green*, rewriting the statute
rather than allowing an absurdity to stand, as a recognition that his approach to interpretation has limits. "I'm an originalist and a textualist, not
a nut," he told NPR's Nina Totenberg in 2008.[15]

Yet compare his approach in *Green* with his approach in *King v. Burwell*,
the Obamacare case. In *King*, under Scalia's relentlessly literal reading of
the Affordable Care Act, people on federal health care exchanges would
have been denied subsidies (authorized by Congress in the law for those on
exchanges "established by the state") for their insurance premiums, causing the system to enter what experts called a "death spiral."

Why does he find it permissible for the Court to insert a "qualification
. . . that could understandably have been omitted by inadvertence" into Rule
609 but not into the Affordable Care Act? If it is absurd to read the Federal
Rules of Evidence to allow a small, asymmetrical, and unfair advantage to
civil defendants over civil plaintiffs, is it any less absurd to read a single
clause in a twenty-seven-hundred-page law—one of the most important
pieces of legislation Congress has enacted in the past few decades, affecting
the health care of millions of Americans—to contain the seeds of its own
destruction, despite other parts of the law that presume those on federal exchanges will get subsidies? Why was Scalia willing to jettison his principles
in a relatively unimportant case but not in such an important one?

⚖

Scalia tempered his textualism not only with appeal to textual canons
(like *ejusdem generis*) but occasionally with what are called "substantive canons," rules of thumb based on policy, such as the "rule of lenity," which
calls for criminal statutes to be construed in favor of criminal defendants.
He called these substantive canons "a lot of trouble" to "the honest textu-

alist," saying they led to "unpredictability, if not arbitrariness" in judicial decisions, and questioned "where courts get the authority to impose them." He doubted that courts can "really just decree we will interpret the laws that Congress passes to mean more or less than they fairly say."[16]

Yet he recognized the validity of some traditional substantive canons. For instance, speaking of the avoidance canon, which tells courts to construe statutes, when fairly possible, to avoid constitutional problems, he argued that "constitutional doubt may validly be used to affect the interpretation of an ambiguous statute." And he called the rule of lenity, which gives criminal defendants the benefit of the doubt when the statutory language is ambiguous, "valid by sheer antiquity" given that the canon "is almost as old as the common law itself." Tradition, and values, over text alone, could win the day in a close statutory case.[17]

In the end, despite his rhetoric, Scalia seemed less disturbed by the use of substantive canons generally than by *particular* substantive canons. He took aim at those he considered especially indeterminate or unwise, such as an old canon holding that statutes which change common law rules which had been developed by judges incrementally through deciding cases should be read narrowly.[18] This selective acceptance is no aberration. Scalia's most important opinions show that despite some notable exceptions, in the important cases his conservative values trumped his jurisprudential commitments. This is true not just in statutory cases but in constitutional ones as well.

But inconsistency in application is only one of textualism's problems.

⚖

The greatest failing of textualism, and particularly Justice Scalia's strict version of it, is its hubris. There is an unwarranted sense of certainty in his statutory interpretation opinions and academic writings on interpretation. The theory rests on the idea that judges can find the right answer to questions about statutory language. It hearkens back to "formalist" judicial philosophy of eighteenth-century legal thinkers such as William Blackstone, who believed that legal questions had right substantive answers, which it was a judge's duty to discover.

Textualism is different. Scalian formalism puts its faith not in an immutable law of nature but in linguistic analysis. Parse the words carefully enough and apply just the right canon of construction when appropriate, Scalia assures us, and most legal questions can be solved with a grammar lesson. Or it might be worse than that. Law and linguistics expert Lawrence Solan describes Scalia's version of textualism as a kind of "parlor game" that "intentionally eschews many of the contextual and cognitive cues that make language meaningful."[19]

This description calls to mind a 1990 opinion, *United States v. Marshall*, written by Frank Easterbrook, a judge on the United States Court of Appeals for the Seventh Circuit. Easterbrook is another leading textualist and former colleague of Scalia's at the University of Chicago. At issue was a federal sentencing rule that imposed a mandatory minimum sentence "for selling more than one gram of a 'mixture or substance containing a detectable amount' of LSD, ten years for more than ten grams." LSD is so potent it is sold in tiny amounts, typically after being dissolved onto "blotter paper" or into a gelatin cube or some other substance. One of the defendants in *United States v. Marshall* had sold LSD on blotter paper, which weighed much more than the drug itself, potentially triggering the mandatory minimum sentence based on the combined weight of both the drug and the paper. Should the sentence be based on the weight of the LSD alone, or on the LSD and the blotter paper?[20]

Easterbrook, writing for a majority of the court, held that LSD dissolved on blotter paper was a "mixture . . . containing a detectable amount" of LSD, thereby kicking in the mandatory minimum sentence. As he saw it, using parlor-game textualism: "You cannot pick a grain of LSD off the surface of the paper. Ordinary parlance calls the paper containing tiny crystals of LSD a mixture."

More pragmatic theories view judging as an exercise in judgment and discretion. Judge Richard A. Posner, a pragmatist who also sat as a Seventh Circuit judge on the case (and was a frequent sparring partner of Scalia in the world of public intellectuals), dissented, noting the absurdity of counting the blotter paper in determining a drug sentence: "A person who sells LSD on blotter paper is not a worse criminal than one who sells the same number of doses on gelatin cubes, but he is subject to a heavier punishment. A person who sells five doses of LSD on sugar cubes is not a worse person than a manufacturer of LSD who is caught with 19,999 doses in pure form, but the former is subject to a ten-year mandatory minimum no-parole sentence while the latter is not even subject to the five-year minimum. If defendant Chapman, who received five years for selling a thousand doses of LSD on blotter paper, had sold the same number of doses in pure form, his Guidelines sentence would have been fourteen months. And defendant Marshall's sentence for selling almost 12,000 doses would have been four years rather than twenty."

Posner is surely right, but Easterbrook's analysis also fails on its own terms. What ordinary speaker of English would refer to LSD-laced blotter paper as a "mixture" of drug and paper? How is that "ordinary parlance" for anyone not playing the textualist parlor game?

Rigid textualist interpretation unsurprisingly can lead to harsh results, but this is an inevitable product of a relentlessly linguistic approach. As Justice Kennedy (himself no rigid textualist), writing for the Court in a bankruptcy case from 2004, *Lamie v. United States Trustee,* warned: "Our unwillingness to soften the import of Congress' chosen words even if we believe the words lead to a harsh outcome is longstanding." Justice Scalia relied on *Lamie* in his dissent in *King v. Burwell,* espousing the view that would have led Obamacare down a death spiral.

Lower courts relying on *Lamie* have approved some harsh results through chary readings of statutes in all kinds of run-of-the-mill cases that do not get the attention of the media or scholars.[21]

- A district court in Kentucky held that an immigrant to the United States from Ghana could be removed from the United States after immigration officials had tried to remove him a second time while his appeal of the government's first removal attempt was ongoing: "It may seem harsh to force [the immigrant] to obey a removal order while his appeal is still pending. But—save for extreme cases implicating constitutional protections—it is not for the courts to moderate the choices that Congress has made." The court, citing *Lamie,* ruled that the words of the statute compelled the court to permit the immigrant's removal during his pending appeal.[22]
- The United States Court of Appeals for the Sixth Circuit held that a

non-profit hospital that was entitled to a refund from the Internal Revenue Service of over $9 million for overpayment of taxes got interest on those payments at a lower rate than individuals because the hospital was treated like a for-profit corporation under the tax code. "No doubt, it is strange that Congress reduced the interest rate on overpayments for *all* corporations, whether for profit or not. We have considerable sympathy for the Medical Center on this score. Congress has created a regime in which a nonprofit hospital receives a lower interest rate on its FICA tax overpayments than Warren Buffett does on his individual tax returns." But the court, in an opinion by Judge Jeff Sutton, a former Scalia clerk and well-respected member of the Sixth Circuit, relied on *Lamie* in holding it could not construe the word "corporations" to exclude non-profit corporations.[23]

- The United States Court of Appeals for the D.C. Circuit, in an opinion by then judge (and later United States chief justice) John Roberts, citing *Lamie,* held that a whistleblower could not bring a claim and collect damages under the federal False Claims Act against a company that defrauded the U.S. railway company Amtrak, because the statute allowed a person seeking such damages to present the claim of misuse of federal funds only to "an officer or employee of the United States Government," and "Amtrak is not the government." Judge Merrick Garland, whom President Obama later unsuccessfully nominated to fill the seat on the Supreme Court that opened when Justice Scalia died, dissented. He accused the court of "surrounding itself on all sides with 'canons' of statutory construction, which serve here as 'cannons' of statutory destruction." Garland agreed with the government's position that "the interpretation the court adopts today will significantly restrict the reach of the False Claims Act in a manner that Congress did not intend, withdrawing False Claims Act protection with respect to a broad swath of false claims inflicting injury on the federal fisc."[24]

Scalia defended textualism as taking away judicial discretion, but these cases show that treating judgments as mere word games neither increases certainty nor assures fundamental justice. There is about as much certainty in hard statutory cases achieved through a textualist approach as there is under an approach looking at legislative history or more eclectic theories of interpretation.

In appellate courts, textualist arguments may come down to a battle of dictionaries, with justices citing competing definitions of a word to make their points. "Dictionary shopping" has become *de rigueur* for lawyers arguing before the Supreme Court and justices writing opinions. It is kind of like picking out your friends at a party, if your friends are historical dictionaries found in law libraries rather than committee reports.[25]

Consider: Can a criminal get five years added to his prison term under the United States Sentencing Guidelines for "carrying a firearm" to a drug deal when the weapon was in the glove compartment of the car he drove to the scene but he made the deal while out of the car? The Supreme Court divided 5–4 on this question. Justice Stephen Breyer's majority opinion, with heavy emphasis on grammar and text, held that the sentencing enhancement applied to the drug dealer caught with a gun in his car but not on his person. By having the gun in his glove compartment, Breyer reasoned, the defendant "carried" it to a drug deal. Justice Ruth Bader Ginsburg, joined by Justice Scalia and two other justices, dissented, saying the weapon had to be on the defendant's person for the sentencing enhancement to apply.

Both sides pointed to many sources on the meaning of "carry." Justice Ginsburg cited the King James Bible, Rudyard Kipling, Charles Bronson in the film *The Magnificent Seven,* and even a speech by the character "Hawkeye" (played by Alan Alda) on the television show *M*A*S*H:* "I will not carry a gun. . . . I'll carry your books, I'll carry a torch, I'll carry a tune, I'll carry on, carry over, carry forward, Cary Grant, cash and carry, carry me back to Old Virginia, I'll even 'hari-kari' if you show me how, but I will not carry a gun!"[26]

One does not have to be Harry Blackmun to be troubled by the reduction of serious legal disputes to word games. Aside from the unfair results that such an approach might yield, it seems not at all in line with how legislators and their staffs who write the statutes view their jobs.

In an extensive survey of the staffers most involved in assisting senators and representatives in drafting legislation, Professors Abbe Gluck and Lisa

Schultz Bressman found only mixed support for the textual canons as an appropriate means of interpretation. These bill-writers said that they did not consult dictionaries for meanings when drafting statutes and were unaware of some of the most important canons used by courts, such as the requirement that federal statutes contain "clear statements" when infringing on state sovereignty. Indeed, "despite the decades of judicial squabbling over it, legislative history was overwhelmingly viewed by our Democratic and Republican Respondents alike as the most important tool of interpretation after statutory text."[27]

Perhaps more important, in the modern administrative state, these drafters saw themselves as primarily in dialogue with agencies and the massive federal bureaucracy, not the courts, but they still expected courts to sort out disputes. As to the lodestone of textual analysis, the statutory language chosen by congressional drafters was far from a dry linguistic exercise: "respondents [to the survey] told us that statutes are sometimes drafted in contorted ways to guard committee jurisdiction and agency oversight; that committee staff, leadership staff, Legislative Counsel, and personal staff all draft statutes, but that each type of staff has different goals and varied drafting practices; that legislative history plays different roles in omnibus, appropriations, and single-subject legislation; that the congressional budget score [explaining the financial impact of legislation] has an enormous impact on statutory language; and that whether a statute goes through committee or not—and *which* committee—should affect the interpretive presumptions applied."[28]

Given the way bills are drafted, text cannot fairly be the only consideration for judges determining how to apply a statute in a concrete situation. Robert A. Katzmann, a judge on the United States Court of Appeals for the Second Circuit, whose book *Judging Statutes* is an impressive response to the modern textualist movement, seemed to get right to the nub of the problem: "excluding legislative history when interpreting ambiguous statutes is just as likely to expand a judge's discretion as reduce it. When a statute is unambiguous, resort to legislative history is generally not necessary; in that circumstance, the inquiry ordinarily ends. But when the statute is ambiguous, barring legislative history leaves a judge only with words that could be interpreted in a variety of ways without contextual guidance as to what legislators may have thought. Lacking such guidance increases the probability that a judge will construe it in a manner that the legislators did not intend."[29]

⚖️

Despite these criticisms, textualism has had enormous influence in the courts and among lawyers and legal scholars. When Justice Kagan declared in 2015 at Harvard's "Scalia Lecture" that "we are all textualists now," she did not mean that most judges agree with Scalia's strict version of textualism, which eschews all reliance on legislative history or consideration of practicality or fairness. She meant that, at least in the less controversial cases, textual analysis is usually the starting point, and sometimes the ending point, for deciding cases involving disputed statutes.

Case in point: the Supreme Court's fierce debate from 2014 about, of all things, whether a fish is a "tangible object."[30]

John Yates is a commercial fisherman who caught undersized red grouper in federal waters off the Gulf of Mexico. After he had a crew member toss the fish in the sea so that federal authorities could not confirm his illegal fishing, he was convicted of violating two federal criminal statutes, including one calling for penalties against anyone who "knowingly alters, destroys, mutilates, conceals, covers up, falsifies, or makes a false entry in any record, document, or tangible object with the intent to impede, obstruct, or influence the investigation or proper administration of any matter within the jurisdiction of any department or agency of the United States . . ." The government argued that Yates violated the statute by having his crew "destroy" the grouper, a "tangible object."

On a 5–4 vote, the Supreme Court overturned the conviction. Justice Ginsburg, writing for herself and three other justices, explained the problem with the conviction: The statute in question "was enacted as part of the Sarbanes-Oxley Act of 2002, legislation designed to protect investors and restore trust in financial markets following the collapse of the Enron Corporation. A fish is no doubt an object that is tangible; fish can be seen, caught, and handled, and a catch, as this case illustrates, is vulnerable to destruction. But it would cut [the statute] loose from its financial-fraud mooring to hold that it encompasses any and all objects, whatever their size or significance, destroyed with obstructive intent. Mindful that in Sarbanes-Oxley, Congress trained its attention on corporate and accounting deception and cover-ups, we conclude that a matching construction . . . is in order: A tangible object . . . , we hold, must be one used to record or preserve information."

Justice Samuel Alito, writing only for himself, provided the fifth vote for the result, with reasoning similar to Ginsburg's.

Justice Kagan wrote a dissent for herself and Justices Kennedy, Scalia, and Thomas. "A fish is, of course, a discrete thing that possesses physical form. See generally Dr. Seuss, *One Fish Two Fish Red Fish Blue Fish* (1960). So the ordinary meaning of the term 'tangible object' in [the statute], as no one here disputes, covers fish (including too-small red grouper)."

What is remarkable about *Yates* is not that the justices' disagreement cuts across ideological lines, with liberals Ginsburg and Kagan going head-to-head. That is not unheard of in the less ideological cases. It is how all of the justices writing opinions focused primarily upon textual analysis. Justice Ginsburg and Justice Kagan simply differ about the linguistic meaning of "tangible object" in the context of the other statutory language. A big question in the case was whether the textual canons of *ejusdem generis* and its cousin, *noscitur a sociis* ("a word is known by the company it keeps") properly applied: must the "tangible object" be like "any record" or "document"? If so, then the defendant wins because a fish is not like a record or document. Word games.

Legislative history appeared in both the Ginsburg and Kagan opinions, but it did little work. Perhaps to keep Scalia on board with her dissenting opinion, Kagan prefaced her brief legislative history discussion with this piquant line: "And legislative history, for those who care about it, puts extra icing on a cake already frosted."

Despite cases like *Yates*, it is important not to overstate Scalia's triumph. While all of the justices embrace a kind of soft textualism, most of them, even the conservative ones (aside from Justice Thomas), want that extra icing of legislative history even as they have recognized its limits.[31]

In a 2006 case involving the Speedy Trial Act, for example, Justice Alito—who by some measures is more conservative than Scalia was—included a section relying on legislative history to solve a statutory interpretation problem, even though, by doing so, he drew a separate concurrence from Scalia, who wanted to distance himself from that part of the opinion. "It may seem that there is no harm in using committee reports and other such sources," Scalia wrote, "when they are merely in accord with the plain meaning of the Act. But this sort of intellectual piling-on has addictive consequences."[32]

⚖

Textualism is doing better in the lower courts. Since its publication, Scalia and Garner's *Reading Law,* with all of its canons and maxims of interpretation, had been cited by state and federal courts over 520 times (including eleven times by the Supreme Court, sometimes against Scalia's positions).[33]

Justice Neil Gorsuch, when he sat as a judge on the United States Court of Appeals for the Tenth Circuit, wrote an opinion for that court sitting en banc (as a whole) which could have been written by Scalia himself. In a case from 2015, *United States v. Rentz,* the court considered interpretation of a federal criminal statute imposing higher penalties for those who use guns in committing violent crimes or drug offenses. The statute had spawned a host of interpretation issues, and the question before the court in *Rentz* was, "What is the statute's proper unit of prosecution? The parties before us agree that Philbert Rentz 'used' a gun only once but did so 'during and in relation to' two separate 'crimes of violence'—by firing a single shot that hit and injured one victim but then managed to strike and kill another. In circumstances like these, does the statute permit the government to charge one violation or two?" The difference in how that issue was resolved would determine whether Rentz would be sentenced to a five-to-ten year term alone or have a mandatory twenty-five-years-to-life sentence tacked on top of it.[34]

Most of Gorsuch's opinion's read like a grammar lesson, full of talk of verbs and prepositional phrases. He sided with Rentz, believing "his reading of the statute—like most good ones—flows from plain old grade school grammar." He rejected the government's textual reading as requiring "sophisticated syntactical somersaults" and its argument that the statute's legislative history compelled a different result: "This may be a shaky enough claim on which to stake any statutory interpretation in the face of adverse textual evidence," and it failed on its own terms in this case. Finally, to the extent any ambiguity in the statute's meaning remained, Gorsuch explained that "we don't default to the most severe possible interpretation of the statute but to the rule of lenity."

During his confirmation hearings Gorsuch got grilled about another textualist interpretation, this time in *TransAm Trucking v. Administrative Review Board,* the so-called "frozen trucker" case. The 2016 case before a three-judge panel of the Tenth Circuit concerned a trucker whose brakes froze while driving a rig through subzero temperatures in Illinois in 2009. "After reporting the problem to TransAm and waiting several hours for a repair truck to arrive, [the trucker] unhitched his truck from the trailer and drove away, leaving the trailer unattended. He was terminated for abandoning the trailer." The trucker claimed protection under a whistleblower statute making it unlawful for an employer to discharge an employee who "refuses to operate a vehicle because . . . the employee has a reasonable apprehension of serious injury to the employee or the public because of the vehicle's hazardous safety or security condition." The Tenth Circuit majority sided with a federal agency which concluded that the trucker could take advantage of the whistleblower statute. Judge Gorsuch dissented, refusing to defer to the agency's interpretation and holding that when the trucker drove his truck away without the trailer to avoid freezing to death, he was "operating"—rather than "refusing to operate"—his vehicle.[35]

As Gorsuch's confirmation hearing, Senator (and former comedian) Al Franken ripped Judge Gorsuch's "plain meaning" interpretation in *TransAm:*

> What you're talking about here is the plain meaning rule. Here's what the rule means. When the plain meaning of a statute is clear on its face, when its meaning is obvious, courts have no business looking beyond the meaning to the statute's purpose. And that's what you used, right?. . .
>
> But the plain meaning rule has an exception. When using the plain meaning rule would create an absurd result, courts should depart from the plain meaning. It is absurd to say this company is in its rights to fire him because he made the choice of possibly dying from freezing to death or causing other people to die possibly by driving an unsafe vehicle. That's absurd.
>
> Now, I had a career in identifying absurdity. And I know it when I see it. And it makes me—you know, it makes me question your judgment.[36]

Already in his first few months as a Supreme Court justice, Gorsuch took up Scalia's textualist mantle. In his first majority opinion for the court in a case involving who counts as a "debt collector" under a federal statute, the new justice relied heavily upon principles of grammar, citing a dictionary and two books of English usage. In one of his first dissents, in a case involving the proper jurisdiction for certain complaints regarding federal employment called *Perry v. Merit Systems Protection Board,* Gorsuch, joined by Justice Thomas, disagreed with an opinion of Justice Ginsburg regarding the proper interplay of federal rules. During oral argument in the case, Justice Alito noted how difficult he thought the statutory interpretation question was. "Who wrote this statute? Somebody who takes pleasure out of pulling the wings off flies?" He added: "The one thing about this case that seems perfectly clear to me is that nobody who is not a lawyer, and no ordinary lawyer, could read these statutes and figure out what they are supposed to do." But Justice Gorsuch thought the case was easily resolved by applying textual rules of interpretation, and his approach was better than the approach of seven colleagues. He snarkily admonished the majority: "If a statute needs repair, there's a constitutionally prescribed way to do it. It's called legislation."[37]

Gorsuch's approach is typical for how textualist-oriented judges approach statutory questions like word games thanks to the work of Justice Scalia. And lawyers have learned too: a good lawyer writing a brief to a court in a case that turns on the meaning of a statute knows to start with the words of the statute and offer an argument about the meaning of the text, even if that brief will later turn to other tools of interpretation, such as arguing about legislative history, or deference to the statute's interpretation given by an agency, or the best or fairest result. Scalia's relentless focus on the text has changed the discourse of cases, and likely influenced the result of cases like *Yates.* And yet . . .

In the most important cases that turn on the meaning of statutes, it does not appear that textualism or any other set of interpretive rules will restrict judicial discretion. It is not just that textualism does not appear to have led to more unanimous opinions, although that is certainly true: if linguistic analysis yields determinate answers, why was *Yates* not unanimous? It is that in the most important cases, outcomes seem to be driven by ideology and a sense of fair results. Think again of the second Obamacare case turning on the meaning of "established by the state."

In an address she gave at Northwestern University Law School in 2015, Justice Kagan told a public audience that when the justices get together in conference to discuss cases following oral argument, they spend more time talking about the less controversial cases than about the more controversial ones. On the controversial cases, further discussion would just "irritate" colleagues and change no one's mind. There is no reason to believe that textualism is any more effective than other forms of reasoning in persuading opposing justices, or that it constrains them more than fidelity to legislative history or any other method.[38]

⚖

Some conservative lower court judges and members of the academy find Scalia's textualism, if anything, too restrained. The conservative farm team that now stands ready to be appointed to the Supreme Court and the lower courts will likely take his jurisprudence several steps further.

Judge Brett Kavanaugh, for instance, is a very able, very conservative judge sitting on the United States Court of Appeals for the D.C. Circuit. In a recent review of Robert Katzmann's book taking on Scalian textualism, Kavanaugh argued not only that textualism can solve most statutory interpretation problems but took it further than Scalia did, rejecting even some of the canons, such as *ejusdem generis,* because they do not help to discern meaning.[39]

In making his defense of textualism, Kavanaugh endorsed Blackstone's notion of a statutory truth that can be "found" by sufficiently careful textual analysis: "courts should seek the best reading of the statute by interpreting the words of the statute, taking account of the context of the whole statute, and applying the agreed-upon semantic canons. Once they have discerned the best reading of the text in that way, they can depart from that baseline if required to do so by any relevant substantive canons—for example, the absurdity doctrine. . . . The current situation in statutory interpretation, as I see it, is more akin to a situation where umpires can, at least on some pitches, largely define their own strike zones. My solution is to define the

strike zone in advance much more precisely so that each umpire is operating within the same guidelines. If we do that, we will need to worry less
about who the umpire is when the next pitch is thrown."[40]

To put it another way, Kavanaugh believes, as Scalia preached, that by
committing to a set of linguistic guidelines for deciding cases, judges can
remove most of the discretion they now have in deciding how to apply statutes to real-world problems. These neutral principles would allow judges
to transcend their ideological and political commitments and decide cases
based only on some ideal "best reading" of the statute.

Even the absurdity exception, which Scalia put in play in Paul Green's
case against the Bock Laundry Machine Company, Judge Kavanaugh would
confine to a very narrow set of cases: "After all, one person's reasonableness
may be another person's absurdity." He described *King v. Burwell,* the second Obamacare case, as being about "mistake," not "absurdity" (though I
do not understand how to draw that line and the categories may overlap),
and he strongly suggested (though he would not directly say so, perhaps
because it would complicate any confirmation hearings for the Supreme
Court) that the Court reached the wrong result. The upshot is that Kavanaugh, like Scalia, would allow Obamacare to enter a "death spiral" on the
basis of a "mistake."[41]

Kavanaugh's criticism of the absurdity doctrine drew on the work of Harvard Law School dean (and former Scalia clerk) John Manning. In a long and
influential *Harvard Law Review* article, "The Absurdity Doctrine," Manning
urged serious textualists to all but abandon it: "Following such a course
would more often require judges to accept seemingly odd or awkward
results in particular cases, but doing so would serve important systemic
values implicit in the constitutional structure—legislative supremacy, the
evenhanded application of statutes, respect for legislative compromise, and
the conception of limited judicial power implicit in rationality review."[42]
Although Manning mentions *Green v. Bock Laundry Machine* only once,
disapproving of Justice Scalia's invocation of the absurdity exception in that
case, the whole article is fairly read as repudiating Scalia's softness on the
question.

For the next generation of textualists, the word games will be more intense, and it will be the beginning and end of efforts at understanding a statute's meaning. Scalia may not have been a "nut" when it comes to textualism, but the logic of his arguments can lead to nutty outcomes, like adding many years to someone's prison sentence not for reasons of culpability but because of dictionary definitions of the word "mixture."

3

From Faint-Hearted to Full-Throated

"WELL, I THINK WHAT JUSTICE SCALIA wants to know is what James Madison thought about video games," Samuel Alito deadpanned. "Did he enjoy them?"

The audience in the Supreme Court gallery laughed. They were listening to oral argument in a November 2010 case pitting the video gaming industry against the State of California, which had enacted a ban on the sale of violent video games to minors. Scalia quickly shot back, "No, I want to know what James Madison thought about violence. Was there any indication that anybody thought, when the First Amendment was adopted, that . . . there was an exception to it . . . for speech regarding violence?"[1]

It was an extraordinary exchange between the two of the Court's conservative justices: Scalia, appointed by President Ronald Reagan, and Alito, appointed by George W. Bush. In the Court's term for 2010–2011, the two justices disagreed on the bottom-line judgment in only 14 percent of decided cases, and on the sixteen 5–4 cases they disagreed only once. By contrast, Scalia disagreed with Ruth Bader Ginsburg 35 percent of the time that term, and they split in fifteen of the sixteen cases decided 5–4. The 2010 term was no aberration: Scalia and Alito disagreed in only 12 percent of cases in the 2011 term, 23 percent in the 2012 term, 10 percent in the 2013 term, and 22 percent in the 2014 term.[2]

But despite the critics who began referring to Justice Alito as "Scalito" when he joined the Court in 2006, the two men had fundamental disagreements on jurisprudential methods. We saw in the previous chapter that Alito, rejecting Scalia's strict textualism, sometimes relies on legislative history to determine the reach and meaning of statutes. His comment about Madison's view of video games shows that the two justices also disagreed over how to read the United States Constitution. Scalia has been one of the most important voices espousing the theory of "originalism" for interpreting the Constitution, and Alito's snarky remark was a slam on this method.[3]

Roughly speaking, originalism is the idea that the meaning of a constitutional provision is fixed at the time it is adopted and it cannot be changed through judicial interpretation. The only avenue for change is a constitutional amendment. The First Amendment means what it meant when it was adopted in 1791, and the Fourteenth Amendment means what it meant when it was adopted in 1868.

Scalia did not create the theory of originalism as a means of constitutional interpretation, just as he did not create textualism for statutory interpretation. Professor Johnathan O'Neill traces originalist ideas back to the Founding, and saw the approach fade by the 1930s only to rise again. Justice Hugo Black, who was on the Court from 1937 to 1971, was a precursor of the modern originalists.[4]

But the idea took off in the 1980s, with the prodding of the Federalist Society, then a new group of lawyers, law students, academics, and judges, that eventually rose to prominence as a network of elite conservative lawyers. President Reagan's attorney general, Edwin Meese, and Robert Bork, a judge of the United States Court of Appeals for the D.C. Circuit whom Reagan nominated to the Supreme Court, both argued extensively for originalism, and the Federalist Society supported their ideas. Scalia, a key early adviser to the group, refined and relentlessly promoted the originalist approach to constitutional interpretation. As Professor (and former Scalia clerk) Gary Lawson put it after the justice's death, "Justice Scalia was the first prominent jurist to set forth a systematic methodology for understanding the content of legal texts by reference to their original public communicative meanings. That was a revolutionary development."[5]

Roughly speaking, under Justice Scalia's view of originalism, the Constitution's words should be interpreted based upon the "original public meaning" of a constitutional provision when it was enacted: The Constitution means what it meant to "intelligent and informed" people, including the Framers, at the time of adoption. "What I look for in the Constitution is precisely what I look for in a statute: the original meaning of the text, not what the original draftsmen intended."[6]

This version of originalism differs from some earlier incarnations, which focused on getting into the minds the Framers of the Constitution to ask how they would have resolved a case before the Court. Alito's crack in the *Brown v. Entertainment Merchants Association* case seemed to be pinning Scalia with the "original intent" version of originalism.[7]

There are many similarities between Scalia's views on textualism and those on originalism. He justified both theories as part of a judge's constitutional obligation to enforce "the law" as written. Both depend upon the meaning of the words at the time of enactment, and he offered both as "neutral" principles for deciding cases. He derided the idea of an evolving or "living" Constitution in which courts decide cases based on contemporary values or understandings. He was fond of saying that he likes his Constitution "dead, dead, dead."[8]

But there is one significant difference between the two theories. In applying original public meaning analysis, Scalia did not just care what the *words* of the Constitution meant when adopted but how people alive at the time would have understood *its application to particular questions.*

For example, the Eighth Amendment prohibits "cruel and unusual punishment." In deciding whether flogging is cruel or unusual, Scalia would not have stopped at asking what the words "cruel" and "unusual" meant in 1791, when the Constitution was ratified; he would have gone on to ask whether people in 1791 would have considered flogging either cruel or unusual. That approach, while usually not focused on the specific intent of the Framers, employs general social understandings from the time of the Eighth Amendment's adoption to decide its contemporary meaning. Sometimes the justice asked how people like the Framers would have understood the text in a specific context, and the closer we come to trying to answer the contextual question, the closer we come to trying to read the Framers' minds.

Although Scalia was not always consistent in applying originalist doctrine—sometimes, for example, he cared more about tradition than text, and sometimes he ignored originalism entirely—this comes closest to the description of the theory he set for himself.[9]

His approach in the *Brown* case, which concerned violent video games, nicely illustrates that original-public-meaning originalism is not a pure linguistic exercise. It is more a marriage of linguistics and constitutional history. The question was whether a California law banning the sale of violent video games to minors violated the First Amendment. Is a state law banning "violent video games" an abridgement of the freedom of speech? (Under the Fourteenth Amendment, the First Amendment's prohibition on restricting free speech applies to the states as well as to Congress.)

California did not pass the law in a vacuum. Its lawmakers knew that artistic expressions such as video games generally receive First Amendment protection, and they drafted the gaming statute so that it had the best chance to survive judicial challenge. The law covered games "in which the range of options available to a player includes killing, maiming, dismembering, or sexually assaulting an image of a human being, if those acts are depicted" in a manner that "a reasonable person, considering the game as a whole, would find appeals to a deviant or morbid interest of minors," is "patently offensive to prevailing standards in the community as to what is suitable for minors," and "causes the game, as a whole, to lack serious literary, artistic, political, or scientific value for minors."

Those three limiting clauses were borrowed from a New York statute that had banned the sale of sexually obscene materials to minors. In a 1968 case, *Ginsberg v. New York,* the Supreme Court upheld that statute as a permissible exercise of New York's police powers and not a First Amendment violation. In *Brown,* California argued that New York's approach to keeping sexually obscene materials away from minors could also extend to its effort to ban violent video games.[10]

Scalia was unpersuaded. Since 1791, he wrote in his majority opinion, the First Amendment had been generally understood to prevent the government from restricting expression based on its content. But throughout that time, a few categories of speech—"obscenity," "fighting words," and "incitement"—had been categorically exempted from the rule barring restrictions on content. All other content restrictions are subject to strict judicial scrutiny, which they rarely survive.

In upholding New York's law barring obscene materials for minors, the *Ginsberg* decision built upon these precedents establishing obscenity as a category of unprotected speech. New York successfully created a test to separate obscene expression from other, protected expression.

In *Brown*, Justice Scalia concluded that California could not rely upon *Ginsberg*, because California's law was aimed at regulating violent expression, not obscenity, and the First Amendment had not traditionally been seen to contain an exception for violence as it did for obscenity. This is why Scalia said at oral argument that the question for him was not what James Madison thought about video games but whether there was "any indication that anybody thought, when the First Amendment was adopted, that . . . there was an exception to it . . . for speech regarding violence?"

After holding there was no such exception under the First Amendment, Scalia held that California's law failed strict scrutiny and was an unconstitutional restriction on content. In reaching this conclusion, he relied heavily on a case from the year before, *United States v. Stevens,* in which the Court struck down on First Amendment grounds a federal law barring the distribution of "crush videos"—videos showing small animals being crushed to death, which some people liked to watch for sexual pleasure.[11]

Scalia's originalist approach in *Brown* was not a pure linguistic exercise in which he simply considered what the words "abridgement" and "freedom of speech" meant in 1791. That is how he would have approached the question under textualism, if the First Amendment were a statute. Instead, to understand the First Amendment's meaning, he incorporated the social meaning and values of people alive in 1791, and asked how they would have understood whether the First Amendment would contain a categorical exemption for violent expression. He came closer to trying to get into James Madison's mind than he likely would have admitted.

Although Alito is at least as conservative as Scalia was, he believes originalism is wrongheaded. At the oral argument, he rejected the suggestion that understandings about the meaning of the First Amendment in 1791 should determine the regulation of expressions of violence in video games: "we have here a new . . . medium that cannot possibly have been envisioned at the time when the First Amendment was ratified. It is totally different from—it's one thing to read a description of . . . one of these video games is promoted as saying, 'What's black and white and red all over? Perhaps the answer could include disposing of your enemies in a meat grinder.' Now, reading that is one thing. Seeing it as graphically portrayed . . ." He certainly would have finished that thought with "is quite another," but he was interrupted by Justice Scalia saying that someone actually doing those things would be a third different thing.

In the end, Alito, who was the only justice in the *Stevens* case voting to uphold the ban on crush videos, agreed with Scalia and the Court majority that California's law banning the sale of violent video games to minors was unconstitutional. But he joined only in the Court's result and not its reasoning. Alito's problem with the law was not that it violated free speech but that it was unconstitutionally vague under the Fourteenth Amendment's Due Process Clause, which bars arbitrary treatment by the government: game manufacturers and retailers would not know under California's law which video games were violent enough to fall under the statute. But he left open the possibility that a better-drafted statute could be constitutional, given the potential social harms he saw in these games.

Justice Alito pointed to the "astounding" violence in some of these games. "Victims by the dozens are killed with every imaginable implement, including machine guns, shotguns, clubs, hammers, axes, swords, and chainsaws. Victims are dismembered, decapitated, disemboweled, set on fire, and chopped into little pieces. They cry out in agony and beg for mercy. Blood gushes, splatters, and pools. Severed body parts and gobs of human remains are graphically shown."

The games were also anti-social, such as one in which a player could "take on the identity and reenact the killings carried out by the perpetrators of the murders at Columbine High School and Virginia Tech. The objective of one game is to rape a mother and her daughters; in another, the goal is to rape Native American women. There is a game in which players engage in 'ethnic cleansing' and can choose to gun down African-Americans, Latinos, or Jews." Justice Alito concluded there was a reasonable basis for thinking the experience of playing these games was "quite different from the experience of reading a book, listening to a radio broadcast, or viewing a movie.

And if this is so, then for at least some minors, the effects of playing violent video games may also be quite different."[12]

⚖

One might have expected Justice Clarence Thomas to side with Scalia in the *Brown* case. Thomas is not only a more committed originalist but also a great defender of the First Amendment: he believes, for instance, that virtually all campaign finance laws, even those requiring the disclosure of political campaign donors, are unconstitutional—a position Scalia rejected.[13]

Thomas and Scalia, both deeply conservative justices, often found themselves in agreement. In the 2010 term, they disagreed on the bottom-line judgment in only 14 percent of decided cases, and in sixteen cases decided by 5–4 votes they disagreed only once (the same as Alito and Scalia). Scalia and Thomas disagreed on only 7 percent of decisions in the 2011 term, 14 percent in the 2012 term, 5 percent in 2013, and 22 percent in 2014.[14]

But in *Brown*, Justice Thomas wrote a dissent that took an unexpected originalist direction, arguing that under the original understanding of the Constitution, people had no right to direct speech to a minor without permission from the minor's parent. This theory was not discussed by either party in their briefs or at oral argument, and barely addressed in one amicus brief. Thomas did not mention his theory at oral argument: following his customary practice, he asked no questions at all.[15]

Thomas's dissent gave a long history of the treatment of minor children in colonial and early American history, citing books on Puritan childrearing from as early as 1648, the writings of Rousseau and John Locke, the papers of John Adams, books detailing Thomas Jefferson's approach to childrearing (though apparently not the rearing of his children born out of wedlock), Blackstone's writings on minors' rights, and early American cases involving limits on the rights of minors. From this historical canvass, Thomas concluded: "In light of this history, the Framers could not possibly have understood 'the freedom of speech' to include an unqualified right to speak to minors. Specifically, I am sure that the founding generation would not have understood 'the freedom of speech' to include a right to speak to children without going through their parents. As a consequence, I do not believe that laws limiting such speech—for example, by requiring parental consent to speak to a minor—'abridg[e] the freedom of speech' within the original meaning of the First Amendment."[16]

Scalia's majority opinion in *Brown* dismissed Thomas's arguments in a single footnote. After noting that his fellow justice's views were inconsistent with *Erznoznik v. Jacksonville,* a 1975 Supreme Court case recognizing that minors have "a significant measure of First Amendment protection," he rejected Thomas's history lesson as unpersuasive.[17] Scalia said it was "true enough" that "parents have traditionally had the power to control what their children hear and say." "And it perhaps follows from this that the state has the power to *enforce* parental prohibitions—to require, for example, that the promoters of a rock concert exclude those minors whose parents have advised the promoters that their children are forbidden to attend. But it does not follow that the state has the power to prevent children from hearing or saying anything *without their parents' prior consent.*" He noted that this would mean that parents could keep children under eighteen out of political rallies without their consent, "even a political rally in support of laws against corporal punishment of children, or laws in favor of greater rights for minors." And if this is true, "it could be made criminal to admit a person under 18 to church, or to give a person under 18 a religious tract, without his parents' prior consent." Scalia seemed to reject Thomas's position not because it was historically wrong, but because it went against earlier precedent and was bad policy.[18]

⚖

This dispute between Thomas and Scalia over the original public meaning of minors' First Amendment rights illustrates several key points. First, doing originalism right seems to depend not just upon the ability to summon up the meaning of words from 250 years ago, but also on understanding centuries-old history and social context. Get the history and social context wrong, and you get original meaning wrong. As hard as it is to describe the current meaning of language and social context, it is much harder to construct an accurate historical record, especially for judges who lack the requisite training. Linguists and historians tend to agree that judges are ill-equipped to do this type of analysis.[19]

This version of originalism, unlike a purely linguistic one focused solely on the meaning of the *words* in the constitutional text, exacerbates the problem discussed in the previous chapter: like guests at a party, originalists can pick and choose the relevant historical record to craft a story in line with their conclusions. Why should we expect one justice's armchair history of the meaning of constitutional provisions at the time of enactment to be any more reliable than contemporary legislative history and not a reflection of the judge's ultimate values? And why should anyone believe there was any consensus on social meaning of terms at a particular point in history, much less one than anyone could discover now?

It should be no surprise that Thomas, who embraces originalism more than any other justice on the Court, and Alito, who rejects originalism, came to the same conclusion in *Brown:* that the state has the ability under the First Amendment to shield minors from some violent content. (Recall that Alito's concern was with the clarity of California's violent video game law, not the aim of the law itself.) They reached similar conclusions by different methodologies because they both believe the state has a strong interest in letting parents control the kind of content to which their children are exposed.[20]

Justice Scalia's decisions as well seemed to be driven more by ideology than methodology. Consider his vote in *Texas v. Johnson,* holding that there is a constitutional right to burn an American flag. Although he liked to point to this case as evidence that he was not driven by ideology because conservatives do not like flag burning, his vote in *Johnson* illustrated only that in his ideological hierarchy, even hateful, anti-patriotic expression was better than government censorship. When it came to the First Amendment, he was generally a conservative libertarian, believing in broad protection for personal expression free from government censorship and regulation. As Professor Steven Heyman describes it, the conservative-libertarian approach to the First Amendment aims "to invalidate laws or policies that in their view threatened to subordinate individual liberty to liberal or progressive goals such as political reform, racial and sexual equality, gay rights, secularism, unionization, and anti-smoking efforts."[21]

But for Justices Alito and Thomas in the *Brown* case, and for Alito in *Stevens,* a socially conservative interest protecting some people (or children) from some emotional harm can be more important than protecting free expression. Alito was also the lone dissenter in a case involving the Westboro Baptist Church, in which the Supreme Court overturned damages for emotional distress awarded to the family of an American soldier killed in action. Members of the church had protested at soldiers' funerals, holding up signs saying things like "God Hates the USA/Thank God for 9/11," "America is Doomed," "Don't Pray for the USA," "Thank God for IEDs," "Thank God for Dead Soldiers," "Pope in Hell," "Priests Rape Boys," "God Hates Fags," "You're Going to Hell," and "God Hates You."[22]

The Court, including Justice Scalia, held that these protests, somewhat connected to political ideas, were protected by the First Amendment. Alito responded that "Our profound national commitment to free and open debate is not a license for the vicious verbal assault that occurred in this case."[23]

The divide between Justices Scalia and Thomas in *Brown* shows that originalists have deep disagreements over how much respect to pay Supreme Court precedents that seem inconsistent with originalist analysis. Scalia believed that Thomas's argument about the free speech rights of minors was foreclosed by the Court's *Erznoznik v. Jacksonville* case of 1975; Thomas thought that precedent did not need to be followed to the extent that it was inconsistent with the First Amendment's original public meaning.[24]

A much more serious dispute over originalism and precedent has arisen over what is known as the "selective incorporation" doctrine. This sounds technical, but in coming years it could have profound implications for individual rights and liberties, as well as for the limits of state power.

As originally understood, the Bill of Rights (the first ten amendments of the Constitution) limited only what the federal government could do, but not the states. Imagine a state being able to shut down a newspaper it did not like, or engage in whatever searches government officials pleased, even without probable cause.

Over time the Court started holding states bound by key parts of the Bill of Rights. The way that it did so is controversial to originalists. Recall that in *Brown,* the Court considered whether the State of California violated the First Amendment, but the amendment, by its own terms, applies only to *Congress.* So how could a good originalist view *California* as bound by the First Amendment?

The Fourteenth Amendment prevents states from depriving persons of "life, liberty, or property without due process of law." The Court has long held that the Due Process Clause prevents arbitrary government procedures: recall that this was Justice Alito's objection to California's violent video game law. More controversially, the Court has also read the Due Process Clause to provide certain substantive protections, such as the right of a woman to an abortion in some circumstances. This theory of "substantive due process" is generally anathema to originalists, who believe the clause is only about fair government procedures.

But substantive due process is the route by which the Court has held that portions of the Bill of Rights apply against the states. The Court ruled in a 1925 case, *Gitlow v. New York,* that states became bound to follow the free speech and press guarantees of First Amendment once the country ratified the Fourteenth Amendment in 1868. Under this theory, the "liberty" guaranteed in the due process clause included substantive rights such as the First Amendment's freedom of speech and press.[25]

This "incorporation" of the First Amendment in *Gitlow* did not establish that the entire Bill of Rights applied to the states. The Court uses "selective incorporation," deciding each right separately. Thanks to cases such as *Gitlow,* it was uncontroversial by the time the Court decided *Brown* that the First Amendment's speech and press protections have been incorporated.[26]

The incorporation doctrine presents a huge problem for originalists because it is based on a "substantive due process" analysis that is very nonoriginalist. Although Scalia has acquiesced in *Gitlow*'s incorporation of the First Amendment, Thomas has not. He has even written that the Establishment Clause in the First Amendment, which prevents the federal government from establishing a religion, has not been properly incorporated, so that it might not stop New Jersey, for example, from declaring the Catholic Church (or any other religious organization) its official church.[27]

⚖

A 2010 case over gun rights, *McDonald v. City of Chicago,* illustrates Scalia's and Thomas's dueling approaches to selective incorporation and gives us a glimpse into future battles over the reach of originalism.[28]

McDonald followed a 2008 case, *District of Columbia v. Heller,* in which the Supreme Court ruled for the first time that the Second Amendment protects an individual's right to keep and bear arms. Before this, courts had disagreed over whether the amendment provided any individually enforceable right to own a gun, or whether it concerned only the formation of militias for defense, and there was Supreme Court precedent many read as establishing there was no individual right. *Heller* held that a Washington, D.C., law barring ownership and registration of handguns violated the Second Amendment. Because the District of Columbia is a federal enclave, the Court treated the law as a federal law. It did not discuss whether an individual right to keep and bear arms would be incorporated against the states. That question was left for *McDonald*.[29]

Incorporation of the Second Amendment created a dilemma for conservative originalists, many of whom favored broad gun rights and wanted to find a way to hold states bound by the Second Amendment, but were uncomfortable with selective incorporation via substantive due process. On this question, Scalia and Thomas agreed on the destination—the Second Amendment applies against the states—but divided over the route.

Scalia's analysis of the Second Amendment incorporation question was perfunctory. He joined in Justice Alito's majority opinion recognizing that states are bound to follow the Second Amendment via substantive due process, and that the City of Chicago's gun law, which was similar to the Washington, D.C., law overturned in *Heller,* violated the Second Amendment. But he also wrote a concurring opinion primarily aimed at responding to a dissent by Justice Stevens, in which he began by briefly addressing the incorporation question: "Despite my misgivings about Substantive Due Process as an original matter, I have acquiesced in the Court's incorporation of certain guarantees in the Bill of Rights 'because it is both long established and narrowly limited.' *Albright v. Oliver,* 510 U.S. 266, 275 (1994) (SCALIA, J., concurring). This case does not require me to reconsider that view, since straightforward application of settled doctrine suffices to decide it."[30]

These two sentences masked a huge effort by some originalists to get Scalia to accept a different, more radical route for requiring states to follow the Second Amendment: the "Privileges or Immunities Clause." That clause, like the Due Process Clause, appears in the Fourteenth Amendment: "No state shall make or enforce any law which shall abridge the privileges or immunities of citizens of the United States." These originalists contend that the individual right to bear arms was a "privilege or immunity" of citizenship at the time of the ratification of the Fourteenth Amendment, and states are therefore bound by it. Whether or not this is a sensible historical understanding of the clause, the Supreme Court shut the door to this interpretation in 1873 in the *Slaughter-House Cases,* which essentially read Privileges or Immunities out of the Constitution. Yet Alan Gura, the lawyer who brought both *Heller* and *McDonald* to the Supreme Court, tried to push the theory at the Supreme Court oral argument in *McDonald.*[31]

It is a theory that would open a Pandora's box, because no one really knows what the "privileges or immunities of citizenship" were in 1868, when the Fourteenth Amendment was ratified, or more to the point, what privileges or immunities an originalist Supreme Court would choose to recognize today. Gura argued that there were many "unenumerated" privileges or immunities that individuals could claim against government action. Unenumerated rights are rights of citizenship that society would have recognized in 1868 even though they are not listed in the Bill of Rights. Their existence is acknowledged in the Ninth Amendment, an almost moribund amendment stating that the Constitution's "enumeration . . . of certain rights, shall not be construed to deny or disparage others retained by the people."

Justice Scalia was having none of this. At oral argument in *McDonald* he interrupted Justice Ginsburg's questioning of Gura about the scope of unenumerated rights under the Privileges or Immunities Clause. Ginsburg asked Gura to "just tell us the dimensions of what it is. I mean, we have the eight amendments, so I know you say that's included. Keep and bear arms would be included even absent the Second Amendment. What unenumerated rights would we be declaring privileges and immunities under your conception of it?"[32]

Justice Scalia then asked Gura if he thought "it's at all easier to bring the Second Amendment under the Privileges and Immunities Clause than it is to bring it under our established law of substantive due process?" When Gura said no, Scalia asked "why are you asking us to overrule 150, 140 years of prior law, when . . . you can reach your result under substantive due—I mean, you know, unless you're bucking for a . . . place on some law school faculty . . . what you argue is the darling of the professoriate, for sure, but it's also contrary to 140 years of our jurisprudence. Why do you want to undertake that burden instead of just arguing substantive due process? Which, as much as I think it's wrong, . . . even I have acquiesced in it."

$$⚖$$

Justice Thomas was less concerned about adhering to 140 years of precedent, and more willing to embrace what he saw as the original meaning of the Constitution. Although Thomas wrote that he recognized the importance of adhering to precedent, he concluded that precedent had to give way to (what he viewed as) correct interpretation.

Thomas's concurring opinion in *McDonald* takes up fifty-three pages, much of it historical, rejecting the *Slaughter-House Cases* at least insofar as they applied to the right to bear arms. He left the question of unenumerated rights under the Privileges or Immunities Clause for another day. By taking the Privileges or Immunities route, rather than the substantive due process route, to incorporation of the Second Amendment, Thomas deprived Alito of a fifth vote for a majority holding that the Second Amendment applies to the states through the Fourteenth Amendment's Due Process Clause. But one way or another, there were five votes to make the states respect the Second Amendment.[33]

$$⚖$$

One way of understanding the divide between Justices Scalia and Thomas is that Thomas reaches the kind of decisions Scalia would have reached if he had the courage of his convictions (though Thomas too has sometimes deviated from originalism without explanation). Thomas feels less constrained by the "wrong" precedent and more willing to be aggressive in interpreting the Constitution. He is willing to say that states are not bound by the Establishment Clause and can set up their own state religion, and to throw out decades of jurisprudence in areas from free speech to takings. His jurisprudence is the logical conclusion of Scalia's ideas.

Thomas's originalism is the opposite of classic conservative "judicial restraint," the call for courts to decide less and to leave more issues to the political branches. It calls instead for what some critics pejoratively call "conservative judicial activism" (which some originalists have now repackaged as "judicial engagement"), with courts reining in legislatures, especially when they pass laws protecting consumers and workers from a fully free economic market.[34]

These labels, however, obscure more than they illuminate. A better way of framing the issue is to recognize that a cadre of originalist thinkers are willing to strike down many constitutional precedents and, using their views of original constitutional public meaning, drastically rework the scope of the Constitution, the rights of individuals against the government, and the balance of power between the states and the federal government. Constitutional law and the United States would be very different, and swayed in a very conservative direction, in a Court with five Justice Thomases.

Nonetheless, lack of courage might not explain why Scalia failed to side more often with Thomas on issues like the Privileges or Immunities Clause. A more charitable reading is that Scalia believed that restraint furthered other constitutional values he favored, such as stability and respect for precedent. His "acquiescence" in the use of substantive due process in the narrow context of incorporating the Bill of Rights against the states shows that he tried to choose his battles carefully and was opposed to fundamentally remaking constitutional law. As he wrote in *A Matter of Interpretation,* "Originalism, like any other theory of interpretation put into practice in an ongoing system of law, must accommodate the doctrine of *stare decisis;* it cannot remake the world anew."[35]

It might seem odd to think of Justice Scalia as in any way "restrained," given his outsize personality, his strongly worded opinions (especially the dissents), and his defense of originalism. Yet when he's compared with many other originalists, restraint is the appropriate description.

He expressed his compromise positions in typically uncompromising language. When he told NPR's Nina Totenberg that he was an originalist and textualist "but not a nut," he appeared to be separating himself from Thomas and the implications of a more radical originalism. He also, in a speech he made before joining the Court, famously called himself a "faint-hearted originalist." Even though flogging would not have been thought "cruel and unusual" punishment at the time the Constitution was adopted, he said, he would vote against that original understanding and hold flogging a violation of the Eighth Amendment.[36]

Scalia tried to have it both ways, by describing himself as bound by strong neutral principles, and then bending those principles to adhere to other principles, such as ideology or respect for precedent. In 2011, perhaps seeking to cement a reputation as a stronger originalist, he took back his earlier self-description in an interview with Marcia Coyle: "In his chambers that late summer afternoon in 2011, Scalia said he had 'recanted' being a 'faint-hearted originalist.' 'I think I would vote to uphold it if there were a state law providing for notching of ears. I would think it is a stupid idea but it is not unconstitutional. You have to be principled and I try to be. The only other thoroughgoing originalist is Clarence [Thomas].'"[37]

As Coyle notes, "Some of Scalia's fans question whether he has truly recanted. True believers in original public meaning originalism call him out for not joining originalist opinions by Thomas or, at the very least, for failing to explain why he did not join Thomas in those opinions."[38]

One of his unexplained silences came in the area of property rights, an issue close to many libertarians' hearts. The Fifth Amendment's Takings Clause bars the government from taking private property for public use without offering just compensation. As Professor Ilya Somin has explained, Scalia was widely credited with expanding the law of "takings" to protect private property owners when government regulations deprived their property of much of its value. And he joined Justice O'Connor's dissent in *Kelo v. City of New London,* a 2005 case reading the term "public use" broadly. In the years that followed, Scalia twice called on the Court to overturn the decision, but he did not join in Thomas's originalist dissent in *Kelo,* nor did he ever engage in sustained originalist arguments on the meaning of the Takings Clause. Somin ascribes this failure to a lack of originalist scholarship on the clause's meaning, as well as the "potentially radical implications" of Thomas's *Kelo* dissent.[39]

Other committed originalists have judged Scalia much more harshly. Professor Randy Barnett has essentially accused him of picking and choosing among originalist interpretations, support for precedent, and reliance on tradition and other theories to reach whatever result conformed with his ideology. As we will see in Chapter 5, Professor Nelson Lund believes Scalia held back on true originalist analysis in recognizing an individual right to bear arms in the *Heller* case. Liberals have accused him of completely ignoring originalist arguments when it suited his ideological disposition.[40]

When publicly pressed about his inconsistent use of originalism in certain cases, he usually demurred. For example, Harvard Law professor Alan Dershowitz asked him in a 2008 forum about his failure to use originalism in a 2003 case, *Chavez v. Martinez,* involving the Fifth Amendment right against self-incrimination. According to Dershowitz, there was a rich historical record that, if consulted, "would have led to the opposite result in the case." Scalia answered, "I don't remember the details of the opinion, but what did Sarah Palin say? 'I'll get back to you on that.'" So far as we know, he never did; nor did he set out any general rules for when he would choose to ignore his chosen methodology. Indeed, in 2015 Scalia refused an invitation from the *University of Chicago Law Review* to review Jack Balkin's book, *Living Originalism,* revealingly explaining that he would "follow Disraeli (never complain, never explain)" and leave it to others to "point out the errors of Prof. Balkin's ways. (If there are any such; since I cannot respond to criticisms, neither do I read them)."[41]

Scalia's views on the role of tradition in originalist constitutional interpretation unquestionably changed over time. In a 1989 case, *Michael H. v. Gerald D.,* he wrote a majority opinion for the Court upholding a California law creating an irrebuttable presumption that a child born to a married woman living with her husband is a child of the marriage. Rejecting the true biological father's claim to parental rights, Scalia wrote that the scope of the Due Process Clause depended on American tradition and "our traditions have protected the marital family."[42]

But in the 2000 case of *Troxel v. Granville,* the role of tradition apparently disappeared from parental rights. In *Troxel,* a Court majority, over Scalia's dissent, struck down a Washington State law giving individuals such as grandparents the right to petition for visitation rights with children, even if the parents objected to the visits. The Court held that the law violated the substantive due process rights of a mother who opposed grandparent visitation. But Scalia rejected the claim of parental traditional control as a matter of constitutional law, even while recognizing it as an "inalienable right" that the Declaration of Independence protects and an "unenumerated right" mentioned in the Ninth Amendment. "I do not believe that the power which the Constitution confers upon me *as a judge* entitles me to deny legal effect to laws that (in my view) infringe upon what is (in my view) that unenumerated right."[43]

The Fourteenth Amendment's treatment of race and sex discrimination is perhaps the best example of Scalia's complex dance with originalism. In the infamous *Plessy v. Ferguson* case of 1896, the Supreme Court upheld "separate but equal" facilities for whites and African Americans under the Fourteenth Amendment's Equal Protection Clause, a decision reversed in 1954 by *Brown v. Board of Education*. Originalists have gone through contortions to try to show that *Brown*, not *Plessy*, represented the true original public meaning of the Equal Protection Clause, even though in 1868, when the Fourteenth Amendment was ratified, separate but equal facilities were fully accepted. The same Congress that passed the Fourteenth Amendment also voted to segregate the District of Columbia's public schools, rendering an originalist interpretation supporting *Brown* problematic.[44]

In defending this position, Scalia ignored the original public meaning of the Equal Protection Clause and focused on a more purely textualist analysis. As he and Garner wrote in *Reading Law*: "The text of the Thirteenth and Fourteenth Amendments, and in particular the Equal Protection Clause of the Fourteenth Amendment, can reasonably be thought to prohibit all laws designed to assert the separateness and superiority of the white race, even those that purport to treat the races equally. Justice John Marshall Harlan took this position in his powerful (and thoroughly originalist) dissent in *Plessy v. Ferguson*." When law professor and head of the National Constitution Center Jeffrey Rosen confronted Scalia "at a convivial dinner" about the social practices at the time of ratification and the conflict with *Brown*, Scalia "replied, with a belly laugh, that no theory is perfect." As he did with Professor Dershowitz and others, Scalia deflected Rosen's legitimate questioning of selective use of originalism with a joke.[45]

Judge Posner notes that Scalia and Garner's reading of this history has been disputed by historians, and the source the authors relied upon for their originalist case, an article by Professor Michael McConnell, is not merely at odds with most of the historical evidence. Its analysis is based "on the legislative history of the Fourteenth Amendment, which should be anathema to Scalia."[46]

Scalia's position on affirmative action was even less originalist. When it came to separate but equal, he at least tried to justify his position on originalist understandings of the Fourteenth Amendment. On affirmative action, though, he was a firm opponent, even though at the very time of the passage of the Fourteenth Amendment, there was wide acceptance of laws giving legal advantages to African Americans, newly freed slaves who needed state aid in becoming self-sufficient. The original understanding of the Equal Protection Clause was that it did not bar raced-based remedies to ameliorate the effects of past discrimination. But Justice Scalia ignored this contemporaneous understanding and instead fell back on a purely textualist reading of the Equal Protection Clause as color-blind and forbidding almost all racial classifications.[47]

The dispute over race and the Equal Protection Clause shows that Scalia's originalism sometimes turned on purely textual analysis, while at other times he looked at contemporaneous understandings. If it matters whether people in 1789 thought the First Amendment contained an exemption for violent speech (as Scalia said in the violent video case, *Brown*), it should matter whether people in 1868 thought the Equal Protection Clause contained an exemption for laws helping past victims of discrimination.

Scalia was willing to look at understandings of the Equal Protection Clause at the time of enactment when it came to sex discrimination. He believed the Fourteenth Amendment did not bar discrimination on the basis of gender, because people in 1868 did not believe it did so (regardless of what the text of the amendment said). Consider his interview with Professor Calvin Massey in 2011, when Massey asked the justice whether the Fourteenth Amendment prohibits sex discrimination or sexual orientation discrimination given that in 1868, when Congress approved the Fourteenth Amendment, no one would have thought so:

> Yes, yes. Sorry, to tell you that. . . . But, you know, if indeed the current society has come to different views, that's fine. You do not need the Constitution to reflect the wishes of the current society. Certainly the Constitution does not require discrimination on the basis of sex. The only issue is whether it prohibits it. It doesn't. *Nobody ever thought that that's what it meant. Nobody ever voted for that.* If the current society wants to outlaw discrimination by sex, hey we have things called legislatures, and they enact things called laws.

You don't need a constitution to keep things up-to-date. All you need is a legislature and a ballot box. You don't like the death penalty anymore, that's fine. You want a right to abortion? There's nothing in the Constitution about that. But that doesn't mean you cannot prohibit it. Persuade your fellow citizens it's a good idea and pass a law. That's what democracy is all about. It's not about nine superannuated judges who have been there too long, imposing these demands on society.[48]

Scalia never fully resolved the tensions in his approach to originalism, but his writings inspired the emergence of an originalism industry, a network of law professors, judges, and lawyers dedicated to furthering conservative political causes through originalist methodology. This industry has produced a farm team of judges who, if appointed to the Supreme Court, might find Scalia too "faint-hearted."

Some liberals have also tried to coopt originalism, and even among conservative originalists, disputes about how to resolve difficult cases threaten to undermine the enterprise. The originalism industry, even as it grows in membership, is losing its message that it can provide definitive neutral answers to difficult constitutional questions.

In 2007, celebrating the twenty-fifth anniversary of the Federalist Society, Scalia remarked on the growth of originalism among law professors. "In the law schools . . . originalism has gained a foothold. I used to be able to say, with only mild hyperbole, that one could fire a cannon loaded with grapeshot in the faculty lounge of any major law school in the country and not strike an originalist. That is no longer possible. . . . Not all law schools, or even a majority of law schools have originalist professors; but being an originalist is no longer regarded as intellectually odd, if not un-intellectual."[49]

If anything, this statement undersold the growth of originalist ideas in legal scholarship. From 1980 to 1984, just 15 law review articles mentioned the term "originalism." From 1995 to 1999, there were 913 mentions, and from 2010 to 2014, there were 2,351. During the time Scalia was its most prominent advocate and (part-time) practitioner, mentions of originalism increased dramatically.[50]

The Federalist Society too has grown enormously. Professor Amanda

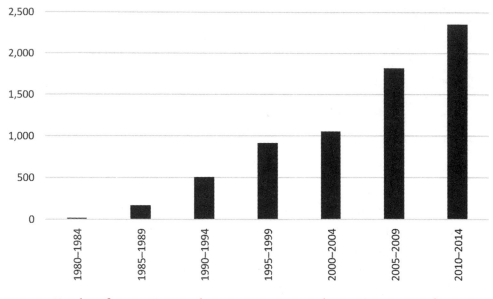

Number of Law Review Articles Mentioning "Originalism" (Five-year periods)
[Source: Author's examination of Westlaw database, 2017]

Hollis-Brusky reports that "the Federalist Society has matured into a nationwide network of more than forty thousand academics, practitioners, judges, politicians, and law students dedicated to reshaping America's institutions to reflect conservative and libertarian values." Its revenues exceeded $18 million in 2015.[51]

Originalists debate among themselves the original understandings of the meanings of constitutional clauses; what to do in cases when the original understanding is not definite enough to resolve a constitutional question, and the difference between "interpretation" of originalist provisions and a "construction zone" for judicial gap-filling; and how to resolve a conflict, as in *McDonald,* between originalist understanding and Supreme Court precedent. They take these debates very seriously, and judges who follow originalism do so as well.

Law professors and Federalist Society lawyers draft originalist arguments, which then get picked up by originalist judges and justices such as Clarence Thomas. Professor Hollis-Brusky has shown how originalist ideas in amicus briefs submitted by Federalist Society–networked lawyers make it into Justice Thomas's opinions, and this transmission of originalist analysis happens in state supreme courts and lower federal courts as well. The group's co-founder, Steven Calabresi, has said that the Federalist Society has "'absolutely' helped keep Justices such as Scalia, Thomas, Roberts, and Alito in check."[52]

Yet if you read enough originalist scholarship, you begin to see that originalist arguments may be employed to support a wide range of results, many of which likely would be anathema to Justice Scalia. For example, Scalia certainly believed that the Constitution contained no right of same-sex couples to marry, a position once echoed by Steven Calabresi. Now originalist scholars have crafted originalist cases for same-sex marriage, a development that might have Scalia turning in his grave. Indeed, even Calabresi in the past few years has changed his tune and made an originalist case for same-sex marriage. As (non-originalist) law professor Orin Kerr explained, these originalist arguments only appear to work if one considers issues of the meaning of "freedom" and "liberty" at the time of the enactment of the Fourteenth Amendment at a very high level of generality.[53]

This malleability of the theory has been noted by critics. As the former Stanford Law School dean Larry Kramer put it, "it is impossible to talk about the notion of an original public meaning, because at that point you really are just making it up from the top down. You are deciding what principles should have been used in the eighteenth century to determine public meaning, because those principles were never settled. You then use those principles, from which you can generate a variety of plausible interpretations, to pick one you think makes sense. Whatever that accomplishes, it is *not* ascertaining what would have been the original public meaning of the constitutional text at the time that text was adopted." He added that "most originalist work reads to me like essays people write about America in French or German papers. They may not misstate facts, but they are very far off in nuance and feel."[54]

Originalism has become so well established that liberals have seen the benefit in coopting it, if only to offer potentially appealing arguments to judicial originalists. The liberal constitutional scholar Jack Balkin has crafted a liberal approach to originalism as a kind of transgressive appropriation of the originalist project. No doubt in an effort to troll Justice Scalia, he titled his book *Living Originalism*. We know from Scalia's response in 2015 to the *University of Chicago Law Review* that he never intended to read it.[55]

A liberal public interest law firm, the Constitutional Accountability Center, has set itself the task of providing "text and history" arguments in *amicus curiae* briefs, remaking originalist ideas with a liberal hue. Justice Stevens, in his dissent in the controversial *Citizens United v. Federal Election Commission* case in 2010, offered an originalist argument as to why the founders would have allowed limits on corporate money in politics, provoking a strong response from Scalia. Law professor Larry Solum, testifying in favor of Justice Gorsuch's confirmation to the Supreme Court, aided this mainstreaming of originalism by claiming, incorrectly I believe, that it cabined discretion and should be embraced by progressives and liberals.[56]

As originalism flourishes among conservative law professors, its future relevance in the courts depends in part on who wins presidential elections and whom those presidents appoint to office. The example of Justice Alito shows that not all conservative jurists are originalists, and a Republican president could well appoint conservative non-originalists. In spite of efforts by Professors Akhil Reed Amar and Solum, neither are most liberals likely to adopt originalism except for strategic ends.

But President Trump's first appointment to the Supreme Court penned an ode to Justice Scalia and his modes of interpretation shortly after Scalia's death. Justice Neil Gorsuch wrote that "the great project of Justice Scalia's career was to remind us of the differences between judges and legislators." While legislators "may appeal to their own moral convictions and to claims about social utility to reshape the law," judges should not do so. They should instead "strive (if humanly and so imperfectly) to apply the law as it is, focusing backward, not forward, and looking to text structure, and history to decide what a reasonable reader at the time of the events in question would have understood the law to be—not to decide cases based on their own moral convictions or the policy consequences they believe might serve society best."[57]

Not only did Justice Gorsuch pledge fidelity to the Scalian originalist project. He also believed that these language-based tools could provide definitive answers to most questions. He wrote that "the amount of indeterminacy in the law is often (wildly) exaggerated," pegging the number of hard cases as very small, maybe 0.014 percent of all cases. In Gorsuch, Scalia seems to have found a worthy heir.[58]

No one knows how many justices each president will get to appoint, and Democratic presidents are less likely to appoint either originalists or conservatives. But originalism could still flourish on the Supreme Court, as well as state supreme courts and lower federal courts. With a young Justice Gorsuch on the Court, it is hard to see any reason for the originalism industry to reduce its prodigious output.

⚖️

The notion that judges can use originalist methods to "find" or "discover" the law, rather than make it, has proven to be an illusion. Instead, originalism looks like a subconscious crutch or, worse, a fig leaf, a pretext justifying a result that lines up with one's ideology. Should it surprise anyone that the originalist analyses of the liberal Justice Stevens in the *Citizens United* and *Heller* cases supported more liberal results than the originalist analyses of Justice Scalia? No doubt Scalia's response would be that Stevens was misusing originalism, while he was not. But with so much malleability to the approach, who could say? It certainly seemed as malleable as other constitutional approaches.

Much of original understanding is in the eye of the beholder. In cases involving vaguely worded constitutional terms and deep ideological divisions, we should expect judicial decisionmaking to be influenced more by ideology and values than methodology.

Scalia was not more ideologically driven or results-oriented than his fellow justices. In *Bush v. Gore*, for example, the controversial case that ended the recount of votes in Florida in the presidential election of 2000 and thus gave the election to the Republican candidate, George W. Bush, all of the conservative justices embraced a liberal reading of the Equal Protection Clause that favored Bush, and all of the liberal justices embraced a conservative reading of the same clause, which favored Gore.[59] Scalia, however, held himself out as better than the other justices because he applied allegedly neutral principles. He promised that his brand of originalism and textualism would free judges from imposing their values on society.

At this point in history, the project appears to have failed.

4

Mr. Justice Scalia, the Fish

PAUL CLEMENT, ONE OF THE NATION'S leading Supreme Court litigators, had a great fish tale to share at the Federalist Society's National Student Symposium in Charlottesville, Virginia, in 2016, just a few weeks after Antonin Scalia's death.[1]

Clement, a former Scalia clerk and solicitor general of the United States who has argued more than eighty cases before the Supreme Court, was not the first to tell the story. He attributed it to Judge Jay Bybee of the United States Court of Appeals for the Ninth Circuit. Bybee, formerly a professor at Louisiana State University and the University of Nevada at Las Vegas and later a Bush Justice Department official who was involved in approving the use of "enhanced interrogation techniques" on detainees at Guantánamo Bay military prison, assured Clement the story was true. Clement related it with great detail and good humor, using it to make a point about Scalia's relationship with the other justices.[2]

Here is how Clement told it:

> So a few years back, Justice Scalia visited LSU's Law School where Judge Bybee was then teaching. Now it's not every day that a Supreme Court Justice makes it to Baton Rouge. Think there was good hunting there. But this event was quite an event on campus and numerous law students gathered for their chance to meet the Justice. But there was one student in particular who was really intent on meeting the Justice because he was a particularly big fan.

Now there was a reception line and the Justice in his gracious and inimi-table way was talking briefly to all of the students [as they] funneled passed him. And this one student who was really intent on meeting the Justice came through the line and Judge Bybee happened to be right behind him so he could overhear this interaction. And this law student was pretty nervous, frankly, about having the chance to meet his judicial idol.

So he . . . sheepishly came up to the Justice and said, "Mr. Justice, it's re-ally a pleasure to meet you." And you know, the Justice had probably heard that a hundred times that night already and so very graciously shook his hand and . . . wished him luck.

And then the student had one other line that actually . . . Justice Scalia hadn't heard . . . earlier that night. And . . . the student said to the Justice, "Justice, I'm such a big fan of you and your jurisprudence. I actually named my . . . pet fish after you."

And so the Justice got this twinkle in his eye, and he said, "So you called it 'Nino'?"

And the student said, "No, no. I wouldn't be that familiar. I named my fish 'Mr. Justice Scalia.'"

And the Justice thought this was great. And he talked to the student a little bit more and then . . . they had to get on with the rest of the line. And Judge Bybee was also pretty intrigued by this. So he came up to the student afterwards, and he asked him, "So do you have other fish named after Jus-tices? Do you have the whole court in your fishbowl?"

And the law student said, "No, I only name fish after justices I like." And so then Judge Bybee was understandably intrigued at this point because he wanted to know which justices got a fish and which justices didn't get a fish. And so he asked him, "So . . . which fish do you have . . . named after justices?"

And then the student looked at him and said, "Well actually, Professor . . . Mr. Justice Scalia is the only fish I have left. He killed all the other justices."

As the audience roared with laughter, Clement continued to the point of his story:

I do want to close by noting Mr. Justice Scalia, the Fish, may well have killed the other justices, but one of the great things about Justice Scalia is that he actually got along incredibly well with the other justices. And par-ticularly his friendships with Justice Ginsburg and with Justice Kagan more recently: the sort of friendships . . . across . . . normal voting patterns in some of the most closely watched cases. You know, [it] is really one of the kind of enduring things that he left . . . He gave a model of how you could absolutely destroy somebody in a dissent, and then turn around and invite them to dinner or plan . . . a gathering to the opera.

It is no surprise that the audience cheered the suggestion that Mr. Justice Scalia, the fish, killed all the other judicial fish. In contrast, Mr. Justice Scalia, the person, was held in high regard not only by Clement and his Federalist Society compatriots but also by some important liberal figures. Scalia and Ruth Bader Ginsburg were close friends who spent every New Year's Eve together with their spouses for decades. They were once pictured joyfully riding an elephant together in India, and they were interviewed about attending the opening of an opera about them, "Scalia/Ginsburg." More recently, Elena Kagan, another Court liberal, learned to hunt with Scalia.[3]

Despite these well-publicized friendships, to other liberals Scalia was a polarizing figure who used humor in a demeaning and condescending way, sometimes to punch down at lawyers at oral argument, and often to claim his path or interpretation as the only legitimate one. Love him or hate him, few who followed his words and work lacked an opinion. It was Sonia Sotomayor who perhaps best expressed the ambivalence, saying that Scalia's death was like losing a family member, but jokingly adding, "There are things he said on the bench where if I had a baseball bat, I might have used it."[4]

Justice Scalia was a charmer who often played for laughs at the Supreme Court's oral argument and at public engagements. In Professor Jay Wexler's 2005 study of laughs justices elicited at Supreme Court oral arguments for the previous term, Scalia was at the top of the list, way ahead of the other justices.[5]

An engaging and interesting writer on a Court whose other justices could make even the most pressing social and legal issues seem mind-numbingly boring, Scalia wrote with clarity and panache, reviving unfamiliar terms like "argle bargle" (nonsense) and "jiggery pokery" (trickery). He was a gregarious public intellectual who reinvigorated a tradition of justices acting as public speakers, and then took it to the next level. He transformed the usually sleepy process of oral argument at the Court into a "hot bench" where litigants struggle to get a word in edgewise and Chief Justice John Roberts must play traffic cop.[6]

And yet in his opinions and public appearances, Scalia displayed an unparalleled level of nastiness and sarcasm. Like his namesake fish, he was a killer with his words, especially in his dissents, where his tone and rhetoric were calculated. As he explained in 1994: "It's always more fun to write dissents if we are talking about just sheer fun because you just write for yourself. You know you can be as outrageous as you like because you don't care if anybody joins you or not. Right? Whereas, when you're writing a majority opinion, . . . you're writing for others as well. You have to be sensitive to their wishes and desires. You cannot say things like, you know, substantive due process is ridiculous—you can't do that in a majority opinion. So it's always more fun to write dissents. But you know, it's a strange kind of fun—you cry the whole time you're laughing."[7]

He said that he wrote as he did to get the attention of law students, the next generation of lawyers, as his stinging dissents got picked up disproportionately in casebooks: "They will read dissents that are breezy and have some thrust to them. That's who I write for." He told Clarence Thomas's biographers that he liked to make his dissents "pizzazzy." And it worked. A Harvard Law School student entry in a contest to produce humorous law school music videos featured "Rather Read," about a group of liberal law students who were bored reading cases in casebooks; they would "rather read" Scalia's "snarky" opinions.[8]

But if Scalia's harsh words were intended to cajole his colleagues into adopting his positions, it did not work. Instead, both his opinions and his public comments served to coarsen judicial discourse and may have helped undermine the legitimacy of the institution he appeared to love so dearly.

The best way to convey Scalia's language and sarcasm is to offer some examples from his written opinions. We have already seen his infamous "hide my head in a bag" comment about the *Obergefell* case, in response to Justice Kennedy's majority opinion establishing the constitutional right for same-sex couples to marry—an opinion Scalia described as "couched in a style that is as pretentious as its content is egotistic."[9]

In a case concerning the constitutionality of executing cognitively disa-bled persons, he remarked, "Seldom has an opinion of this Court rested so obviously upon nothing but the personal views of its Members." In a civil rights[case], sticking up for the non-elites he thought were always getting the short end of the stick at the Court, he ended his dissent by stating, "The irony is that these individuals—predominantly unknown, unaffluent, unor-ganized—suffer this injustice at the hands of a Court fond of thinking itself the champion of the politically impotent." In a gender discrimination case, he wrote: "Today's opinion is an inspiring demonstration of how thoroughly up-to-date and right-thinking we Justices are in matters pertaining to the sexes (or as the Court would have it, the genders), and how sternly we dis-approve the male chauvinist attitudes of our predecessors. The price to be paid for this display—a modest price, surely—is that most of the opinion is quite irrelevant to the case at hand."[10]

In an abortion rights case he wrote: "The emptiness of the 'reasoned judgment' that produced *Roe* [*v. Wade*] is displayed in plain view by the fact that, after more than 19 years of effort by some of the brightest (and most determined) legal minds in the country, after more than 10 cases upholding abortion rights in this Court, and after dozens upon dozens of *amicus* briefs submitted in these and other cases, the best the Court can do to explain how it is that the word 'liberty' *must* be thought to include the right to destroy human fetuses is to rattle off a collection of adjectives that simply decorate a value judgment and conceal a political choice." In a concurring opinion in a substantive due process case, he wrote: "Today's opinion gives the lie to those cynics who claim that changes in this Court's jurisprudence are at-tributable to changes in the Court's membership. It proves that the changes are attributable to nothing but the passage of time (not much time, at that), plus application of the ancient maxim, 'That was then, this is now.'"[11]

Dean Erwin Chemerinsky has catalogued other caustic statements, espe-cially in dissents: "Justice Scalia describes the majority's approaches as 'noth-ing short of ludicrous' and 'beyond the absurd,' 'entirely irrational,' and not 'pass[ing] the most gullible scrutiny.' He has declared that a majority opin-ion is 'nothing short of preposterous' and 'has no foundation in American constitutional law, and barely pretends to.' He talks about how 'one must grieve for the Constitution' because of a majority's approach. He calls the approaches taken in majority opinions 'preposterous,' and 'so unsupported in reason and so absurd in application [as] unlikely to survive.' He speaks of how a majority opinion 'vandaliz[es] . . . our people's traditions.'"[12]

Chemerinsky noted that much of the sarcasm in these opinions was aimed at Scalia's colleagues. At various times, Scalia called other justices' arguments "bizarre," "grotesque," and "incoherent."[13]

⚖️

These examples tell only part of the story. It was not only that Scalia was caustic and sarcastic; it is that his sarcasm greatly exceeded anything coming from other justices and made him an outlier on a Court whose members often went out of their way to appear courteous and to understate the full extent of their emotions over disagreements.

In a database of thousands of law review articles, a search for descriptions of any justice's opinion as "sarcastic" or "caustic" turns up references to 134 cases decided between 1986, when Scalia joined the Court, through 2013. Seventy-five of the opinions described as "sarcastic" or "caustic" were Justice Scalia's. The next highest total belongs to Justice Stevens, who had 9. The median justice had 3.5 such references. Chief Justice Roberts and Justice Sotomayor had none.

Raw numbers tell only part of the story, because justices' terms on the Court vary in length. By calculating the number of opinions per year labeled sarcastic or caustic, we can generate a "Sarcasm Index." This shows us that Justice Scalia's sarcasm is off the charts (though not off this one): he has more than five and a half times the number of the next most sarcastic justice, and more than fifteen times the median.

Of the 75 sarcastic Scalia opinions referenced in law journals, 42 appear in (at least partially) dissenting opinions and 15 appear in (at least partially) concurring opinions.

Perhaps these statistics overstate things. Law review authors, who are mostly law professors, skew liberal, and perhaps they were more apt to call a conservative justice's comments "sarcastic" than a liberal's. As former Scalia clerk Ed Whelan put it in a panel discussion, "Sarcastic is the liberal word for a conservative who's funny."[14]

But none of the other justices—liberal, conservative, or otherwise—came

Sarcasm Index: Average Number of Justices' Opinions Labeled Sarcastic or Caustic per Year, Through 2013

Justice	Opinions Labeled "Sarcastic" or "Caustic"	Years on Court through 2013	Sarcasm Index (Sarcastic opinions per year)
Scalia	75	27	2.78
Alito	3	7	0.43
Blackmun	8	24	0.33
Kagan	1	3	0.33
Stevens	9	35	0.26
Rehnquist	8	33	0.24
Thomas	5	22	0.23
Souter	4	19	0.21
White	6	31	0.19
Marshall	4	24	0.17
Brennan	5	34	0.15
Kennedy	2	25	0.08
Powell	1	15	0.07
Breyer	1	19	0.05
Ginsburg	1	20	0.05
O'Connor	1	25	0.04
Sotomayor	0	4	0
Roberts	0	8	0

Source: Richard L. Hasen, "The Most Sarcastic Justice," 18 *Green Bag* 2d 215 (2015)

close to Scalia on the Sarcasm Index even though some of them do try to be funny. Justice Thomas is more conservative than Scalia, yet in twenty-two years of opinions he wrote only five that are described as sarcastic. He has an index of 0.23, compared to Scalia's 2.78.

Scalia saw himself as "a snoot . . . Snoots are nit-pickers for the *mot juste*, for using a word precisely the way it should be used." But that definition does not capture the harsh irony he so often employed. He admitted in 2013 that his "tone is sometimes sharp. But I think sharpness is sometimes needed to demonstrate how much of a departure I believe the thing is. Especially in my dissents . . ."[15]

This sharpness was accompanied by a remarkable lack of self-awareness. He told an interviewer in 2013: "One of the things that upsets me about modern society is the coarseness of manners. You can't go to a movie—or watch a television show for that matter—without hearing the constant use of the F-word—including, you know, *ladies* using it. People that I know don't talk like that! But if you portray it a lot, the society's going to become that way. It's very sad." In an interview in 2006, he lamented the loss of our "decent, respectful culture."[16]

Scalia was not reported to have used foul language in public, though he caused controversy in 2006 with a gesture to a reporter that some considered obscene. A Supreme Court spokesperson later described it as "a hand off the chin gesture that was meant to be dismissive." Foul language or hand motions, though, are not the only ways to be coarse or disrespectful. As Professor Adam Winkler wrote in response to Scalia's 2006 complaint, "While Scalia may be right about the underlying development in American culture—even though the discourse from earlier eras, such as the pre–Civil War days, was also quite coarse—what makes this complaint so funny is that it comes from the Supreme Court Justice who has made rude, mocking rebuttal of other Justices' arguments an art form."[17]

⚖

Did Scalia's unusually sharp rhetoric influence the Court's decisions, its reputation, or the greater legal culture? He maintained in an interview from 2013 that he never regretted his tone: "It never cost me a majority. And you ought to be reluctant to think that any justice of the Supreme Court would make a case come out the other way just to spite Scalia. Nobody would do that. You're dealing with significant national issues. You're dealing with real litigants—no."[18]

Despite rumors to the contrary, this statement does not appear to be contradicted by anything that has come out of other justices' court papers. Professor Jeffrey Rosen noted in 2006 that "some scholars argued that Scalia's relentless personal attacks on O'Connor and Kennedy dissuaded them from overturning *Roe v. Wade*" in a 1992 opinion, *Planned Parenthood v. Casey*. But those claims do not mesh with what we know about the drafting of the joint opinion in the case by Justices Kennedy, O'Connor, and Souter. At most, Scalia failed to persuade Kennedy to change his mind.[19]

A much harder question to answer is whether Scalia could have written more majority opinions and achieved greater Court acceptance of his theories of textualism and originalism, had he not been so strident. Some argued that Scalia pushed O'Connor and Kennedy from the right to the center. At the very least, human nature suggests that his constant personal barbs questioning his colleagues' intelligence and integrity made them less receptive to his ideas.

This claim is hard to evaluate. Professor Mark Tushnet doubts that Scalia's tone and rhetoric mattered: "The effect of personal relations among the justices has to be swamped by their effect on those positions, except occasionally and mostly at the margins." He described Scalia's style as "the sound bite style of *Crossfire,* highly quotable, reducing complex issues to simple—and often misleading—phrases." Some justices publicly brushed off concerns about tone, with Stevens writing of Scalia's "wonderfully spontaneous sense of humor." Even privately, some justices who disagreed strongly on the merits of decisions got along personally with Scalia, at least at times. He and the liberal Harry Blackmun rarely agreed on outcomes in the controversial cases, but they bonded as the grammar police, exchanging notes as members of "The Chancellor's English Society" whose aim was "to identify and stamp out illiteracies and barbaric neologisms in legal writing—or at least to commiserate about them."[20]

Ginsburg's statement about Scalia, presaging Sotomayor's "baseball bat" comment, furthered his image as an incorrigible curmudgeon: "I love him. But sometimes I'd like to strangle him." Other judgments were harsher. Justice Lewis Powell's biographer, John C. Jeffries, Jr., wrote: "Politically Powell and Scalia were not so far apart but personally they were like oil and water. . . . His volubility struck Powell as bad manners. In Scalia's first oral argument, he asked so many questions that Powell whispered . . . 'Do you think he knows that the rest of us are here?'" O'Connor was clearly irritated with Scalia's insults to her jurisprudence, such as when he called one of her opinions "irrational." Joan Biskupic reports that such comments "got under O'Connor's skin," though "for the most part she could take it—or at least appear to take it. 'Well it is better than a punch in the nose,' she said when one of her clerks brought her a draft of a Scalia opinion concurring in her bottom-line judgment but offering a competing legal rationale."[21]

Some justices worried about how Scalia's criticism of O'Connor affected the Court. Once, after reading a draft Scalia dissent attacking O'Connor, Chief Justice Rehnquist called Scalia to admonish him: "Nino, you are pissing off Sandra again. . . . Stop it!" For his part, Scalia brushed off the concern. "Sandra may not have liked an occasional barb in one of my opinions, but I considered her a good friend and I think she considered me a good friend."[22]

Even within the confines of the Court, out of public view, Scalia was no shrinking violet. According to Edward Lazarus, he would sometimes fire off "what several other Justices (some fondly and others not) referred to as a Ninogram—generally a one-or two-page, single-spaced and always colorful legal polemic on a pending case."[23]

While we may never know the extent to which Scalia squandered his opportunity for influence by trying to catch flies with vinegar rather than honey, his rhetoric may have adversely affected the tone of legal argument generally as well as the Court's legitimacy. As Chemerinsky argued: "No doubt, [Scalia's sarcasm] makes his opinions among the most entertaining to read. He has a great flair for language and does not mince words when he disagrees with a position. But I think this sends exactly the wrong message to law students and attorneys about what type of discourse is appropriate in a formal legal setting and what is acceptable in speaking to one another." He reports that students and lawyers became much more likely to emulate Scalia's harsh language in legal briefs. Even students who are not swayed by Scalia's legal arguments try to imitate his pungency.[24]

What's worse, Scalia's rhetoric took aim at the legitimacy of the Supreme Court's decisionmaking. His sarcasm was rarely *ad hominem* but more often made the point that the majority was usurping judicial power. The justices on the other side of the issue were sometimes described as not even acting as judges, but instead acting in bad faith as politicians in robes.

Consider, for example, another statement from Scalia's *Obergefell* dissent, which some observers mistakenly interpreted as a call for greater diversity on the Court. He wrote that the majority's interpretation of the Fourteenth Amendment to include a right of same-sex couples to marry "is a naked judicial claim to legislative—indeed, *super*-legislative—power; a claim fundamentally at odds with our system of government. Except as limited by a constitutional prohibition agreed to by the People, the States are free to adopt whatever laws they like, even those that offend the esteemed Justices' 'reasoned judgment.' A system of government that makes the People subordinate to a committee of nine unelected lawyers does not deserve to be called a democracy."

He then tied this point to the question of the lack of diversity among the judiciary and what he viewed as its elite biases:

> Judges are selected precisely for their skill as lawyers; whether they reflect the policy views of a particular constituency is not (or should not be) relevant. Not surprisingly then, the Federal Judiciary is hardly a cross-section of America. Take, for example, this Court, which consists of only nine men and women, all of them successful lawyers who studied at Harvard or Yale Law School. Four of the nine are natives of New York City. Eight of them grew up in east- and west-coast States. Only one hails from the vast expanse in-between. Not a single Southwesterner or even, to tell the truth, a genuine Westerner (California does not count). Not a single evangelical Christian (a group that comprises about one quarter of Americans), or even a Protestant of any denomination. The strikingly unrepresentative character of the body voting on today's social upheaval would be irrelevant if they were functioning as *judges,* answering the legal question whether the American people had ever ratified a constitutional provision that was understood to proscribe the traditional definition of marriage. But of course the Justices in today's majority are not voting on that basis; *they say they are not.* And to allow the policy question of same-sex marriage to be considered and resolved by a select, patrician, highly unrepresentative panel of nine is to violate a principle even more fundamental than no taxation without representation: no social transformation without representation.[25]

Scalia's key point here, as Ed Whelan noted, is not the need for greater diversity on the Court. It is that "if the justices 'were functioning as *judges*'" (Scalia's emphasis), their "strikingly unrepresentative character . . . would be irrelevant." Diversity is only required, according to Scalia, because the Supreme Court justices are functioning not as judges but as "super-legislators."

Scalia also cannot resist a dig at liberal California, which "does not count" as the American West.[26]

Scalia's dismissal of his fellow justices' good faith in reaching conclusions contrary to his views contributed to popular cynicism about Supreme Court decisionmaking. A harder question is whether it moved public opinion. While Scalia was a member of the Court, the public's opinion of the institution declined. In January 2001, right after the controversial decision in the *Bush v. Gore* case ending the disputed Florida election of 2000, Gallup measured the Court's public approval rating at 59 percent, with disapproval at 25 percent. By July 2016, its approval was 42 percent and its disapproval 52 percent.[27]

It is impossible to say whether Scalia's coarsening rhetoric contributed to the decline, but it certainly could not have helped. His constant claims that the majority's decisions were illegitimate, and not even true acts of judging, served as a model for populist denunciations of elitist Court decisions. It was a position later echoed by many of his followers, including Whelan, who writes a regular column for *National Review Online* entitled "This Day in Liberal Judicial Activism." As partisan talk about the Court has increased, public opinion about the Court has grown increasingly polarized. Republicans in 2016 were much less likely than Democrats to approve of the job the Supreme Court was doing (26 percent approving, versus 67 percent for Democrats), with two-thirds of Republicans telling pollsters that the Court is too liberal.[28]

The question of the relationship of Scalia's rhetoric to public approval of the Court is complex. No doubt, other factors contribute to the Court's falling approval rating, including a general decline in trust in all government institutions. In recent years, approval of the Supreme Court seems higher among those in the president's party than among those in the opposition. Another factor might be public approval or rejection of particular Supreme Court decisions. Here the evidence is mixed. Public support for same-sex marriage has been steadily increasing, even after *Obergefell*, while support for the Court has decreased. But a large majority of Americans believe that *Citizens United*, which freed corporate money in candidate elections, was wrongly decided. The public disapproved of *Citizens United* soon after the decision was announced, and continues to disapprove of it.[29]

Justice Scalia was thus on the wrong side of public opinion in both the same-sex marriage and campaign finance cases, but it may have been the Court's decisions, rather his rhetoric, driving public opinion.

⚖⚖

Justice Scalia's tirades against the legitimacy of more liberal Court decisions helped to put him in the spotlight and create a new role for the justices: partisan celebrities. He styled himself a reluctant one, even as he hammed it up for audiences. In a 2008 interview on C-SPAN, interviewer and Scalia friend Brian Lamb asked him how he felt about a bobblehead doll of him being offered by the lighthearted legal journal *Green Bag* and about the sale of T-shirts featuring his name. Scalia noted that his was the most popular of all the Supreme Court justice bobbleheads ("maybe people are using it for dart practice," he quipped), and then turned to his role as a celebrity. With what Court reporter Tony Mauro described as an "air of resignation," Scalia said: "Well, frankly, Brian, that's one reason I've sort of come out of the closet—and in recent months done more interviews and allowed my talks to be televised more than I did formerly. I've sort of come to the conclusion that the old common law tradition of judges not making public spectacles of themselves and hiding in the grass has just broken down. It's no use. I'm going to be a public spectacle whether I come out of the closet or not, beyond T-shirts and bobblehead dolls and what-not. So if, you know, I'm going to be a public figure, I guess the public may as well get their notion of me firsthand rather than filtered through people such as Brian Lamb."[30]

When asked whether his celebrity was like "Greta Garbo joining Facebook," Scalia again demurred: "Come on. It hasn't been that—you know, part of it is I have a book I'm trying to promote but some of it is just that I, at the urging of friends and family members, I've decided to be less reclusive."[31]

Scalia was hardly reclusive before 2008. He made at least 178 publicly reported appearances between 1986, when he joined the Court, and 2014. But there is no question that these appearances came in waves, with an initial early set, followed by a period of very few appearances, followed by what was called the "charm offensive" corresponding to the release of his books in 2008 and 2012. The number of his publicly reported appearances and interviews peaked in 2012 at 23.[32]

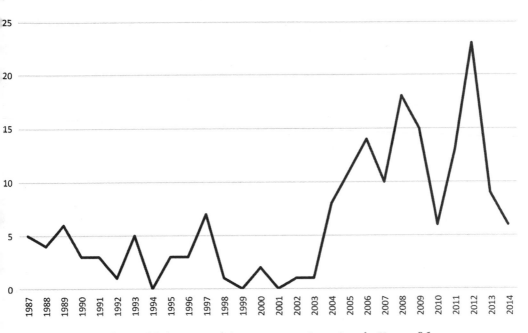

Justice Scalia's Publicly Reported Appearances or Interviews by Year, 1986–2014
[Source: Author's compilation of data, as derived from Richard L. Hasen, "Celebrity
Justice: Supreme Court Edition," 19 *Green Bag* 2d 157 (2016)]

Although he was off the charts on the Sarcasm Index, Scalia was not
such an outlier when it came to the number of publicly reported appearances and interviews. Looking at all justices on the Court from 1960 to
2014, nine of the top ten in public appearances were members of the Court
at the time Scalia died in 2016, and among that group, he was in the middle
of the pack.

Collectively, justices' public appearances have cycled from moderate to
low to very high. In the 1960s, William Douglas, Arthur Goldberg, and
Chief Justice Earl Warren engaged in a fair bit of extrajudicial speech, perhaps because they had been politicians and public figures before serving on
the Court. Some of the drop in the 1970s may have been due to a change of
chief justice. Chief Justice Burger discouraged oral dissents, and perhaps
extrajudicial speech as well.[33]

Appearances really took off once Scalia joined the Court. My research
identified 192 publicly reported appearances or interviews for all the sitting

Publicly Reported Appearances and Interviews of Supreme Court Justices, 1960–2014

Justice	Total Reported Appearances/ Interviews	Years on Court, 1960–2014	Celebrity Index
Sotomayor	65	5	13
Breyer	214	20	10.7
Goldberg	31	3	10.33
Ginsburg	194	21	9.24
Thomas	174	23	7.57
Scalia	178	28	6.36
Alito	52	9	5.78
Roberts	51	9	5.67
Kennedy	139	27	5.15
Kagan	20	4	5
Burger	74	17	4.35
Fortas	16	4	4
Rehnquist	130	34	3.82
Clark	25	7	3.57
Douglas	56	16	3.5
Warren	29	9	3.22
Stevens	61	35	1.74
O'Connor	37	24	1.54
Souter	27	19	1.42
Marshall	31	24	1.29
Brennan	37	31	1.19
Blackmun	26	24	1.08
Frankfurter	3	3	1
Powell	12	15	0.8
Whittaker	2	3	0.67
White	16	31	0.52
Black	6	12	0.5
Stewart	8	22	0.36
Harlan	4	12	0.33

Source: Richard L. Hasen, "Celebrity Justice: Supreme Court Edition," 19 *Green Bag* 2d 157 (2016)

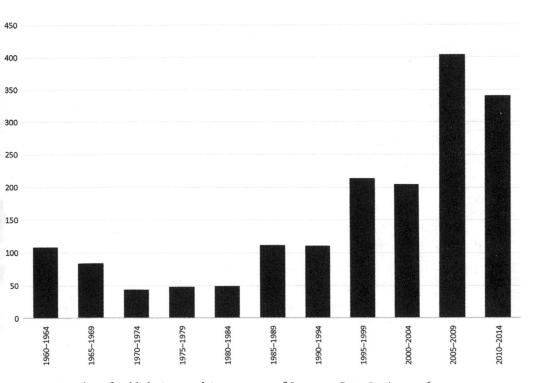

Number of Publicly Reported Appearances of Supreme Court Justices, 1960–2014
[Source: Richard L. Hasen, "Celebrity Justice: Supreme Court Edition," 19
Green Bag 2d 157 (2016)]

justices between 1960 and 1969. This number fell by more than half (to 91) in the 1970s. But it nearly doubled in each successive decade from the 1970s to the 2000s, and in the last decade of Scalia's life (2005–2014), it rose to 744, an eightfold increase since the 1970s.

How responsible was Scalia for this trend? Although he was not the most prolific public speaker, the nature and tone of his appearances could well have inspired others to counter him. When he did speak, he pulled no punches. No modern justice had spoken so candidly and provocatively. And as he put out books on jurisprudence, others did as well, leading not only to extra income for the justices but to book tours and other talks.

Scalia set a tone of outrageousness in public speaking just at the time that social media made it much easier for such comments to be shared, praised, and criticized. The country moved from *Green Bag* bobbleheads to the deification and memeification of justices—Scalia by those on the right and Justice Ginsburg, now known as the "Notorious R.B.G." (after the late rap star Notorious B.I.G.) on the left—and the demonization of justices on the opposite side of the aisle. Perhaps this polarization is what emboldened Ginsburg to break protocol and publicly oppose the election of Donald Trump in 2016.[34]

Although Scalia could dish it out, he did not take criticism as well. At a 2009 appearance in Florida, a college student asked him why he opposed cameras in the Supreme Court's courtroom even though justices were willing to speak to public audiences to promote their books. He dismissed the perfectly reasonable query as a "nasty, impolite question," and a week later told the journalist Joan Biskupic: "I do not mind difficult questions. The part of any appearance I enjoy the most is the Q-and-A. But hers was not just a hard question. It was intentionally nasty [and] calculated to embarrass. I'm doing her a favor to answer her question. I shouldn't have to put up with her abuse."[35]

By the mid-2000s, justices were in full celebrity mode. Sonia Sotomayor, while publicizing her book *My Beloved World,* appeared with the Muppets on *Sesame Street.* She and Samuel Alito each threw out the first pitch at baseball games. Sotomayor and Clarence Thomas were active in speaking to high school groups, especially in poor and minority areas, preaching a message of education and opportunity.

While much of this activity helped to demystify the Court, other activities were more partisan, especially in an era when all the conservative justices on the Court have been appointed by Republican presidents and all the liberals by Democrats. Liberals were incensed when Scalia told them to "get over" *Bush v. Gore.* Conservatives believe Ginsburg says too much about pending cases and should recuse herself. Alito's appearances before conservative groups raising funds have drawn liberal criticism.

Liberals may feel that conservative justices' appearances at Federalist Society events undermine the rule of law, and conservatives may see liberal justices' appearances at American Constitution Society events the same way. It probably does not help that only conservative justices speak at the annual Federalist Society events and only liberal ones at the American Constitution Society. This politicization started with Scalia's role in helping the

Federalist Society get off the ground. Other justices were not making such political appearances before he did.

Scalia's public outspokenness extended to the Court itself. He ratcheted up the rhetoric at oral argument, turning the Court's sleepy discussions into more lively affairs. A study in 2013 found that he asked the most questions at oral argument, an average of twenty-two questions per case. The study also found that Justice Breyer "is the wordiest Justice and Scalia is the second wordiest." Biskupic described him at oral argument as "a showman, a streetwise guy, and a pulverizer—as aggressive an advocate as any of the lawyers who stood at the lectern to make their cases."[36]

⚖️

In April 2015, a few weeks before oral argument in the *Obergefell* case, a group called 99Rise, made up of left-wing activists unhappy with the Supreme Court's campaign finance decisions, engaged in a rare series of protests inside the Court. They would stand during the Court's very formal oral argument and shout slogans such as "one person, one vote" until they were escorted out by marshals. During the arrests in the courtroom, Scalia could be heard muttering that they should get "stiff, stiff sentences."[37]

Another protester showed up at the *Obergefell* oral argument, but he was of a different political persuasion. Just as the plaintiffs' lawyer Mary L. Bonauto finished her argument in favor of a constitutional right of same-sex couples to marry, and before United States solicitor general Donald Verrilli began his argument, the protestor began shouting something that sounded like this: "People who support gay marriage, you will burn in hell for eternity . . . It is an abomination from God!"[38]

Chief Justice Roberts gave Verrilli a moment to gather his thoughts before his presentation as Supreme Court marshals removed the protestor. Scalia, who often cracks jokes at oral argument, said before Verrilli began: "It was rather refreshing, actually." The Court's small public audience of reporters, lawyers, and spectators (some of whom had paid up to $6,000 to companies that hire people to stand in line for them so they could get a rare public seat at the high-profile argument) laughed heartily at Scalia's joke. Others took offense.

New Yorker columnist Jeffrey Toobin wrote that Scalia, not the protestor, was the real embarrassment, because he appeared to endorse the protestor's message. Toobin, a noted critic of the justice, said that Scalia "further established his reputation as the Fox News Justice."[39] More likely, Scalia the class clown meant only that it was nice to hear from a right-wing protester after all the leftist interruptions from 99Rise.

By the end of his life, whatever filter Scalia had used to self-censor his comments seemed to be fraying. A few days after the Court issued the *Obergefell* ruling, it had a public session to announce an opinion in a totally unrelated case, *Glossip v. Gross.* In *Glossip,* the five most conservative justices, including Scalia, held that Oklahoma's drugs used for lethal injections did not violate the Eighth Amendment's prohibition on cruel and unusual punishment.[40]

When a justice is particularly unhappy with the result in a case, that justice may present a spoken dissent from the bench in addition to issuing the traditional written dissent. In *Glossip,* both Justice Sotomayor and Justice Breyer gave oral dissents, and Breyer, joined by Justice Ginsburg, took the position that the death penalty itself was unconstitutional.

In a very unusual move for a justice concurring in a majority opinion, Scalia chose to speak after the dissenters spoke, and his topic was *Obergefell.* *Slate* reporter Dahlia Lithwick, who was in the courtroom for the *Glossip* announcement, described the scene: "Scalia announced—*after* the reading of the dissents—that he was concurring in the majority opinion but had some things to say about the dissents. [He] deviated from his written concurrence in some really odd ways. And while I don't want to spend too much more time on Scalia acting oddly, this was *very* odd. He opened his statement—which seemed not to have been written down, and didn't really track his written opinion—with: 'Last Friday five justices of this court took the issue' of same-sex marriage away from the voters based on their 'policy preferences' and then noted that today two justices sought to do that again, with the call to abolish the death penalty. In case you were wondering, he isn't over *Obergefell.*"[41]

Lithwick continued: "Weirder? He concluded with the oral statement that 'not often in the law is it the case that so few have changed so much.' The latter may not be as pointed an indictment as the zinger at the end of his written concurrence, which accuses Breyer (but not his partner in crime,

Ginsburg) of rejecting, well, 'the Enlightenment.' But it's a deliberate echo of Breyer's lament in reading his dissent aloud in the 2007 Seattle schools case, that, 'It is not often in the law that so few have so quickly changed so much.' This is really a doubly strange accusation since of course the two dissenters—unlike the majority in the schools case—have in fact changed nothing at all, since they are the only two willing to do away with the death penalty."[42]

The unfiltered Scalia near the end of his life offered more bite, and less play, than his earlier incarnation. Anger, not humor, was more apt to carry the day.

⚖

Scalia the person, unlike Justice Scalia the fish, inflicted only non-lethal barbs on his enemies and his friends who strayed from his positions. No doubt he saw his harsh rhetoric and sharp humor as a tool to get his message across, especially to law students, and believed that his way with words did much more good than harm.

His rhetoric and style undoubtedly got attention for his ideas and entertained readers of sometimes dreadfully dull Supreme Court opinions. But it also changed the Court and the legal culture in some ways that he never acknowledged and even denied.

Elena Kagan appeared to borrow from the Scalia playbook in a 2011 campaign finance case, *Arizona Free Enterprise Club's Freedom Club PAC v. Bennett*. In *Bennett*, the chief justice's majority opinion claimed to have found "smoking guns" showing that Arizona voters had passed a campaign law with the goal of leveling the electoral playing field, a constitutionally forbidden interest under the majority's view of the First Amendment. Kagan retorted in her dissent that "the only smoke here is the majority's, and it is the kind that goes with mirrors." It is hard to imagine Kagan, a very talented writer, writing so nasty a response had Scalia not paved the way.[43]

And while we cannot necessarily attribute every snarky remark on the Court to the presence of Scalia, there is a definite feeling that things have gotten much sharper since he joined the Court. Consider Justice Alito's comments in *United States v. Windsor*, a 2013 case considering the constitutionality of the federal Defense of Marriage Act. In his dissenting opinion,

Justice Alito noted that in an earlier gay rights case, a trial court had made factual findings about the nature and history of marriage, and that a group of constitutional scholars submitted a brief suggesting that the Supreme Court should defer to those factual findings unless they were "clearly erroneous." Justice Alito wrote that "only an arrogant legal culture that has lost all appreciation of its own limitations could take such a suggestion seriously."[44]

Or consider the extraordinary exchange among the justices in *Schuette v. Coalition to Defend Affirmative Action,* a case from 2014 raising the question whether Michigan voters violated the Constitution's Equal Protection Clause in barring race-conscious preferences such as affirmative action plans in admissions to state universities. The Supreme Court, in a set of divided opinions, upheld the initiative against challenge.

Justice Scalia's opinion for himself and Justice Thomas put forward his long-held view that all affirmative action plans violate the Constitution, rendering the Michigan initiative perfectly acceptable. This led Justice Sotomayor to write a long and impassioned dissent about why "race matters," and accusing the majority of being "out of touch with reality." Responding to the statement of Chief Justice Roberts from an earlier case that "the way to stop discriminating on the basis of race is to stop discriminating on the basis of race," Justice Sotomayor retorted: "The way to stop discrimination on the basis of race is to speak openly and candidly on the subject of race, and to apply the Constitution with eyes open to the unfortunate effects of centuries of racial discrimination. As members of the judiciary tasked with intervening to carry out the guarantee of equal protection, we ought not sit back and wish away, rather than confront, the racial inequality that exists in our society. It is this view that works harm, by perpetuating the facile notion that what makes race matter is acknowledging the simple truth that race *does* matter." This in turn prompted the chief justice to object that Sotomayor was questioning the conservative justices' good faith: "People can disagree in good faith on this issue, but it similarly does more harm than good to question the openness and candor of those on either side of the debate." It is hard to imagine the justices using the tone in this debate had it not been for Scalia's example.[45]

Despite his protests against the coarsening of American culture and his belief that his principles and methods of jurisprudence could move the Court toward greater legitimacy, Scalia's tone both coarsened and delegitimized. He appeared, at least for the time being in American law, to undermine the respectful tone that the country's best lawyers use to communicate with one another, and perhaps to make the public view the Supreme Court as a more politicized, and more political, institution.

It is a legacy much more mixed than the moral of Paul Clement's fish tale.

5

Kulturkampf

IAN SAMUEL COULD NOT COME RIGHT out and say it, because doing so would have breached confidentiality and professional legal norms. But he came as close as he could to admitting he helped tone down Justice Scalia's harsh anti-gay rhetoric in a 2012 case, *United States v. Windsor.*[1]

Soon after Scalia's death, Samuel wrote a law review essay on the justice's use of "counter-clerks." Before every Supreme Court term, each justice normally hires four recent law school graduates, usually those fresh from a year-long stint with a federal appeals court judge, to assist in legal research and in drafting opinions. Scalia sometimes chose a left-leaning recent law school graduate as one of his four. Samuel was one of these "counter-clerks," a "token liberal," as he said he was often called. Many of these counter-clerks, such as Harvard Law School professor Lawrence Lessig, later became prominent legal scholars, lawyers, and judges.

In 2013, soon after Samuel's clerkship ended, Scalia explained to a reporter why he wanted a counter-clerk in his chambers: "I've said often in the past that other things being equal, which they usually are not, I like to have one of the four clerks whose predispositions are quite the opposite of mine—who are social liberals rather than social conservatives. That kind of clerk will always be looking for the chinks in my armor, for the mistakes I've made in my opinion. That's what clerks are for—to make sure I don't make mistakes. The trouble is, I have found it hard to get liberals like that, who pay attention to text and are not playing in a policy sandbox all the time."[2]

Scalia's death in 2016 prompted some of these counter-clerks to come forward with their remembrances. At least one, from Harvard Law School professor Bruce Hay, was very harsh. Hay wrote in *Salon* that Scalia's "own weapon was the poison-barbed word, and the battleground was what he once labeled the *Kulturkampf,* the culture war. The enemy took many forms. Women's rights. Racial justice. Economic equality. Environmental protection. The 'homosexual agenda,' as he called it. Intellectuals and universities. The questioning of authority and privilege. Ambiguity. Foreignness. Social change. Climate research. The modern world, in all its beauty and complexity and fragility."[3]

More typical were the words of NYU School of Law's Rachel Barkow, who concluded her glowing *Harvard Law Review* tribute with a recollection of Scalia's laugh: "Indeed, of all the memories I have, the sound of Justice Scalia's laugh is the most prominent. He had a contagious laugh that spread pure joy to those who hear it. Now when someone reacts negatively to hearing that I clerked for Justice Scalia, that laugh echoes in my mind. And the joke is on anyone who doesn't realize that working with Justice Scalia was the greatest job a lawyer could have."[4]

University of Michigan law professor Gil Seinfeld offered a nuanced view in "The Good, the Bad, and the Ugly: Reflections of a Counter-Clerk," an essay for the *Michigan Law Review*'s online companion. The "good" was the justice's good-humored mentoring and occasional open-mindedness. The "bad" was his failure to be a consistently principled originalist despite having sold himself that way to the public. The "ugly" was his rhetoric, especially in dissent: "The fact is that the strident contemptuousness of so many of Justice Scalia's dissenting opinions and public comments served no worthy purpose. It was just an angry man railing against a world that was changing around him in ways he found profoundly unsettling. Most disappointing, the Justice's rhetoric taught a generation of law students precisely the opposite of what he taught me (through his words and his actions) during our year's work together: that deep ideological disagreement can play out with civility—that you can think a person profoundly misguided and still treat him not just with respect, but with genuine warmth. It is a shame."[5]

Samuel discussed Seinfeld's essay in his own, noting the passage in

which Seinfeld explained that he asked for (and graciously received) permission from Justice Scalia not to work on *Lawrence v. Texas*, a 2003 Supreme Court case about the constitutionality of a Texas law criminalizing
gay sex. Scalia issued a bitter dissent from the Court opinion striking down
the law, a dissent full of language seen as strongly anti-gay. "Even before
I read the Justice's opinion, I knew I'd want no part of it. I didn't want to
help hone the Justice's arguments or improve his prose. I didn't even want
to point out a typo or a citation error."[6]

Samuel explained why the *Lawrence* dissent bothered a lot of people: "In
particular, its closing section, which begins this way: 'Today's decision is
the product of a Court, which is the product of a law-profession culture,
that has largely signed on to the so-called homosexual agenda, by which I
mean the agenda promoted by some homosexual activists directed at eliminating the moral opprobrium that has traditionally attached to homosexual
conduct.' The fat, juicy target in that sentence is obvious: the use of the
phrase 'homosexual agenda,' which was (even in 2003) so politically loaded
that the rest of the sentence might as well not be there, for most readers
will not get to it."

Samuel also pointed to this statement by Scalia: "I have nothing against
homosexuals, or any other group, promoting their agenda through normal
democratic means." Samuel wrote that "the quotation is easy (too easy) to
shorten to the groan-worthy 'I have nothing against homosexuals.' And the
dissent observes that 'many Americans do not want persons who openly
engage in homosexual conduct as partners in their business, as scoutmasters for their children, as teachers in their children's schools, or as boarders
in their home,' because they view that 'lifestyle' as 'immoral.' Maybe, but
. . . yikes."[7]

Samuel, however, thought that by removing himself from the opinion-
drafting process in *Lawrence*, Seinfeld lost a key opportunity. He noted that
Scalia's views were "capable of being expressed in a much different way.
During my Term, the Court decided *United States v. Windsor*, which inval-
idated the so-called Defense of Marriage Act. To no one's surprise, Justice
Scalia dissented. His substantive principle was the same as in *Lawrence:*
that the issue of gay rights was one of those issues left to democratic resolution. But the tone was very different." Samuel noted that Scalia said the

issue had "inspired 'passion by good people on all sides,' and that passion had prompted 'plebiscites, legislation, persuasion, and loud voices—in other words, democracy.'" Scalia "disagreed with the idea that 'this story is black-and-white: Hate your neighbor or come along with us.' He spoke of 'our fellow human beings, our fellow citizens, who are homosexual,' and how terrible it was that the majority had accused the authors of the law of acting with 'the purpose' to 'degrade' or 'humiliate' gay people. In a lament I think Seinfeld might cheer, he observed how 'hard' it is 'to admit that one's political opponents are not monsters.'" Samuel believed that the *Lawrence* dissent "created for some a misimpression: a man who did not believe that the rights of gay people were to be settled via the political process, but who had *personal* animus toward gay people *qua* people."

Samuel thought Seinfeld could have improved Justice Scalia's prose and taken off the harsh edges. "I genuinely wonder what would have happened if someone had said: 'Justice, not for nothing, but if you say "homosexual agenda," that's where half of people will stop reading.' Would a *Lawrence* dissent with a counter-clerk's touch have been any different?" Samuel demurred on whether he spoke up in *Windsor,* but the implication is that he did: "It would be fair to ask, at this point: 'So, did *you* ever have a "homosexual agenda" moment—a time when you had to stand athwart an opinion shouting "stop"? Did you speak up?' Unfortunately, the ethical obligations of clerkships forbid discussing one's work in any detail. I will say only that there were times when we disagreed, times when I persuaded him, and times when he persuaded *me.*"

Left unsaid by Samuel was whether it was the counter-clerk's job to stop Scalia from being insensitive, as opposed to making sure he stayed true to his methodological commitments despite his conservative instincts. Scalia's comments on the counter-clerk's job to look for "chinks in [his] armor" suggested the justice intended to employ the counter-clerks for critique of substance, not style.

⚖

Samuel's story illustrates both the extent to which Scalia sought to keep an open mind and the limits of others' influence over his disposition of the cases that appeared to matter to him most: abortion, same-sex marriage, affirmative action, guns, and religion. While his tone may have varied, de-pending on which clerks were working for him that year—and it is hard to read Samuel as suggesting anything other than that he did speak up and get Scalia to tone down his *Windsor* dissent—the outcome in these culture war cases always followed Scalia's conservative instincts, not the views of his counter-clerks or the consistent application of originalist methodology.

There is no indication that a counter-clerk ever changed Scalia's position or vote in any of these cases. There is no way even to know for sure that, as Samuel claimed, the belief that Scalia harbored an anti-gay animus was a *mis*impression. Perhaps Samuel's efforts to tone down the justice's lan-guage were about suppressing his true feelings so as not to alienate his future law student readers.

Scalia reportedly had friends who were gay, but he said nothing publicly I could find offering support for gay individuals. Perhaps he was simply from a generation and a traditional Roman Catholic culture where these issues simply were not discussed, and the "homosexual lifestyle" (as Scalia called it) simply ignored or dismissed as foreign. The closest evidence showing he lacked anti-gay animus was his vote in a 2013 case, *Hollingsworth v. Perry,* dismissing on technical standing grounds a challenge to a lower court deci-sion holding California's ban on same-sex marriage unconstitutional. The upshot of *Hollingsworth,* a 5–4 decision with Scalia in the majority, was to require same-sex marriages in California. But a year before, at a book event at Princeton, he was confronted by a gay student who said he was offended by Scalia's statements in earlier cases comparing homosexual acts to besti-ality and murder. Justice Scalia responded: "If we cannot have moral feel-ings against homosexuality, can we have it against murder? Can we have it against other things? I don't apologize for the things I raise."[8]

In a 2013 interview Scalia declined to state his personal feelings on the subject but said he would write again what he wrote in *Lawrence* about some people believing a homosexual lifestyle to be "immoral and destruc-tive": "I would write that again. But that's not saying that I personally think it's destructive. Americans have a right to feel that way. They have a dem-ocratic right to do that, and if it is to change, it should change democrati-cally, and not at the ukase of a Supreme Court." In that same interview, he acknowledged that future generations could view him as "standing athwart" the march of gay rights, or "at least standing athwart it as a constitutional entitlement." The "at least" hangs there as a big question mark.[9]

Scalia's supporters have to look elsewhere—perhaps to some of his criminal law opinions—for evidence of his giving neutral methodology precedence over conservative ideology. The one constant in the culture wars cases is that Scalia always ended up—with fellow conservatives Alito, Rehnquist, and Thomas—on the hard-conservative side, in line with where you would expect someone with his political, social, and religious commitments to be.

⚖

Before the same-sex marriage debate, nothing better encapsulated the *kulturkampf* at the Supreme Court than the abortion cases. Beginning with the Court's *Roe v. Wade* decision in 1973, recognizing a woman's constitutional right to have an abortion in some circumstances, the fight between the Court's liberals and its conservatives over abortion has lasted more than forty years.[10]

The Constitution does not mention abortion, and since *Roe* the fight has been not only over *whether* such a right exists, but if so *where* in the Constitution such a right is to be found and *how far* it extends. There is an extra-legal question as well: would it have been better for abortion rights supporters to let the issue be resolved through the political process? This debate was reprised decades later in the more recent legal fight over same-sex marriage.

The *Roe* decision was not made in a vacuum. It followed earlier rulings recognizing certain rights of privacy and reproductive autonomy. In the *Skinner v. Oklahoma* case in 1942, the Court struck down a law allowing state courts to order sterilization of certain criminals, holding that the law violated the Equal Protection Clause and that procreation was a fundamental right.[11]

In 1965, the Court decided *Griswold v. Connecticut,* striking down a Connecticut law banning the use and distribution of contraceptives. Justice Douglas, writing for the Court, found a right to privacy that protected access to contraception not in any particular clause of the Constitution but—in one of the most criticized constitutional analyses of the past century—existing in the "penumbras" and "emanations" of various parts. Concurring justices in *Griswold* believed the right to privacy came from either the Fourteenth Amendment's Due Process Clause or from the Ninth Amendment, which provides that "The enumeration in the Constitution, of certain rights, shall not be construed to deny or disparage others retained by the people." The dissenters, Hugo Black and Potter Stewart, believed the Constitution contained no right to privacy.[12]

In later cases, the Court expanded on this right, striking down a Massachusetts law barring distribution of contraceptives to unmarried people, and a New York law banning the sale or distribution of contraceptives to some minors and the advertising and displaying of contraceptives.[13]

Roe built on these reproductive autonomy cases in considering the constitutionality of a Texas law banning all abortions except those needed to save the life of the mother. Justice Harry Blackmun wrote an extensive (and deeply controversial) majority opinion weighing history, medical information, and constitutional analysis to conclude that the liberty interest in the Constitution's Due Process Clause protected a right to privacy which encompassed a woman's right to have an abortion in some circumstances. *Roe* is the most controversial modern example of the Court using "substantive due process" (a reading of the Due Process Clause to guarantee not just fair procedures, but certain substantive protections) to protect a fundamental right not traditionally recognized by the courts. (The Court also gave a nod to the Ninth Amendment, but not to Justice Douglas's "penumbras" and "emanations.")

The *Roe* decision directed courts to balance a woman's fundamental right to abortion against the state's interests, such as protecting prenatal life. The Supreme Court concluded that before the point of fetal viability (when a fetus could survive outside the womb), a woman's right was paramount to the state's interests, but after this point the interest shifted to the state. This led Justice Blackmun to adopt a trimester approach, with no limitation on abortion during the first trimester of pregnancy, some regulation permissible during the second trimester, and an abortion ban permissible during the final trimester, except if the mother's health or life was endangered.[14]

Roe was controversial when it was decided. Dissenting Justices William Rehnquist and Byron White, as well as the eminent constitutional scholar John Hart Ely, rejected it as unmoored to the Constitution. But the logic

of the criticism of *Roe* extended beyond abortion to all reproductive autonomy cases. As constitutional law scholar Erwin Chemerinsky put it, "The
Court has safeguarded the right to marry, the right to custody, the right to
keep the family together, the right to control the upbringing of children,
the right to procreate, the right to purchase and use contraceptives, the
right to refuse medical treatment, and the right to engage in private, adult
homosexual activity even though these liberties are not mentioned in the
Constitution and were not intended by the framers."[15] Why should abortion
be treated any differently?

Justice Ruth Bader Ginsburg later attacked *Roe* from a different angle,
arguing that it should have been decided under the Equal Protection Clause
as a case of sex discrimination, and suggesting the Court should have let
the political process play itself out longer before recognizing a right to abortion (an argument which has proven to be controversial). But given the
existing decision, she has been a reliably strong voice for abortion rights.[16]

In the years since *Roe,* abortion jurisprudence changed considerably, but
the Court has never overruled it despite the considerable efforts of conservatives on and off the Court. In the 1989 case *Webster v. Reproductive Health
Services,* four justices (Kennedy, Rehnquist, Scalia, and White) seemed
ready to overturn *Roe.* Justice Sandra Day O'Connor provided a fifth vote
to uphold a strict Missouri abortion law, but she refused to reconsider *Roe.*
By 1992, in *Planned Parenthood v. Casey,* the Court reaffirmed *Roe's* central holding that women have the right to an abortion before viability, even
while rejecting the trimester framework. In a rare jointly authored opinion by Justices Kennedy, O'Connor, and then-new justice David Souter, the
Court held that state regulation of abortion in the pre-viability period was
unconstitutional when it imposed an "undue burden" on the exercise of
that right.[17]

The meaning of "undue burden" has shifted over time, as the Court considered a number of abortion regulations. In the years after *Casey,* many
stricter abortion regulations survived the undue burden test, thanks in part
to Justice Kennedy's vote. In a case involving the constitutionality of the
federal Partial Birth Abortion Act, Kennedy voted to uphold the law, finding
that it did not pose an undue burden for a "large fraction of women." In an
opinion that many saw as patronizing, he remarked that "it seems unex-

ceptional to conclude some women come to regret their choice to abort the infant life they once created and sustained. Severe depression and loss of esteem can follow."[18]

Then, in a majority opinion written by Justice Stephen Breyer and joined by Justice Kennedy months after Justice Scalia's death, the Court refined the "undue burden" test yet again, this time making it quite difficult for states to enforce restrictive abortion laws. In the 2016 *Whole Woman's Health v. Hellerstedt* case, the Court rejected two Texas requirements related to abortion, one requiring that doctors performing abortions have admitting privileges at a nearby hospital, and the other mandating that abortion facilities meet the standards under Texas law for ambulatory surgery centers. The Court saw this for what it was: a measure not to protect women's health but to make it difficult to perform (or obtain) abortions. It concluded that "neither of these provisions confers medical benefits sufficient to justify the burdens upon access that each imposes. Each places a substantial obstacle in the path of women seeking a previability abortion, each constitutes an undue burden on abortion access."[19]

Whether the new "undue burden" test, and even *Roe*'s core holding that women have the right to an abortion pre-viability, will survive depends on whether future justices embrace this reading of the Constitution or the alternative reading forcefully put forward by Scalia, referenced in Justice Thomas's dissent in *Whole Woman's Health*. A true five-justice conservative majority could throw it all out and send the issue back to the states, some of which could then ban abortion outright.

From the beginning of his time on the Court, Scalia rejected any constitutional right to abortion or belief that continued adherence to *Roe* was justified by *stare decisis*, the respect for precedent that justices usually (but not always) give to earlier opinions.

In the 1989 *Webster* case, his first major abortion case on the Court, Scalia concurred separately, arguing that the Court's primary opinion had essentially overruled *Roe* but should have done so more explicitly. He argued against the idea that the majority's minimalism was an act of statesmanship: it "needlessly [prolonged] this Court's self-awarded sovereignty over a field where it has little proper business since the answers to most of the cruel questions posed are political and not juridical—a sovereignty which therefore quite properly, but to the great damage of the Court, makes it the object of the sort of organized public pressure that political institutions in a democracy ought to receive." In language some considered sexist, he added that Justice O'Connor's call for judicial restraint "cannot be taken seriously."[20]

Scalia frequently returned to the theme that the abortion question was divisive and best left to the political processes, both for the good of American democracy and for the Court's legitimacy. But he also emphatically rejected the idea that the right to an abortion could be a constitutionally protected liberty interest. As he wrote in *Casey*: "Laws against bigamy, for example—with which entire societies of reasonable people disagree—intrude upon men and women's liberty to marry and live with one another. But bigamy happens not to be a liberty specially 'protected' by the Constitution."

He wrote that the issue was not "liberty" in the "absolute sense; or even whether it is of great importance to many women. Of course it is both." It was whether it was an interest the Constitution protected. "I am sure it is not." He mockingly quoted the joint *Casey* opinion in saying he did not rely on any "exalted views" of the "concept of existence, of meaning, of the universe, and of the mystery of human life." "Rather, I reach it for the same reason I reach the conclusion that bigamy is not constitutionally protected—because of two simple facts: (1) the Constitution says absolutely nothing about it, and (2) the longstanding traditions of American society have permitted it to be legally proscribed."[21]

This key move confined the meaning of "liberty" to those interests, as Scalia put it in a 1990 case, "found in the longstanding traditions of our society [or] logically deduced from the text of the Constitution." As we saw in Chapter 3, this on-again, off-again elevation of tradition as a means of interpreting constitutional provisions was at odds with the pure textualism he applied in other areas of law.[22]

Scalia defended "tradition" as a touchstone for constitutional analysis, rejecting the argument that reliance on it would, for instance, require the Court to accept state bans on interracial marriage (which were declared unconstitutional in the *Loving v. Virginia* case in 1967). Such bans, he wrote, violated the text of the Equal Protection Clause; but "There is, of course, no comparable tradition barring recognition of a 'liberty interest' in carrying one's child to term free from state efforts to kill it."[23]

In his writings, he frequently reflected on what he saw as the barbarity of abortion, as when he dissented in the 2012 case *Stenberg v. Carhart*, involving the constitutionality of Nebraska's ban on "partial birth" abortion. He wrote that he was "optimistic enough" to believe that one day the case "will be assigned its rightful place in the history of this Court's jurisprudence beside" *Korematsu*, which upheld the internment of American citizens of Japanese descent during World War II, and *Dred Scott*, which held that descendants of African American slaves were not protected as citizens under the Constitution. "The method of killing a human child—one cannot even accurately say an entirely unborn human child—proscribed by this statute is so horrible that the most clinical description of it evokes a shudder of revulsion."[24]

But if tradition and his personal abhorrence lined up with how Scalia voted in the abortion cases, what of the argument that to reject the liberty interest in *Roe* means rejection of other rights of privacy and reproductive autonomy, such as the right to access to contraceptives recognized in *Griswold*? Aside from noting that *Griswold* itself was not based in the Due Process Clause, Scalia had a more fundamental answer, given in this exchange with *Fox News Sunday*'s Chris Wallace in 2012:

> WALLACE: What about the right to privacy that the court found in . . . 1965?
> SCALIA: There is no right to privacy. No generalized right to privacy.
> WALLACE: Well, in the *Griswold* case, the court said there was.
> SCALIA: Indeed it did, and that was—that was wrong.[25]

⚖

The fight over gay rights and same-sex marriage neatly parallels the fight over abortion, with essentially the same division of justices along ideological lines and the same debate over whether our understanding of the Constitution's protections of individual rights should evolve over time. Only this time, it is not clear that the gay rights fight will be as unending as that over abortion. It will be more likely to focus on the intersection of gay rights and the religious liberty of those opposed to such rights.

In the 1986 case of *Bowers v. Hardwick*, on a 5–4 vote, the Court held that Georgia could criminally punish individuals for engaging in gay oral or anal sex (leaving open the question whether a state could criminalize heterosexual oral or anal sex). In an opinion by Justice Byron White, the Court rejected the argument that reproductive autonomy and privacy cases such as *Griswold* or *Roe* established a right to engage in "consensual homosexual sodomy."[26] White recognized that some cases had read the liberty provision of the Due Process Clause to include substantive protection of rights, but he refused to apply this right as protecting private gay sexual conduct. Such recognition, he wrote, should be limited to those liberties recognized by American tradition, and laws against homosexual conduct have "ancient roots." "To claim that a right to engage in such conduct is 'deeply rooted in this Nation's history and tradition' or 'implicit in the concept of ordered liberty' is, at best, facetious." White also raised the dangers of judicial illegitimacy stemming from overuse of substantive due process, pointing to the era in the first half of the twentieth century when the Court used substantive due process to strike down New Deal economic legislation. These are all themes Scalia would raise later.[27]

Bowers was controversial when it was decided, and within thirty years the Court had not only reversed it but recognized a right of same-sex couples to marry. Such a dramatic turnaround in such a short time is highly unusual and reflects both social upheaval and the Court's own role in it. Scalia saw the Court's path to same-sex marriage coming early on, which is why he seemed to fight so hard against gay rights in the early cases.

The break with *Bowers* began in the 1996 case *Romer v. Evans. Romer* struck down a voter-initiated state constitutional amendment in Colorado that repealed state and local laws barring discrimination against gays, lesbians, and bisexuals. In an opinion by Justice Anthony Kennedy, the Court held that the amendment violated the Fourteenth Amendment's Equal Protection Clause. It denied gays and lesbians certain legal protections, such as protection against housing discrimination, with no rational basis for doing so. The Court concluded the law must have been motivated by anti-gay animus.[28]

Scalia, for himself, Chief Justice Rehnquist, and Justice Thomas, dissented, beginning by declaring:

The Court has mistaken a Kulturkampf for a fit of spite. The constitutional amendment before us here is not the manifestation of a "'bare . . . desire to harm'" homosexuals, but is rather a modest attempt by seemingly tolerant Coloradans to preserve traditional sexual mores against the efforts of a politically powerful minority to revise those mores through use of the laws. That objective, and the means chosen to achieve it, are not only unimpeachable under any constitutional doctrine hitherto pronounced (hence the opinion's heavy reliance upon principles of righteousness rather than judicial holdings); they have been specifically approved by the Congress of the United States and by this Court.

Scalia wrote that the decision contracted *Bowers* "and places the prestige of this institution behind the proposition that opposition to homosexuality is as reprehensible as racial or religious bias." He believed the Constitution said "nothing about this subject," and argued it should be "resolved by normal democratic means, including the democratic adoption of provisions in state constitutions. This Court has no business imposing upon all Americans the resolution favored by the elite class from which the Members of this institution are selected, pronouncing that 'animosity' toward homosexuality is evil. I vigorously dissent."[29]

Scalia argued that if a state has the right to criminalize homosexual conduct, as recognized in *Bowers*, it could impose lesser restrictions like those contained in the Colorado amendment. Having decriminalized the conduct, Scalia maintained, Colorado was now being prohibited from imposing these lesser restrictions, and the Court was taking away this ability because of the growing political power of gay individuals. As he put it, applying a stereotype of gay lifestyles, "The problem (a problem, that is, for those who wish to retain social disapprobation of homosexuality) is that, because those who engage in homosexual conduct tend to reside in disproportionate numbers in certain communities, have high disposable income, and, of course, care about homosexual-rights issues much more ardently than the public at large, they possess political power much greater than their numbers, both locally and statewide. Quite understandably, they devote this political power to achieving not merely a grudging social toleration, but full social acceptance, of homosexuality."[30]

Scalia saw early on (as did many others) that *Romer* would lead the Court down the path (happily for many, but unhappily for him) to full legal equality for gay, lesbian, and bisexual Americans. He faulted the Court for elitism and political correctness: "When the Court takes sides in the culture wars, it tends to be with the knights rather than the villeins—and more specifically with the Templars, reflecting the views and values of the lawyer class from which the Court's Members are drawn. How that class feels about homosexuality will be evident to anyone who wishes to interview job applicants at virtually any of the Nation's law schools." He challenged the Court to explain how it could strike down the Colorado amendment while still upholding laws against polygamy.[31]

It took only seven more years for the Court to overrule *Bowers,* in *Lawrence v. Texas,* the case decided in 2003 that Scalia permitted the counter-clerk Gil Seinfeld not to work on, and which counter-clerk Ian Samuel described as containing some of Scalia's most insensitive language toward gays, lesbians, and the "homosexual agenda."

In *Lawrence,* the Supreme Court on a 6–3 vote struck down a Texas law barring sexual activity between people of the same sex. Justice Kennedy, writing for five justices, held that the law violated the liberty interest of the Due Process Clause. The decision explicitly overruled *Bowers.*[32] In explaining why the Court did so, Kennedy wrote that the Constitution is a living document, with its meaning changing along with social mores. He noted that the case did not involve minors, persons who might be in abusive or nonconsensual relationships, or public conduct or prostitution. "The case does involve two adults who, with full and mutual consent from each other, engaged in sexual practices common to a homosexual lifestyle. The petitioners are entitled to respect for their private lives. The State cannot demean their existence or control their destiny by making their private sexual conduct a crime. Their right to liberty under the Due Process Clause gives them the full right to engage in their conduct without intervention of the government. . . . The Texas statute furthers no legitimate state interest which can justify its intrusion into the personal and private life of the individual."

Kennedy recognized principles of a living Constitution: "Had those who drew and ratified the Due Process Clauses of the Fifth Amendment or the Fourteenth Amendment known the components of liberty in its manifold possibilities, they might have been more specific. They did not presume to have this insight. They knew times can blind us to certain truths and later generations can see that laws once thought necessary and proper in fact serve only to oppress. As the Constitution endures, persons in every generation can invoke its principles in their own search for greater freedom."

Scalia's arguments in dissent followed the familiar path. He derided the slippery slope ("State laws against bigamy, same-sex marriage, adult incest, prostitution, masturbation, adultery, fornication, bestiality, and obscenity are likewise sustainable only in light of *Bower*'s validation of laws based on moral choices. Every single one of these laws is called into question by today's decision; the Court makes no effort to cabin the scope of its decision to exclude them from its holding."). He noted what he saw as the disproportionate political power of gay individuals ("Today's opinion is the product of a Court, which is the product of a law-profession culture, that has largely signed on to the so-called homosexual agenda, by which I mean the agenda promoted by some homosexual activists directed at eliminating the moral opprobrium that has traditionally attached to homosexual conduct"). He signaled moral opprobrium, though couching it in what "many Americans" think ("Many Americans do not want persons who openly engage in homosexual conduct as partners in their business, as scoutmasters for their children, as teachers in their children's schools, or as boarders in their home. They view this as protecting themselves and their families from a lifestyle that they believe to be immoral and destructive."). He advocated leaving the matter in the political process ("What Texas has chosen to do is well within the range of traditional democratic action, and its hand should not be stayed through the invention of a brand-new 'constitutional right' by a Court that is impatient of democratic change."). And he lamented what he saw as the lack of a principled stopping point for the scope of constitutional rights ("it is the premise of our system that those judgments are to be made by the people, and not imposed by a governing caste that knows best."). Scalia concluded his *Lawrence* dissent by signaling once again that the Court was on its way to recognizing same-sex marriage, a move that would take only another decade.[33]

In *United States v. Windsor*, decided in 2013, the Court struck down a part of the federal Defense of Marriage Act, which defined marriage under federal law to exclude same-sex couples. Edith Windsor, who married her same-sex partner in Canada, challenged the federal government's failure to recognize her marriage, requiring her to pay estate taxes she would not have had to pay if her marriage were recognized. Echoing *Romer*, Justice Kennedy and the four liberal justices (Breyer, Ginsburg, Kagan, and Sotomayor) held the law unconstitutional as based on animus toward gays and lesbians in violation of due process and equal protection guarantees. Chief Justice Roberts and Justices Alito, Scalia, and Thomas dissented. Scalia raised his familiar arguments, but (likely thanks to Ian Samuel's efforts), with a much less vituperative edge than before.[34]

The Court officially struck state bans on same-sex marriage in *Obergefell v. Hodges*, decided in 2015 during Scalia's last full term on the Court. The case featured the usual duel between Kennedy and Scalia and the same 5–4 divide as in *Windsor*. Kennedy, relying on reproductive autonomy cases such as *Griswold* and *Eisenstadt*, held that the Constitution protected "certain personal choices central to individual dignity and autonomy, including intimate choices that define personal identity and beliefs."[35]

Kennedy reiterated that the Court's determination of how to understand the scope of liberties should evolve over time. "The nature of injustice is that we may not always see it in our own times. The generations that wrote and ratified the Bill of Rights and the Fourteenth Amendment did not presume to know the extent of freedom in all of its dimensions, and so they entrusted to future generations a charter protecting the right of all persons to enjoy liberty as we learn its meaning. When new insight reveals discord between the Constitution's central protections and a received legal stricture, a claim to liberty must be addressed." Same-sex couples, he concluded, were entitled to "equal dignity in the eyes of the law," and state laws banning same-sex marriages were unconstitutional.[36]

Scalia's dissent was brief. He joined in a lengthier dissent by Chief Justice Roberts as well as a dissent by Justice Thomas, and also wrote "separately to call attention to this Court's threat to American democracy." And he excoriated what he saw as the ponderousness and pretentiousness of the majority opinion. Indeed, his ire was not directed at gay people or the gay "lifestyle," but instead at Justice Kennedy and his opinion.[37]

On the merits, he reaffirmed his view that text and tradition limited the Court's power to recognize protected liberties. It was enough for him that when the states ratified the Fourteenth Amendment in 1868, each state limited marriage to one man and one woman, "and no one doubted the constitutionality of doing so. That resolves these cases. When it comes to determining the meaning of a vague constitutional provision—such as 'due process of law' or 'equal protection of the laws'—it is unquestionable that the People who ratified that provision did not understand it to prohibit a practice that remained both universal and uncontroversial in the years after ratification."

He concluded: "We have no basis for striking down a practice that is not expressly prohibited by the Fourteenth Amendment's text, and that bears the endorsement of a long tradition of open, widespread, and unchallenged use dating back to the Amendment's ratification. Since there is no doubt whatever that the People never decided to prohibit the limitation of marriage to opposite-sex couples, the public debate over same-sex marriage must be allowed to continue."[38]

As Scalia left the Court, the next frontier was the question of how to reconcile same-sex marriage rights with religious objections. The battle was presaged in the 2014 case of *Burwell v. Hobby Lobby Stores.* Justice Scalia was in a conservative majority of five justices upholding the right of a closely held corporation to be exempt from federal health law requirements to provide no-cost contraception for employees. (The employees could still get the contraception directly through the employer's insurance company.) Cases involving religious wedding photographers and cake bakers who did not want to provide services for gay weddings but faced liability under state anti-discrimination laws waited in the wings after Scalia's death.[39]

⚖

Scalia's contention that the Fourteenth Amendment's due process and equal protection clauses are vague, and that because of this vagueness it is appropriate to look at contemporaneous practice and understanding at the time of the Fourteenth Amendment's ratification, well explains his position in the abortion and gay rights cases. One can agree or disagree with his rejection of evolving constitutional rights and his reliance on tradition, but at least his positions are consistent.[40]

But his contention about how to read the Fourteenth Amendment does not explain how he treated the key question of affirmative action. There, as we saw in the last chapter, he ignored evidence of special programs for newly freed slaves at the time of ratification, which indicated contemporaneous understandings of the amendment's scope.

Generally speaking, laws that discriminate on the basis of race, such as those providing for separate schools or housing for people of different races, are inherently suspect under the equal protection clause. On this point, all current justices now agree (although it was not always so). More controversial is how to evaluate the constitutionality of laws that give preferences to prior victims of discrimination, such as race-conscious college admissions or employment programs. These "affirmative action" measures have divided the Supreme Court for decades.

Some liberals would subject such laws to a lesser scrutiny and uphold more of them, under the view that laws helping victims of discrimination and their descendants are more justified than laws hurting them. The Court's conservatives, including Scalia, have won the battle over whether these affirmative action plans are subject to the same strict scrutiny as laws that discriminate against racial minorities. In *Fisher v. University of Texas*, a case challenging the use of race as a factor in the admissions program at the University of Texas, Justice Kennedy explained for the Court that "strict scrutiny requires the university to demonstrate with clarity that its purpose or interest is both constitutionally permissible and substantial, and that its use of the classification, is necessary . . . to the accomplishment of its purpose."[41]

The conservatives have divided, however, on the question of what interests and plans satisfy strict scrutiny. Chief Justice Roberts and Justices Thomas and Alito generally view the Fourteenth Amendment as requiring a "color-blind" Constitution and reject virtually all government laws or rules that take race into account, even to ameliorate past discrimination or serve other benign social goals. Scalia took this position as well. In the college admissions context, for example, these justices would not accept achieving racial diversity or a "critical mass" of minority students a sufficient basis for race consciousness. Scalia wrote in a challenge to Michigan Law School's race-conscious admissions program dismissing the "educational benefit" of "cross-racial understanding" or better preparation of students "for an increasingly diverse workforce and society." He mocked the concept: "This is not, of course, an 'educational benefit' on which students will be graded on their law school transcript (Works and Plays Well with Others: B+) or tested by the bar examiners (Q: Describe in 500 words or less your cross-racial understanding). For it is a lesson of life rather than law—essentially the same lesson taught to (or rather learned by, for it cannot be 'taught' in the usual sense) people three feet shorter and 20 years younger than the full-grown adults at the University of Michigan Law School, in institutions ranging from Boy Scout troops to public-school kindergartens."[42]

His views dismissing the value of diversity did not garner a majority on the Supreme Court while he was alive, but they could well do so after his death as more justices like Neil Gorsuch join the Court. In the 2003 Michigan case, Justice O'Connor provided the crucial fifth vote (over the dissent of Scalia and the other conservatives) to uphold the University of Michigan's race-conscious admissions programs, although she accompanied her opinion with a caveat that as racial equality continued to advance, the Court expected such programs to be no longer constitutionally acceptable in another twenty-five years.[43]

Fisher, the University of Texas case, made its way to the Supreme Court a few times. In its final trip, heard while Scalia was still alive but decided after his death, Justice Kennedy joined with the Court's liberals (except for Kagan, who recused herself presumably because she worked on the case in the United States solicitor general's office before joining the Court) to uphold the University of Texas's plan. Although Kennedy had dissented in the earlier University of Michigan case, he relied on it in finding that the University of Texas had a compelling interest in "a race-conscious admissions program as a means of obtaining 'the educational benefits that flow from student body diversity.' As this Court has said, enrolling a diverse student body 'promotes cross-racial understanding, helps to break down racial stereotypes, and enables students to better understand persons of different races.' Equally important, 'student body diversity promotes learning outcomes, and better prepares students for an increasingly diverse workforce and society.'" While rejecting quotas, Kennedy concluded that the University of Texas plan survived strict scrutiny, for now.[44]

Had he lived, Scalia would have written a pungent dissent. At the *Fisher* oral argument a few months before his death, he advanced a controversial theory when questioning the attorney for the University of Texas, the former U.S. solicitor general Gregory Garre, as to why affirmative action in college admissions was not good for minority students:

> JUSTICE SCALIA: There are . . . those who contend that it does not benefit African-Americans to . . . get them into the University of Texas where they do not do well, as opposed to having them go to a less-advanced school, a less—a slower-track school where they do well. One of . . . the briefs pointed out that . . most of the black scientists in this country don't come from schools like the University of Texas. . . . They come from lesser schools where they do not feel that they're . . . being pushed ahead in . . . classes that are too . . . fast for them.
> MR. GARRE: This Court—
> JUSTICE SCALIA: I'm just not impressed by the fact that . . . the University of Texas may have fewer. Maybe it ought to have fewer. And maybe some—you know, when you take more, the number of blacks, really competent blacks admitted to lesser schools, turns out to be less. And . . . I don't think it . . . stands to reason that it's a good thing for the University of Texas to admit as many blacks as possible. I just don't think—
> MR. GARRE: This Court heard and rejected that argument, with respect, Justice Scalia, in the *Grutter* case, a case that our opponents haven't asked this Court to overrule. If you look at the academic performance of holistic minority admits versus the top 10 percent admits, over time, they . . . fare better.[45]

The exchange about "really competent blacks" certainly clarified one reason why Scalia thought affirmative action might be bad policy. It was a long-held belief. Reflecting back on how his opposition to race-conscious policies began, he told Joan Biskupic in 2009 that "I had no idea that I would be cast in the role of having to decide things of this sort. . . . But I certainly felt that the Lewis Powells of the world were not going to bear the burden they were creating. It wasn't their kids. It was the Polish factory worker's kid who was going to be out of a job." Here was Justice Scalia, again seeing the elites sticking it to working-class whites.[46]

But his view of color blindness under the Fourteenth Amendment appeared to be at odds with the original understanding of the Equal Protection Clause. Scalia the originalist found a way to completely ignore the point that the Reconstruction Amendments (the Thirteenth Amendment, barring slavery, the Fourteenth Amendment, guaranteeing equal protection and other protections, and the Fifteenth Amendment, barring racial discrimination in voting rules) were aimed to help newly freed slaves achieve political freedom and equality in American society. Following those amendments, the federal government gave preferential treatment on the basis of race to help former slaves.

Indeed, in his essay "The Good, the Bad, and the Ugly," Gil Seinfeld counted as "bad" Scalia's failure to grapple with the original understanding of the Fourteenth Amendment. "Commentators pointed to a robust body of evidence indicating that, in the years following the Civil War and the ratification of the Reconstruction Amendments, Congress routinely enacted measures conferring benefits on blacks as a group. And they noted that none of the opinions authored or joined by Justice Scalia in [this area] makes a remotely serious effort to engage with the relevant historical record."

Seinfeld reports that as a counter-clerk he called these issues to the justice's attention, hoping for at least a reasoned response in an opinion, but to no avail: "If the Justice could show why the measures enacted by Reconstruction era Congresses were inapposite to the question of whether modern affirmative action policies are permissible under the Fourteenth Amendment, so be it."

He continued: "If there was evidence that courts were skeptical of Reconstruction era legislation that conferred benefits exclusively on blacks, fine. Or, if the Justice felt that his commitment to originalist constitutional interpretation ought to give way to other considerations, he could identify those considerations and explain his position. But if he could not do any of these things, it seemed to me, the Justice needed to be on the other side of these cases. And I told him so."

Seinfeld noted that the opinions in the affirmative action cases that year did not show that the intervention was of any consequence. "Not one of these opinions contains even a syllable of originalist argument." Seinfeld added: "Perhaps the Justice believed that the Court abandoned originalism in connection with race and equal protection in *Brown v. Board of Education,* and that there could be no turning back. Perhaps the Justice thought that the race-conscious measures enacted by the Reconstruction Congress were distinguishable from the sorts of affirmative action policies that came before the Court during his tenure, and that the historical record therefore did not speak clearly to the questions at hand. We do not know. His opinions shed no light on the matter." Seinfeld found this "gravely disappointing, and it gives the lie to those who regard the Justice as an unfailing champion of adjudicative rectitude."[47]

⚖️

Scalia showed off his originalist and textualist jurisprudence most forcefully in the area of gun rights, where he was able to write on a cleaner slate (though there was a precedent from 1939, *United States v. Miller,* contrary to his position, a case he managed to brush off). The debates over abortion, gay rights, and affirmative action were already in progress when he joined them, but there was little judicial debate before 2008, when the Supreme Court decided *District of Columbia v. Heller,* considering the constitutionality of a ban on handguns in Washington, D.C. Even on the Second Amendment, however, he had to rely on substantive due process—precedent he said he disagreed with as an originalist matter—to extend gun rights to individuals.[48]

The Second Amendment reads in full: "A well regulated Militia, being necessary to the security of a free State, the right of the people to keep and bear Arms, shall not be infringed." Scalia, joined by Chief Justice Roberts and Justices Alito, Kennedy, and Thomas, took the position in *Heller* that the Second Amendment guaranteed an individual right to possess firearms. Justice Stevens, dissenting for himself and Justices Breyer, Ginsburg, and Souter, viewed the amendment as relating only to service in militias.

The majority opinion in *Heller* combines all the elements of a classic Scalia opinion. It carefully parses the "prefatory" clause of the Second Amendment (concerning militias) and contrasts this with its "operative" clause (naming the right to bear arms). It engages in detailed textual exegesis, followed by the history of gun rights from England, to the colonies, and then through American history both before and after the Civil War. It concludes, despite point-by-point rebuttals and citations to text and history from Stevens, that the Constitution created an individual right to bear arms, leaving for another day the appropriate balancing test to apply to federal laws regulating guns: "We are aware of the problem of handgun violence in this country, and we take seriously the concerns raised by the many *amici* who believe that prohibition of handgun ownership is a solution. The Constitution leaves the District of Columbia a variety of tools for combating that problem, including some measures regulating handguns. But the enshrinement of constitutional rights necessarily takes certain policy choices off the table. These include the absolute prohibition of handguns held and used for self-defense in the home. Undoubtedly some think that the Second Amendment is outmoded in a society where our standing army is the pride of our Nation, where well-trained police forces provide personal security, and where gun violence is a serious problem. That is perhaps debatable, but what is not debatable is that it is not the role of this Court to pronounce the Second Amendment extinct."[49]

Scalia viewed the case as one of his biggest triumphs. He told the interviewer Nina Totenberg: "I think *Heller* is my legacy opinion insofar as it is the best example of the technique of constitutional interpretation, which I favor; that is to say, it is a good example of originalism, of going back and seeing what the meaning of the Second amendment was at the time it was adopted . . . I think it is the most complete originalist opinion that I've ever written."[50]

But even *Heller* was not fully originalist. As Sara Anonchick Solow and Barry Friedman explain, it was less originalism than lawyerly interpretation. *Heller* "deals not only with text and original meaning, but with pre- and post-ratification practice, precedent, evolved understandings, normative justification, and consequentialist limitations on the right. It is by surveying this broad array of sources that Justice Scalia locates the ethos of self-defense purportedly at the center of the Second Amendment." Or, as Professor Laurence Tribe and Joshua Matz put it, "Focusing . . . on how *Heller* works—the sources it cites, the logic, the scope of the rights it creates— we discover a ruling exquisitely attuned to the living constitutionalism that Scalia so vehemently disdains."[51]

Professor Nelson Lund goes further, saying that Scalia's reasoning in *Heller* is "at critical points so defective—and in some respects so transparently nonoriginalist—that *Heller* should be seen as an embarrassment for those who joined the majority opinion. It may also be widely (though unfairly) seen as an embarrassment for the interpretive approach that the Court purported to employ. Originalism deserved better from its judicial exponents." Although Lund agreed that Scalia was right on originalist grounds in finding within the Second Amendment an individual right to bear arms, he found the rest of the analysis on the permissibility of the D.C. handgun ban to be both non-originalist and ahistorical.[52]

While Scalia's *Heller* decision got the Court into the business of adjudicating Second Amendment claims, it did not resolve the inevitable balancing of rights and interests. It will fall to future justices to determine how best to balance the newly declared right to own weapons against a government interest in deterring violence. Strict laws banning ownership and possession of guns are likely to remain off the table at least until there is a more liberal majority on the Court. By then, gun rights supporters will argue that *Heller* deserves respect as valid precedent.

In *Heller,* the Court considered the constitutionality of a law in Washington, D.C., part of the federal government. It did not consider whether the Second Amendment applies to state laws restricting individual firearm ownership and usage. As we saw in Chapter 3, however, Scalia signed on to Alito's opinion in the 2010 case *McDonald v. City of Chicago,* holding that the Second Amendment applied against the states under the incorporation doctrine. "Incorporation" of most rights from the Bill of Rights relies on the very same constitutional doctrine that Scalia so heavily criticized in the abortion and same-sex marriage cases—substantive due process. He disagreed with incorporation as an originalist matter but was willing to accept it as a matter of *stare decisis* (unlike his fellow originalist Justice Thomas, who found that the Second Amendment applied to the states through the Privileges or Immunities Clause). He was more willing to rely on substantive due process when it protected a right he liked than when it protected rights he did not like.[53]

⚖

Second Amendment gun rights are perhaps second only to religious freedom among the issues most important to social conservatives like Justice Scalia, and Scalia frequently weighed in on religious freedoms under

the Constitution in ways that seemed to favor greater government entangle-
ment with religion and Christian practices.

Peter Eliasberg, an attorney for the American Civil Liberties Union, had
a very different view from Scalia's about the role of religion in general and
Christianity in particular in American life. In October 2009, Eliasberg was
arguing at the Supreme Court against then–solicitor general Elena Kagan
in *Salazar v. Buono* over whether the federal government violated the First
Amendment's Establishment Clause by transferring to the Veterans of Foreign Wars public land containing a cross to honor dead American veterans. The cross was erected originally in the 1930s in California's Mojave
Desert.[54]

Eliasberg, whose father and grandfather were Jewish war veterans, had
just told the Court that the cross did not honor non-Christian veterans.
That remark got Justice Scalia's attention:

> JUSTICE SCALIA: The cross doesn't honor non-Christians who fought in the
> war? Is that . . .
> MR. ELIASBERG: I believe that's actually correct.
> JUSTICE SCALIA: Where does it say that?
> MR. ELIASBERG: It doesn't say that, but a cross is the predominant symbol of
> Christianity and it signifies that Jesus is the son of God and died to redeem
> mankind for our sins, and I believe that's why the Jewish war veterans—
> JUSTICE SCALIA: It's erected as a war memorial. I assume it is erected in
> honor of all of the war dead. The . . . cross is . . . the most common symbol of
> . . . the resting place of the dead, and it doesn't seem to me—what would you
> have them erect? A cross—some conglomerate of a cross, a Star of David,
> and you know, a Moslem half moon and star?
> MR. ELIASBERG: Well, Justice Scalia, if I may go to your first point. The cross
> is the most common symbol of the resting place of Christians. I have been
> in Jewish cemeteries. There is never a cross on a tombstone of a Jew.
>   (Laughter.)
> MR. ELIASBERG: So it is the most common symbol to honor Christians.
> JUSTICE SCALIA: I don't think you can leap from that to the conclusion that
> the only war dead that that cross honors are the Christian war dead. I think
> that's an outrageous conclusion.
> MR. ELIASBERG: Well, my . . . point here is to say that there is a reason the
> Jewish war veterans came in and said we don't feel honored by this cross. This
> cross can't honor us because it is a religious symbol of another religion.[55]

The Supreme Court ducked the particular question in *Salazar v. Buono*, about the permissibility of the land transfer containing a cross, but during Scalia's decades on the Court it decided dozens of cases concerning religion and the First Amendment. And while the Court's doctrine on both the Establishment Clause (barring Congress from making any law "respecting an establishment of religion") and the Free Exercise Clause (barring Congress from "prohibiting the free exercise thereof") has been convoluted and shifting, Scalia's views were consistent: he was, as Dean Chemerinsky has argued, a strong majoritarian who believed the government could favor or disfavor religion in most ways that a majority would want to do. In a country that is majority Christian, this view has allowed majorities to favor displays of Christian symbols and sectarian public prayers, and accepted laws limiting the activities of smaller religions.[56]

In the 1990 case *Employment Division of Oregon v. Smith,* for example, Scalia wrote an opinion for the Court upholding a decision by the Oregon government to deny unemployment benefits to two employees of a private drug rehabilitation center who used peyote for religious purposes at their Native American Church. The employees argued that the denial of unemployment benefits interfered with their free exercise of religion. In evaluating this claim, Scalia wrote that the government's actions, unlike most actions restricting religious freedom, did not need to be judged under "strict scrutiny."

He instead rejected the employees' arguments under a standard making it much easier to sustain such laws, reasoning: "Precisely because we are a cosmopolitan nation made up of people of almost every conceivable religious preference and precisely because we value and protect that religious divergence, we cannot afford the luxury of deeming *presumptively invalid,* as applied to the religious objector, every regulation of conduct that does not protect an interest of the highest order. The rule respondents favor would open the prospect of constitutionally required religious exemptions from civic obligations of almost every conceivable kind—ranging from compulsory military service, to the payment of taxes, to health and safety regulation such as manslaughter and child neglect laws, compulsory vaccination laws, drug laws, and traffic laws; to social welfare legislation such as minimum wage laws, child labor laws, animal cruelty laws, environmental protection laws, and laws providing for equality of opportunity for the races. The First Amendment's protection of religious liberty does not require this."[57]

Congress disagreed with *Smith,* and through a 1993 statute called the Religious Freedom Restoration Act it made government decisions that burden religion subject to stricter scrutiny than the Court required in *Smith.* In 1997, Scalia and other conservative justices decided in *City of Boerne v. Flores* that the act exceeded Congress's power to regulate the states. Scalia ended his concurrence in *Boerne* by stating that "it shall be people" who decide what religious practices will be exempt from generally applicable laws, even though *Boerne* rejected a law passed by the people's representative, Congress.[58]

Smith allows majorities to burden any religion through a generally applicable law, but in practice, majorities are less likely to pass laws burdening Christianity. While it is thinkable for the public to ban peyote for Native American religious rituals, it is unthinkable that an American legislature would ban sacramental wine for use in Christian services.

Scalia's views on the Establishment Clause were similarly majoritarian. He strongly disagreed with Court's three-part "*Lemon* test" for determining whether a government action touching on religion violated the clause. The *Lemon* test asks whether a challenged law has a secular purpose; whether its primary effect is to advance or hinder religion, and whether it excessively entangles government with religion. Aside from attacking the test's flexibility and muddiness in the *Edwards v. Aguillard* case of 1987, Scalia disagreed with the premise that furthering a religious purpose should somehow be disqualifying for a law, given that religious and secular views can often line up ("we surely would not strike down a law to feed the hungry or shelter the homeless. . . ."). In a 1993 case, *Lamb's Chapel v. Center Moriches Union School District,* he called the *Lemon* test "some ghoul in a late-night horror movie that repeatedly sits up in its grave and shuffles abroad, after being repeatedly killed and buried." He added that the government could endorse religion in general.[59]

In all his time on the Supreme Court, Scalia rejected Establishment Clause challenges in nearly every case. He voted in *Aguillard* to allow Louisiana schools to teach creationism alongside evolution in biology classes. Relying in part on historical practice, he argued that school districts could have clergy offer prayers at public school graduations. He voted in 2005 to allow county courthouses in Kentucky and the Texas State Capitol to display copies of the Ten Commandments. He never found that a legislative majority had gone too far in promoting religion in general, and only once found it went too far in discriminating among religions. In one of his last opinions, in *Town of Greece v. Galloway,* he joined Justice Thomas in concluding that the Establishment Clause was violated only when the government legally coerces religious participation.[60]

Scalia never embraced Thomas's originalist idea that the Establishment Clause may not even bind the states because it was never incorporated against them. But no matter: their differing philosophies led these two conservative justices to reject all Establishment Clause claims against states.

⚖

Soon after Scalia dissented in *Romer v. Evans,* the 1996 case striking down Colorado's Amendment 2 as an act of anti-gay animus, he gave a speech at the Manhattan Institute. University of Arizona professor Toni Massaro recounted part of that speech at a Federalist Society panel in 2016 discussing Scalia's writing and rhetoric. Massaro explained that Scalia told "an appreciative crowd" in 1996 that "'My Court struck [Colorado's law] down as unconstitutional under—I don't know—the 'Homosexuality Clause' of the Bill of Rights, or whatever that is,' and it got a big laugh." Massaro's repetition of the quip did not get a laugh at the Federalist Society (nor was it intended to: she found the remark "dizzying"), and there seemed little appetite at the conference for revisiting the same-sex marriage precedent of *Obergefell.* Times were already changing less than a year after the justice's death.[61]

When an interviewer asked Scalia about his legacy in the gay rights cases, and how Justice Kennedy's role as the "Thurgood Marshall of gay rights" might be perceived in fifty years, he responded with his "at least" comment noted earlier: "I don't know either. And, frankly, I don't care. Maybe the world is spinning toward a wider acceptance of homosexual rights, and here's Scalia, standing athwart it. At least standing athwart it as a constitutional entitlement. But I have never been custodian of my legacy. When I'm dead and gone, I'll either be sublimely happy or terribly unhappy."[62]

6

Home of the Brave

HILLARY: THE MOVIE, A NINETY-MINUTE documentary produced by the conservative group Citizens United, was a hatchet job aimed at Hillary Clinton, then the frontrunner for the Democratic presidential nomination of 2008. Dick Morris, a former Bill Clinton confidante turned enemy, said in the film that Hillary Clinton "is the closest thing we have in America to a European-style socialist." Others in the film, such as conservative firebrand Ann Coulter, were even less complimentary. *Hillary: The Movie* was red meat for those who already hated the Clintons, but it seemed unlikely to convince many others that Clinton was, in the words of the movie, unfit to be commander-in-chief.[1]

A lawsuit over whether funds from for-profit corporations funneled through the Citizens United group could be used to pay for airing the documentary over Comcast cable television's video-on-demand service in the period before the presidential election provided a surprising vehicle for the Supreme Court to overturn precedent and upend the rules for money in U.S. politics. The resulting decision in *Citizens United v. Federal Election Commission* vindicated a position Justice Scalia had hammered on the Court for decades: that corporations have the First Amendment right to spend whatever they want to influence the outcomes of elections. This position fit into his overall disdain for what he saw as intrusive regulation of politics. He was generally content to let the political process run its course, except when legislators or voters acted to limit money in politics or protect minority voting rights. When politics had to be regulated, he favored states over the federal government, the executive branch over Congress, and businesses over consumers and unions, with the courts having the last word.

⚖️

Perhaps the most controversial opinion of Scalia's tenure on the Court under Chief Justice John Roberts, *Citizens United v. Federal Election Commission* did more than resolve the dispute over *Hillary: The Movie.* It reversed decades of settled law. The Court held that business corporations have a right under the First Amendment to spend unlimited sums to help elect or defeat candidates for office. *Citizens United* set the stage for other court and regulatory decisions, including those allowing the emergence of "Super PACs" and other groups that can take unlimited sums from wealthy individuals or corporations to fund election-related advertisements and activities. It has led to an explosion of "outside money"—money not spent by candidates or political parties—in U.S. elections.[2]

For those who pay little attention to the Supreme Court, *Citizens United* may have come as a surprise. But the campaign finance issue had divided the Court since the era of post-Watergate restrictions on money in politics. Justices Scalia and Kennedy had been fighting for a decision allowing corporate money into elections since they dissented in a 1990 decision, *Austin v. Michigan Chamber of Commerce.* They divided on social issues such as abortion and same-sex marriage, but here they were united. Once Sandra Day O'Connor left the Supreme Court in 2006, they finally could put together a majority to overturn *Austin.*[3]

Austin concerned a Michigan state campaign finance law, not a law regulating federal elections. Federal campaign finance laws generally do not apply to state and local elections, and it is up to each state to set its own rules. Michigan's law for state elections, like a parallel federal election law, provided that a business corporation could not spend money on election activity from its "general treasury funds," meaning the money the corporation receives from its business activities. The corporation could set up a separate entity, called a "political action committee" (or "PAC"), to engage in election-related activities. The corporate PAC could solicit donations of up to $5,000 from executives, officers, and shareholders of the corporation.

The same limits applied to non-profit corporations, like the United States Chamber of Commerce, that took money from business corporations. Without this rule, business corporations could simply get around limits by sending the money through a non-profit. Although Michigan's law applied to most businesses, it did not apply to media corporations engaged in providing news and commentary. A newspaper or a television station could use all of its resources to support or oppose candidates for office. Further, unlike the federal PAC law, which applied evenly to both business corporations and labor unions, the Michigan PAC law applied only to corporations.

On a 6–3 vote, the Supreme Court held that Michigan's law did not violate the First Amendment guarantees of free speech and association or the Equal Protection Clause of the Fourteenth Amendment.

In an earlier case, *Buckley v. Valeo* (1976), the Court had held that the United States Congress violated the First Amendment when it limited independent spending by individuals on elections. It concluded that limits on independent spending were an infringement on First Amendment rights of free speech and association, and that under the Court's "strict scrutiny" review, the government could justify the limit only by pointing to a "compelling interest" and showing that the law was "narrowly tailored" to meet that interest.[4]

Although the Court recognized that preventing corruption was a compelling interest, it held that that truly independent spending by individuals could not corrupt candidates or create the appearance of corruption. If the candidate and spender could not coordinate, the Court reasoned, there was no chance for bribery or undue influence. This meant that an individual spending limit was unconstitutional because it was not narrowly tailored to the government's anticorruption interest. Further, the Court rejected the idea that the government could limit money in elections for purposes of leveling the playing field. It was "wholly foreign to the First Amendment" for the government to limit the voices of some to enhance the voices of others.[5]

Austin, like *Buckley*, also involved spending limits. But while *Buckley* concerned the permissibility of spending limits applied to individuals, *Austin* concerned spending limits applied to business corporations. In *Austin*, the Court held that the corporate PAC requirement and ban on spending general treasury funds satisfied strict scrutiny. Rather than find that the rules were justified to prevent bribery-like corruption, the *Austin* Court held that Michigan's law was designed to prevent a "different type of corruption in the political arena: the corrosive and distorting effects of immense aggregations of wealth that are accumulated with the help of the corporate form and that have little or no correlation to the public's support for the corporation's political ideas."[6]

Although the Court described this interest as "corruption," its actual concern appeared to be political inequality: it allowed Michigan to prevent wealthy corporations from having disproportionate influence over its elections. The Court did not make this equality point directly, likely because *Buckley* had rejected political equality as a reason to limit spending.

Justice Scalia's pungent dissent rejected the majority's "antidistortion" argument. He began his opinion by focusing on what he saw as the censorship allowed by Michigan's law: "'Attention all citizens. To assure the fairness of elections by preventing disproportionate expression of the views of any single powerful group, your Government has decided that the following associations of persons shall be prohibited from speaking or writing in support of any candidate: ___.' In permitting Michigan to make private corporations the first object of this Orwellian announcement, the Court today endorses the principle that too much speech is an evil that the democratic majority can proscribe."[7]

All the major arguments that conservatives later advanced against campaign finance laws can be found in Scalia's dissent. He argued consistent with his conservative libertarian outlook that limiting how much any person or entity spends in elections counts as unconstitutional censorship. He argued that legislatures often pass campaign laws intending to protect incumbents. He maintained that an incumbent politician who says "he welcomes full and fair debate is no more to be trusted than the entrenched monopolist who says he welcomes full and fair competition." He suggested that the reason Michigan regulated the spending of business corporations and not labor unions was because of the political power of labor unions in Michigan. And he attacked the exemption for the press. Any special danger of "disproportionate" corporate power, he wrote, would apply *especially* to corporations that produce news stories and commentary. "Amassed corporate wealth that regularly sits astride the ordinary channels of information is much more likely to produce the New Corruption (too much of one point of view) than amassed corporate wealth that is generally busy making money elsewhere. Such media corporations not only have vastly greater power to perpetrate the evil of overinforming, they also have vastly greater opportunity."[8]

Scalia did not make this point to suggest that the press could be limited like other corporations. Instead, he argued that the press could be the next entity the government could target for regulation because the Court did not *require* its exemption from campaign finance laws—it only *allowed* Michigan to exempt media corporations. He believed the better solution was to let all corporations spend unlimited sums in elections.

Between 1990 and 2010, Scalia consistently argued that all limits on election spending violated the First Amendment. But until *Citizens United,* he could not find four other votes to support him. In a 2003 case reviewing the constitutionality of the Bipartisan Campaign Reform Act of 2002 (commonly known as the McCain-Feingold law for its two Senate sponsors), *McConnell v. Federal Election Commission,* the Court reaffirmed and extended the *Austin* case on a 5–4 vote.[9]

The Supreme Court majority in *McConnell* advanced a very different view from Scalia's on how the First Amendment related to campaign finance laws. To the *McConnell* majority, large amounts of money flowing into politics raised dangers of corruption and undue influence, even if the money was spent independently. Too much spending from those with the greatest wealth could undermine democracy and the public's faith in democracy. And rather than worry that these laws were passed to protect incumbents, the *McConnell* majority believed the Court should defer to the elected officials who crafted campaign finance laws, because legislators, with experience running for office, had greater expertise than judges on the dangers of money in politics.

McConnell marked the high point of Supreme Court deference toward governments that passed restrictive campaign finance laws to improve the democratic process. In 2006, however, Sandra Day O'Connor retired from the Supreme Court and was replaced by Samuel Alito, whose views on campaign finance are similar to Scalia's. At first, Alito (and the new chief justice Roberts) acted to limit *Austin* and *McConnell* rather than to overrule them.

Scalia criticized their caution as "faux judicial restraint." Then, in the *Citizens United* case decided in 2010, the position Scalia had championed since his *Austin* dissent prevailed, as five justices voted to overturn *Austin* and part of *McConnell*.[10]

Justice Kennedy's opinion in *Citizens United* held that *Austin*'s antidistortion argument was about equality, not corruption, and under the First Amendment, as interpreted in *Buckley*, equality was an impermissible reason to limit money in politics. The *Citizens United* majority accepted all of Scalia's arguments—about the press, about incumbency protection, and about censorship—in holding that any limit on money spent by human or corporate citizens in elections violates the First Amendment. Scalia wrote a brief concurrence, rebutting the argument made by Justice Stevens in dissent that an originalist understanding of the First Amendment allowed Congress to limit corporate spending in campaigns.[11]

Despite this ruling, Scalia had no problem voting just two years later to allow the federal government to ban *all* campaign-related spending by foreign individuals, even those on American soil. The plaintiff in that case, Benjamin Bluman, was a Canadian lawyer living in New York who wanted to spend fifty cents to print flyers at Kinko's supporting President Obama's reelection and pass out those flyers in Central Park. He faced years in jail and up to a $10,000 fine for violating the law barring foreign spending in U.S. elections. If the First Amendment really provided "no foothold" to exclude "any category of speaker," Scalia's vote in *Bluman* made no sense. It made sense only as Scalia's populist nationalism trumping his conservative libertarianism.[12]

The result of *Citizens United* has been dramatic. Outside spending in U.S. federal elections reached about $1.3 billion in 2012 and exceeded $1.4 billion in 2016. In the 2012 elections, one couple, Sheldon and Miriam Adelson, spent between $98 million and $150 million to try to elect Republican candidates. In the midterm elections of 2014, an environmentalist, Tom Steyer, spent $74 million to try to preserve the Democrats' United States Senate majority. In 2016, Steyer and Adelson again topped the list of disclosed donors, with Steyer giving Super PACs over $66 million and Adelson over $42 million.[13]

Even with this explosion in outside money and the great rise of wealthy donors influencing elections, the issue is not settled. Those who favor even less regulation have brought more lawsuits, seeking to get the courts to strike down limits on how much individuals can give directly to political parties and candidates, and to prevent disclosure of these contributions.

Before Scalia's death, these suits appeared likely to succeed, except for those seeking to prevent public disclosure of the sources of campaign financing. Scalia was perhaps the most outspoken justice in favor of campaign finance disclosure, saying that the First Amendment should not be read to allow for anonymous campaign activity. Writing in a 1995 case, he declared: "I do not know where the Court derives its perception that 'anonymous pamphleteering is not a pernicious, fraudulent practice, but an honorable tradition of advocacy and of dissent.' I can imagine no reason why an anonymous leaflet is any more honorable, as a general matter, than an anonymous phone call or an anonymous letter. It facilitates wrong by eliminating accountability, which is ordinarily the very purpose of the anonymity."[14]

In a 2010 case raising parallel issues about the identity of people signing petitions to put an anti-gay-rights measure on the Washington State ballot, Scalia declared the need for "civic courage." "For my part, I do not look forward to a society which, thanks to the Supreme Court, campaigns anonymously and even exercises the direct democracy of initiative and referendum hidden from public scrutiny and protected from the accountability of criticism. This does not resemble the Home of the Brave."[15]

On this question, Scalia parted company with his fellow originalist Justice Clarence Thomas. Thomas, looking to the tradition of anonymous pamphleteering during the American Revolution, found in the First Amendment's cryptic words about freedom of "speech" a right to anonymous political speech. His view remains a decidedly minority one. In *Citizens United,* Thomas alone dissented from the Court's upholding of the laws requiring the disclosure of donors funding television ads promoting *Hillary: The Movie.* But it was Scalia's position rejecting Thomas's originalist argument that prevailed.[16]

⚖️

Scalia's concern that incumbent lawmakers are apt to pass laws protecting their own interests was a major reason for his skepticism about campaign finance limits, but he was much less concerned about incumbency protection and partisan self-dealing in other areas of election law, such as redistricting and the rules for running state and local elections.

The rules regarding legislative districts are important in the United States because voters choose members of Congress, most state legislators, and many local elected officials using winner-take-all voting in single-member districts. Candidates, not parties, run in elections, and the plurality winner in each district wins the single seat. If they can draw the district lines that define each legislator's territory, members of one political party may gerrymander the districts to gain more seats than the party would be entitled to under a purely proportional system of interest representation. The term "gerrymander" comes from a cartoon criticizing districts drawn by a nineteenth-century Massachusetts governor, Elbridge Gerry. One district was said to be shaped like a salamander—"Gerry's salamander," or "gerrymander."[17]

Before the 1960s, Congress and the Supreme Court put few constraints on district-based voting, other than a requirement that each state use single-member Congressional districts. The Court had ruled in the 1940s that it could not hear questions over unequally populated legislative districts, which give voters in districts with smaller populations greater voting power. It said that this was a "nonjusticiable" political question.[18]

But it reversed itself in *Baker v. Carr,* holding that courts *could* rule on such questions. In later cases, including *Reynolds v. Sims,* the Court imposed the one person, one vote rule, which requires equality in populations across districts. Congress passed the Voting Rights Act in 1965 which, as amended in 1982, provides for better representation of racial minority groups, most importantly African American, Latino, and Native American voters. Although the Voting Rights Act requires those who draw legislative districts to be race-conscious in redistricting, the Supreme Court since the 1990s has held that taking race too much into account—making it the "predominant factor" in drawing district lines—violates the Equal Protection Clause of the Constitution.[19]

For many decades, opponents of partisan gerrymandering have tried to get the Court to impose some sort of limit on drawing district lines to favor one political party. In a 1986 case, *Davis v. Bandemer,* the Court agreed that it could hear claims of partisan gerrymandering but held that the district-ing plan in Indiana, where the case arose, did not constitute a partisan ger-rymander. Four justices endorsed one test for partisan gerrymandering and two others took a different approach. But the *Bandemer* standards proved very difficult to meet, and for the next eighteen years there were no success-ful cases brought against partisan gerrymandering.[20]

The Court returned to the issue in 2004 in *Vieth v. Jubelirer*, which in-volved allegations of gerrymandering in the creation of congressional districts for Pennsylvania. The Court divided badly. Scalia, writing for four conserv-ative justices, took the position that *Bandemer* was wrong and that partisan gerrymandering posed a nonjusticiable political question—meaning the courts had no authority to hear such claims. Four liberal justices disagreed both on justiciability and on the standard, but each of them offered a dif-ferent standard for deciding when it is permissible to take party into ac-count in drawing district lines and when it is not. Scalia's opinion rejected each of the dissenters' standards, as well as the standards from *Bandemer* and those proposed by the *Vieth* plaintiffs. All, he wrote, were "judicially unmanageable."[21]

But his position did not represent the majority view of the Court. Jus-tice Kennedy, writing only for himself, argued that the question of partisan gerrymandering is justiciable, meaning courts can hear such cases. But he agreed with Scalia and the other conservative justices that each of the stand-ards proposed by the dissenters and others was improper and judicially unmanageable. The result of this odd 4–1–4 split was that the plaintiffs in *Vieth* lost their case but the issue remained open for future litigation.

Kennedy suggested that litigants in some future case might use com-puter programs, a study of history, or a focus on First Amendment asso-ciational rights to provide a basis for creating a manageable standard for separating the permissible and impermissible consideration of race in re-districting. Scalia dismissed Kennedy's "never-say-never" approach to par-tisan gerrymandering claims, calling Kennedy's position "not an available disposition." In other words, according to Scalia, Kennedy could not both reject the plaintiffs' claims in *Vieth* but also leave open the question of cre-ating a standard for a future case. Yet Kennedy did just that.

Perhaps the most interesting aspect of Scalia's opinion is his admission that extreme partisan gerrymandering may well be unconstitutional, even if the courts do not have the tools to police it: "Much of [Justice Stevens's] dissent is addressed to the incompatibility of severe partisan gerrymanders with democratic principles. We do not disagree with that judgment, any more than we disagree with the judgment that it would be unconstitutional for the Senate to employ, in impeachment proceedings, procedures that are incompatible with its obligation to 'try' impeachments. The issue we have discussed is not whether severe partisan gerrymanders violate the Constitution, but whether it is for the courts to say when a violation has occurred, and to design a remedy." He noted that Justice Stevens had said he erred "in assuming that politics is 'an ordinary and lawful motive'" in redistricting, "but all he brings forward to contest that is the argument that an *excessive* injection of politics is *un*lawful. So it is, and so does our opinion assume."[22]

Since 2004, when the Court decided *Vieth,* it passed up opportunities to reconsider, or at least for Justice Kennedy to reconsider, whether there is a judicially manageable standard for policing partisan gerrymandering. Litigants have brought new cases to try to come up with a standard which would satisfy Kennedy that there is a bright line to draw between permissible consideration of party interests in drawing district lines and unconstitutional partisan gerrymanders. And the Court finally agreed to hear one of those cases, *Gill v. Whitford,* from Wisconsin, in the 2017–2018 term, perhaps the last time the Court will consider such a question before a Kennedy retirement.[23]

A ruling limiting partisan gerrymandering would likely benefit the Democratic Party, at least in the short term. Since many more U.S. legislatures are controlled by Republicans than Democrats, a move to curb partisan excesses would likely lead to more Democratic districts. The number of seats created would likely not be enough, by itself, to swing control of the United States House of Representatives from one party to another, but it might make for a closer balance than the current one.

In the meantime, in the absence of a standard from the Supreme Court, some states have adopted rules to limit partisan gerrymandering. These changes have come in states where voters can adopt rules via the initiative process. Direct democracy has allowed the creation of non-partisan redis-

tricting commissions in California, Arizona, and elsewhere, and a requirement in Florida that legislatures not take partisan advantage into account
in redistricting. Early results show that these methods limit partisan redistricting to some extent.

On this question, too, Justices Kennedy and Scalia divided. Kennedy
sided with the Court's liberals in holding that voters constitutionally could
seek to limit the role of politics in congressional redistricting. Scalia and
four other conservatives viewed the Elections Clause contained in the Constitution's Article I as forbidding voter-initiated action in this area and as
vesting in state *legislatures* alone (subject to congressional override) the
power to set the rules for congressional elections.[24]

⚖️

Scalia was inconsistent on the question of judicial deference to legislative
actions affecting legislators' own political power. He had a hands-off attitude
toward partisan gerrymandering, letting legislators set their own rules affecting their own reelection. Not so when it came to campaign finance laws.

Speech and association issues are at the core of campaign finance challenges but enter only peripherally in partisan gerrymandering cases. Still,
we cannot simply chalk up Scalia's divergent approaches in these cases to
the different First Amendment stakes. In another key First Amendment
area, he was quite willing to ignore a chilling of political activity to allow
victors to get their spoils.

While Scalia was extremely protective of the speech and association rights
of huge corporations and of billionaires to spend unlimited dollars to elect
or defeat their chosen candidates, he believed it was perfectly fine for states
like Illinois to hire, fire, promote, and demote employees just because of
their partisan affiliation. If the Republican governor of Illinois wanted to
fire a state janitor because he was registered as a Democrat, Scalia saw no
First Amendment violation.

This is exactly what gave rise to *Rutan v. Republican Party of Illinois*, a
major case from 1990 holding that patronage hiring, firing, transferring,
and promotion of non-policymaking employees violates the First Amendment. Scalia, in dissent, wrote that patronage greases the wheels of government. It promotes strong political parties, which Scalia found a strong

enough government interest that it overrode employees' First Amendment rights to free association. A janitor or administrative assistant could be fired simply for belonging to the wrong political party. "It may well be that the Good Government Leagues of America were right, and that [George W.] Plunkitt, James Michael Curley, and their ilk were wrong; but that is not entirely certain. As the merit principle has been extended and its effects increasingly felt; as the Boss Tweeds, the Tammany Halls, the Pendergast Machines, the Byrd Machines, and the Daley Machines have faded into history; we find that political leaders at all levels increasingly complain of the helplessness of elected government, unprotected by 'party discipline,' before the demands of small and cohesive interest groups."[25]

⚖

This inconsistency in deference to legislatures over the allocation of political power extended to voting rights. Despite his belief that political actors should have a free hand in drawing districts to perpetuate their own power, and in hiring and firing low-level employees to reward political loyalty, Scalia was often unwilling to accept legislative judgments about the need to protect racial and ethnic minorities' and others' access to the ballot. He believed states could use unsubstantiated fears of voter fraud as an excuse to limit the franchise, and even create special burdens in voting for some citizens.

In 1965, Congress passed the Voting Rights Act to assure that the promise of the Thirteenth, Fourteenth, and Fifteenth Amendments would be fulfilled, allowing African Americans to have full voting rights in fact and not just in theory. A key part of the Voting Rights Act was Section 5, which required that states and localities with a history of racial discrimination in voting get federal approval ("preclearance") before making any changes to their voting rules, such as changing the location of a polling place or redrawing district lines. Under Section 5, the burden fell on the covered jurisdiction to show that the law was not enacted with a discriminatory purpose and that it would not make minority voters worse off. Section 5 was temporary, but Congress kept extending it, citing continued problems with voting rights in the covered jurisdictions. The most recent extension came in 2006, for twenty-five years.

In 1982, Congress significantly strengthened the Voting Rights Act by revising Section 2 to make it easier for minority voters—not just African Americans but Latinos, Native Americans, and Asians—to get representation in Congress and on state and local legislative bodies. Thanks to *Thornburg v. Gingles,* a 1986 decision issued just before Scalia joined the Court, when minority voters could prove that whites and minority voters voted for different candidates in district elections, and that the minority voting group was large enough to elect a candidate of its choice in a district election, "vote dilution" could require the redrawing of district lines to create "majority-minority" districts in which the protected minority group could elect its preferred candidates to office.[26]

Throughout his time on the Court, Scalia showed great hostility to both Section 2 and Section 5 of the Voting Rights Act. He voted with Justice Thomas to hold that few voting decisions made by state and local bodies had to be precleared under Section 5 or could be subject to suit under Section 2. He believed Section 2 should not cover vote dilution claims at all, meaning it would have no application to protect minority rights in redistricting. He wrote a majority opinion for the Court's conservatives narrowly construing what it meant for a covered jurisdiction under Section 5 to act with a racially discriminatory purpose. He sided with the Court's conservatives in creating a new "racial gerrymandering" cause of action under the Equal Protection Clause when jurisdictions or the U.S. Department of Justice drew too many majority-minority districts. He voted to read the scope of Section 2 voting protections narrowly, suggesting that broad interpretations were unconstitutional or not supported by the text of the act.[27]

Most dramatically, Scalia joined the other conservative justices in 2013 to rule that the preclearance provision of the act, which the Court had repeatedly upheld as a constitutional exercise of congressional power to enforce the Reconstruction Amendments, was no longer constitutional. In *Shelby County v. Holder,* Chief Justice Roberts, writing also for Justices Alito, Kennedy, Scalia, and Thomas, held that Congress's failure to update the coverage formula to decide which states had to submit to preclearance violated the "equal sovereignty" of the states not allowing the federal government to treat one state worse than another without a good reason, a phrase found nowhere in the Constitution. Justice Ginsburg, for the four liberal dissenters, objected to this second-guessing of Congress's determination that minority voters continued to need protection in places where racial discrimination in voting had been prevalent, writing: "Throwing out preclearance when it has worked and is continuing to work to stop discriminatory changes is like throwing away your umbrella in a rainstorm because you are not getting wet."[28]

At the *Shelby County* oral argument, Scalia could not conceal his disdain for the Voting Rights Act. He suggested that Congress continued to extend the act because minority voters had too much political power, making legislators afraid to vote against its renewal. Responding to Solicitor General Donald Verrilli's suggestion that Congress was entitled to make the judgment that racial problems in voting remained serious enough to warrant an additional period of preclearance, Scalia responded:

JUSTICE SCALIA: Well, maybe it was making that judgment, Mr. Verrilli. But that's . . . a problem that I have. This Court doesn't like to get involved in . . . racial questions such as this one. It's something that can be left . . . to Congress.

The problem here, however, is suggested by the comment I made earlier, that the initial enactment of this legislation . . . in a time when the need for it was so much more abundantly clear was—in the Senate, there—it was double-digits against it. And that was only a 5-year term.

Then, it is reenacted 5 years later, again for a 5-year term. Double-digits against it in the Senate. Then it was reenacted for 7 years. Single digits against it. Then enacted for 25 years, 8 Senate votes against it.

And this last enactment, not a single vote in the Senate against it. And the House is pretty much the same. Now, I don't think that's attributable to the fact that it is so much clearer now that we need this. I think it is attributable, very likely attributable, to a phenomenon that is called perpetuation of racial entitlement. It's been written about. Whenever a society adopts racial entitlements, it is very difficult to get out of them through the normal political processes.

I don't think there is anything to be gained by any Senator to vote against continuation of this act. And I am fairly confident it will be reenacted in perpetuity unless . . . a court can say it does not comport with the Constitution. You have to show, when you are treating different States differently, that there's a good reason for it.

That's the . . . the concern that those of us who . . . have some questions about this statute have. It's . . . a concern that this is not the kind of a question you can leave to Congress. There are certain districts in the House that are black districts by law just about now. And even the Virginia Senators, they have no interest in voting against this. The State government is not their government, and they are going to lose—they are going to lose votes if they do not reenact the Voting Rights Act.

Even the name of it is wonderful: The Voting Rights Act. Who is going to vote against that in the future?[29]

This was the second time Scalia had questioned the Senate's 98–0 vote for the Voting Rights Act renewal of 2006, and it seemed to mark an exception to his rule that courts should let politicians make the choices about how to divide political power. In 2009, when the Court first considered (and failed to resolve) the constitutional challenge to Congress's renewal of preclearance, Scalia remarked at oral argument: "The Israeli supreme court, the Sanhedrin, used to have a rule that if the death penalty was pronounced unanimously, it was invalid, because there must be something wrong there." The remark led Adam Liptak, the Supreme Court reporter for the *New York Times,* to note that the Sanhedrin comment was "as an offhand reference to an ancient court, and Justice Scalia was not announcing a universal principle. Indeed, he almost certainly does not think that every unanimous legislative act is problematic. In 1986, for instance, the Senate approved Justice Scalia's nomination to the Supreme Court by a vote of 98 to 0."[30]

Putting together his positions in *Shelby County* and in *United States v. Windsor,* in which Justice Scalia dissented from a Court decision striking down part of the federal Defense of Marriage Act as a judicial usurpation of the democratic function, it is hard to escape the conclusion that his deference to democratic acts of legislative bodies depended in good part on how much he liked the underlying law.

⚖

As Ginsburg foresaw, after *Shelby County* several jurisdictions that had been covered under Section 5 passed new restrictive voting laws. This has led to new lawsuits over whether these measures violate the Voting Rights Act. There is little doubt how Justice Scalia would have voted in considering such challenges.[31] Even before *Shelby County*, however, he voted to approve increasingly restrictive voting rules put in place in areas not then covered by the preclearance provisions of the Voting Rights Act.

In 2008, the Court badly divided over the constitutionality of an Indiana law that required voters to produce one of a few acceptable forms of photographic identification for voting. *Crawford v. Marion County Election Board* is important because Indiana was one of the first states to adopt strict voter identification requirements after the disputed presidential election of 2000. Roughly speaking, some states under Republican control, such as Indiana, have enacted laws making it harder to register and vote, while some states controlled by Democrats have adopted laws making registering and voting easier. Both Democrats and Republicans believe that easier voting and registration helps Democrats, because more new voters and less-regular voters are more likely vote Democratic.[32]

The *Crawford* case proceeded without much evidence on either side. The state could point to no evidence that impersonation fraud (where one person goes to the polls claiming to be someone else) was a problem. It conceded there were no known cases of impersonation fraud in Indiana. But the plaintiffs produced few eligible voters who were prevented from voting because they lacked the right identification.

The Supreme Court divided 3–3–3. Justice Stevens, writing for himself, Chief Justice Roberts, and Justice Kennedy, rejected the challenge to the law, holding that most voters faced only a minor burden and the law was justified by important state interests in preventing voter fraud and instilling confidence in the voting process. These interests were acceptable even though the state could point to no modern incidents of impersonation voter fraud. But the Stevens opinion left open the possibility of new lawsuits brought by groups of voters who faced significant burdens, such as those who could not afford the documents needed to get a "free" voter identification card.

Scalia, writing for himself, Justice Alito, and Justice Thomas, took a different view. Like the three justices in the Stevens bloc, he believed the law placed little burden on most voters. On this basis, however, he would have upheld the law against *everyone*, leaving no opening for challenges from voters who faced special burdens in obtaining the right form of identifica-

tion. "The Indiana photo-identification law," he wrote, "is a generally applicable, nondiscriminatory voting regulation, and our precedents refute the
view that individual impacts are relevant to determining the severity of the
burden it imposes."[33]

Under this view, even if some voters faced severe burdens, the law was
constitutional because most people were not burdened. This is an extreme
position. Consider, for example, evidence from Wisconsin, which recently
imposed a new strict voter I.D. law. The state Supreme Court read the state
constitution to require the Department of Motor Vehicles to assist voters
facing burdens to obtain the documents necessary to get an identification
card. Ongoing litigation accuses the department of refusing to grant an
identification card to an otherwise eligible voter who lacked the use of her
hands, because the voter could not sign the form requesting the waiver. The
department refused to accept the signature of the voter's daughter, who had
the legal power to sign for her. And the suit alleges that it took a few years
and considerable effort for someone who was born in a German concentration camp during World War II to establish identity and get a Wisconsin
voter identification card. Justice Scalia would say these voters should have
no chance for judicial relief.[34]

In his *Crawford* opinion, Scalia further worried that allowing lawsuits
to go forward based upon arguments that some voters were burdened by
voting laws would lead to too much litigation. He warned of a flood of future suits: "A State reducing the number of polling places would be open to
the complaint it has violated the rights of disabled voters who live near the
closed stations. Indeed, it may even be the case that some laws already on
the books are especially burdensome for some voters, and one can predict
lawsuits demanding that a State adopt voting over the Internet or expand
absentee balloting."[35]

While Scalia was bothered by the possibility of suits to help assure that
eligible voters could cast a meaningful ballot, the dissenting justices in
Crawford were more concerned about the disenfranchisement of voters facing severe burdens. Justices Souter, Ginsburg, and Breyer in dissent agreed
with Stevens that the courts should use closer scrutiny to examine voting
laws that could burden some voters. But unlike Stevens, they believed that
the law imposed greater burdens on many voters and that the state had

failed to demonstrate that its stated (but unproven) interests in preventing fraud and promoting voter confidence were strong enough to justify those burdens. The dissenters would have struck down the law—for all voters in Indiana.[36]

The Stevens opinion recognized that Indiana might have passed its law for partisan reasons—it passed on a straight party-line vote, with only Republican legislators voting in favor and only Democrats voting against. But Stevens found the law permissible because there were non-discriminatory reasons to pass it as well. Scalia's opinion did not even address partisanship concerns, a sharp contrast to his focus on the issue of incumbency protection in the campaign finance cases. The Court allowed Indiana to enforce its law despite the legislators' likely partisan motivations.

The dissenters, in contrast, saw Indiana as acting in a partisan manner, and its stated reasons for the identification requirement as a pretext for discrimination. Justice Souter wrote that Indiana adopted one of the strictest voter identification laws "without a shred of evidence that in-person voter impersonation is a problem in the state, much less a crisis."

Souter explained that Indiana "hardly even tries to explain its decision to force indigents or religious objectors to travel all the way to their county seats every time they wish to vote, and if there is any waning of confidence in the administration of elections it probably owes more to the State's violation of federal election law than to any imposters at the polling places. It is impossible to say, on this record, that the State's interest in adopting its signally inhibiting photo identification requirement has been shown to outweigh the serious burdens it imposes on the right to vote." He concluded that "if more were needed to condemn this law, our own precedent would provide it, for the calculation revealed in the Indiana statute crosses a line when it targets the poor and the weak."[37]

Shelby County and *Crawford* laid bare an ideological division between conservatives and liberals. In *Shelby County,* the conservatives would not let Congress provide voting rights protections, suggesting that the legislative process was too warped by concerns about "racial entitlements." In *Crawford,* Scalia led the most conservative group of justices to embrace complete deference to state choices about conducting elections, even when those choices are motivated by partisanship and could leave some voters disenfranchised and without recourse. His inconsistent opinions here were of a piece with his views on partisan gerrymandering and political patronage.

⚖⚖

Likely the most controversial Supreme Court decision of Scalia's tenure was the *Bush v. Gore* case in 2000. After the extremely close presidential election between Republican George W. Bush and Democrat Al Gore, the result came down to the electoral votes from the state of Florida, where the candidates were within a few hundred votes of each other.[38]

Elsewhere I have described the long court battle between the parties, the decentralization of American election administration, the role that partisan elected officials played in deciding how to handle Gore's effort to get recounts in some counties, and the controversial decisions of both the Florida Supreme Court and the United States Supreme Court. The latter divided 5–4, with conservatives voting to stop the recount and liberals voting to allow it to continue. Stopping the recount allowed Bush, ahead at the time, to win Florida's electoral votes and the presidency.[39]

The five most conservative justices, including Scalia, held in an unsigned (per curiam) opinion that election judges used inconsistent standards to determine voter intent when examining "punch card" paper ballots, and that this violated the Equal Protection Clause of the Fourteenth Amendment. Different counties, and different election judges within counties, used different methods for deciding what markings on the ballots counted as a valid vote for a candidate. According to the majority, once the Florida legislature gave voters the right to vote for president, the state "may not, by later arbitrary and disparate treatment, value one person's vote over that of another."[40]

Justice Souter and (depending on how one parses his opinion) Justice Breyer accepted the majority's equal protection argument. Justices Ginsburg and Stevens did not, but all four of the dissenting justices agreed that even if there was a constitutional problem with Florida's rules for recounting votes, the case should have been sent back to Florida for a recount. The remedy was to count more and not, as the majority ordered, to end the counting.[41]

Bush v. Gore was controversial for many reasons, including the fact that the conservative majority adopted a liberal reading of the Equal Protection Clause to expand voting rights, while at least two of the liberal dissenters adopted a narrower reading which refused to expand voting rights. Given their ideological commitments, one would have expected the opposite. The role reversal underscored the suggestion that the justices were motivated (one presumes subconsciously) more by their choice of candidates than by a neutral examination of the Constitution's requirements.

Justice Scalia, along with Chief Justice Rehnquist and Justice Thomas, signed on to the majority opinion with this expansive view of equal protection. They likely did it to create five votes for a majority opinion, rather than an opinion for two justices and a separate opinion for three others. But they offered a different reason for siding with Bush, and one suspects they preferred this theory to the equal protection theory embraced by Kennedy and O'Connor. The alternative theory was that under Article II of the Constitution, only the state *legislature* had the power to set the rules for choosing presidential electors. The Florida Supreme Court, by allowing recounts and extending deadlines, was, under this theory, usurping the state legislature's power to set the rules for an election. (Never mind that the state legislature itself contemplated a role for state courts in resolving election disputes, including for presidential elections, and that court intervention and interpretation were thus part of the legislature's intent.)

In his public appearances, Scalia often faced questions about the *Bush v. Gore* decision. He would tell Democrats and others disappointed with the result to "get over it!" But the decision is still debated, just about everywhere except on the Court itself. Throughout the rest of Scalia's tenure, *Bush v. Gore* was never cited or discussed in a majority opinion. The Court did not even discuss it when it was right on point. The dissenters in the 2015 case considering the constitutionality of Arizona's voter initiative to create an independent redistricting commission for congressional elections did not cite *Bush v. Gore*, even though it raised the parallel issue about the power of the state "legislature" to set certain federal election rules. Since 2000, only Thomas has cited *Bush v. Gore*, in a single dissenting opinion in 2013, and not for the case's key holding.[42]

Bush v. Gore demonstrated that we cannot expect the justices to put aside partisan leanings when the stakes are that high. Should there be another disputed presidential election, both the Court and the nation could be even more partisan and divided than they were in 2000. In *Bush v. Gore,* two Republican-appointed justices, Souter and Stevens, were among the liberal dissenters. A division along ideological lines was not also, or by definition, a division along party lines.

Today, however, all of the Supreme Court justices considered liberal were nominated by Democratic presidents, and all of the justices considered conservative were nominated by Republican presidents. This division increases partisan perceptions of the Court. It is not that these justices consciously vote to favor the party of the president who chose them, but that these justices were nominated because their jurisprudential views line up with their party's interests and ideology. But even ideology gave way in *Bush v. Gore* to the politics of the moment, not just for Scalia but for all of the justices.

⚖️

Scalia's vote in the case was odd, not only in endorsing a broad view of equal protection law usually favored by liberals but also in rejecting the power of the state to resolve the election dispute under its own rules rather than turning the question over to the federal courts. Again, politics may be part of the explanation. His vote aligned him against the Democratic-dominated Florida Supreme Court (which he saw as usurping the state legislature's power) and with Jeb Bush, the Republican governor (and the Republican presidential candidate's brother), the Republican secretary of state, Katharine Harris, and the Republican-dominated Florida legislature, which threatened to pick a rival slate of electors had state courts declared Gore the winner.

Scalia took a more typical position on federalism and states' rights in his vote in *Shelby County,* which killed a key part of the Voting Rights Act as a congressional violation of state sovereignty. He almost always voted to favor states over the federal government, as he did in *City of Boerne v. Flores,* when he joined other conservatives in rejecting congressional attempts to require states to accommodate religious objections through the Religious Freedom Restoration Act. He voted the same way in *Printz v. United States,* holding, despite the lack of "constitutional text [on] this precise question," that Congress could not require state governments to assist the federal government in implementing federal laws. The law at issue was the Brady Handgun Violence Prevention Act, and it would have required local law enforcement assistance in running federal background checks for gun purchasers. (It is an opinion that resonates as the Trump administration may conscript local police departments to assist the federal government in immigration round-ups.)[43]

He did not believe in the Court's approach to the "Dormant Commerce Clause," a doctrine which the Court had used over the years to prevent states from passing protectionist trade legislation. He viewed such legislation as a state's prerogative, and in 2015 he called the Court's approach a "judicial fraud" because it was not based directly upon the text of the Constitution. Dissenting with Justice Thomas in his last full term on the Court in *Comptroller of Treasury of Maryland v. Wynne,* he parted company with Thomas on whether to nonetheless follow some earlier precedent in the area despite the doctrine being a "fraud." As expected, Scalia would, and Thomas would not.[44]

In 2012, he dissented bitterly in *Arizona v. United States,* a case holding that parts of Arizona's controversial anti-immigration law, S.B. 1070, were preempted by the federal government's broad immigration powers. Presaging some of the themes that emerged in Donald Trump's 2016 presidential campaign, Scalia wrote that if the federal government chose not to enforce all federal immigration laws, states could do so on their own. He mocked the "looming specter of inutterable horror" if each state could prosecute federal immigration registration violations. It "seems to me not so horrible and even less looming. But there has come to pass, and is with us today, the specter that Arizona and the States that support it predicted: A Federal Government that does not want to enforce the immigration laws as written, and leaves the States' borders unprotected against immigrants whom those laws would exclude. So the issue is a stark one. Are the sovereign States at the mercy of the Federal Executive's refusal to enforce the Nation's immigration laws?"

Scalia then suggested that the states joining the Union at the time of the Constitution's ratification would not have agreed to give up this right of sovereignty to protect their borders to the federal government. But he ended by bemoaning "the country's illegal immigration problem," saying that citizens "feel themselves under siege by large numbers of illegal immigrants who invade their property, strain their social services, and even place their lives in jeopardy. Federal officials have been unable to remedy the problem, and indeed have recently shown that they are unwilling to do so. Thousands of Arizona's estimated 400,000 illegal immigrants—including not just children but men and women under 30—are now assured immunity from enforcement, and will be able to compete openly with Arizona citizens for employment."[45]

Scalia was so protective of states' rights that he was willing to ignore both the plain text of the Constitution and constitutional history to expand state immunity from citizen lawsuits. The Eleventh Amendment states: "The Judicial power of the United States shall not be construed to extend to any suit in law or equity, commenced or prosecuted against one of the United States by Citizens of another State, or by Citizens or Subjects of any Foreign State." Yet Scalia (and Thomas) read it to bar suits by citizens against their own states as well.

As Professor Eric Segall explained, the Eleventh Amendment "quite obviously bars any suit, whether for damages or an injunction, against a state by citizens of 'another' state. Both Justices Scalia and Thomas, however, have interpreted this language to bar lawsuits by citizens of a state against their home state. In other words, they have taken the word 'another' and twisted it to mean 'the same.'" Segall found this distortion of the plain meaning of words inconsistent with any principled originalist theory. It also conflicted with the history of the Eleventh Amendment's adoption. The justices instead were following a non-originalist case from 1890, *Hans v. Louisiana*. And in the 1999 case, *Alden v. Maine*, they were in a Court majority holding that a state cannot be sued in its own courts. Once again, there was no textual basis for the argument. What ties them together is an ideological belief in the virtues of sovereign immunity, the idea that people should not be allowed to sue the government without consent.[46]

The other major exception to Scalia's love of states' rights was his vote in the case of *Gonzales v. Raich* in 2005, concerning the federal government's power to ban the growing of marijuana for personal, medicinal use within the state of California. The majority, in an opinion by Justice Stevens, relied upon New Deal precedent to hold that the federal government had the power under the Commerce Clause to regulate even purely in-state activity because of its effect on interstate commerce. Scalia concurred in the judgment rather than joining in Thomas's originalist dissent. Scalia biographer Bruce Allen Murphy suggests that this vote was an effort to "tailor . . . his votes in certain key areas to appear more acceptable to administration and Senate conservatives" while he was lobbying for the job of chief justice after the death of William Rehnquist (a job President Bush instead offered to John Roberts). In 2008, while fielding questions at an annual conference of the Federalist Society about whether *Gonzales* was inconsistent with his other votes on federalism, Scalia answered simply, "Oh no . . . get another question." It was his typical dodge when confronted with supposed inconsistencies in his jurisprudential approaches.[47]

⚖

Just as Scalia could generally be counted on to side with the states against the federal government, he also could be counted on to side with the president over Congress and over independent entities created by Congress to exercise executive power. He strongly believed in the "unitary executive" theory that no executive power could be exercised that did not answer ultimately to the president. In his *Printz* opinion rejecting the Brady gun control law, these separation-of-powers concerns gave him an alternative basis for finding the statute unconstitutional. The concern was not only the separation of powers between the state and federal governments but also "the separation and equilibration of powers between the three branches of the Federal Government itself." He wrote that the Constitution gave the president and the executive branch the power to faithfully execute the law, but the Brady Act "effectively transfers this responsibility to thousands" of local law enforcement officials in the states, "who are left to implement the program without meaningful Presidential control (if indeed meaningful Presidential control is possible without the power to appoint and remove)."[48]

The themes Scalia sounds in *Printz* echo his famous lone dissent in the *Morrison v. Olson* case from 1988. *Morrison* concerned the constitutionality of the Ethics in Government Act of 1978, which created the Office of the Independent Counsel and gave a panel of the Court of Appeals for the D.C. Circuit the power to appoint a special prosecutor to investigate the executive branch. This prosecutor could be removed by the United States attorney general only for good cause. In a majority opinion by Chief Justice Rehnquist, the Supreme Court on a 7–1 vote upheld this scheme, rejecting arguments that it violated the separation of powers.[49]

As the lone dissenter, Scalia saw the Office of Independent Counsel as a great threat to the separation of powers: "The allocation of power among Congress, the President, and the courts in such fashion as to preserve the equilibrium the Constitution sought to establish—so that 'a gradual concentration of the several powers in the same department,' Federalist No. 51 (J. Madison), can effectively be resisted. Frequently an issue of this sort will come before the Court clad, so to speak, in sheep's clothing: the potential of the asserted principle to effect important change in the equilibrium of power is not immediately evident, and must be discerned by a careful and perceptive analysis. But this wolf comes as a wolf."[50]

In remarks that seemed prescient by 1998, given the controversy over the independent counsel Kenneth Starr's report following an investigation of President Bill Clinton and his affair with Monica Lewinsky, which eventually led to Clinton's impeachment, Scalia thought the separation of powers system itself provided adequate remedies for abuse.[51]

Scalia acknowledged that a "system of separate and coordinate powers necessarily involves an acceptance of exclusive power that can theoretically be abused. . . . While the separation of powers may prevent us from righting every wrong, it does so in order to ensure that we do not lose liberty. The checks against any branch's abuse of its exclusive powers are twofold: First, retaliation by one of the other branch's use of *its* exclusive powers: Congress, for example, can impeach the executive who willfully fails to enforce the laws; the executive can decline to prosecute under unconstitutional statutes; and the courts can dismiss malicious prosecutions. Second, and ultimately, there is the political check that the people will replace those in the political branches (the branches more 'dangerous to the political rights of the Constitution,' Federalist No. 78) who are guilty of abuse. Political pressures produced special prosecutors—for Teapot Dome and for

Watergate, for example—long before this statute created the independent counsel."

And he saw the independent counsel system as likely to lead to abuse. "Unless it can honestly be said that there are 'no reasonable grounds to believe' that further investigation is warranted, further investigation must ensue; and the conduct of the investigation, and determination of whether to prosecute, will be given to a person neither selected by nor subject to the control of the President—who will in turn assemble a staff by finding out, presumably, who is willing to put aside whatever else they are doing, for an indeterminate period of time, in order to investigate and prosecute the President or a particular named individual in his administration. The prospect is frightening. . . ." He thought it would be especially frightening "for the President's high-level assistants, who typically have no political base of support, it is as utterly unrealistic to think that they will not be intimidated by this prospect, and that their advice to him and their advocacy of his interests before a hostile Congress will not be affected. . . ." He concluded that nothing "is so politically effective as the ability to charge that one's opponent and his associates are not merely wrongheaded, naive, ineffective, but, in all probability, 'crooks.' And nothing so effectively gives an appearance of validity to such charges as a Justice Department investigation and, even better, prosecution."[52]

History after *Morrison* and the rise in prosecutions against politicians (such as Senators Ted Stevens and John Edwards) that ended without convictions, or with convictions overturned, vindicated Scalia's position, and no doubt future Supreme Court justices will be more receptive to his analysis. Years later, he called the decision "probably the most wrenching" in his years on the Court, not because he agonized over it but because of how he lost. He told an interviewer in 2013: "To take away the power to prosecute from the president and give it to somebody who's not under his control is a terrible erosion of presidential power. And it was wrenching not only because it came out wrong—I was the sole dissenter—but because the opinion was written by Rehnquist, who had been head of the Office of Legal Counsel, before me, and who I thought would realize the importance of that power of the president to prosecute. And he not only wrote the opinion; he wrote it in a manner that was more extreme than I think Bill Brennan would have written it. That was wrenching."[53]

Scalia did not always side with the president over Congress, and he seemed to grow wary of presidential power and deference to agencies during the presidency of Barack Obama. In the 2014 case *N.L.R.B. v. Noel Canning*, a majority opinion by Justice Breyer held that the president had exceeded his powers in appointing members of the National Labor Relations Board during a three-day break in Senate sessions that the president characterized as a Senate recess. All of the justices agreed that while the president has the power to make recess appointments, a short period between two "pro forma" sessions did not constitute a recess. Scalia, writing for himself, Roberts, Alito, and Thomas, concurred only in the judgment, reading the president's power to make recess appointments much more narrowly.[54]

⚖

An expert in administrative law even before joining the Supreme Court, Scalia told an audience at Duke Law School in 1989 that "administrative law is not for sissies." He wrote and thought often about when and how courts should defer to agency interpretations of federal statutes. His belief in a strong executive branch, including agencies under the president's control, sometimes clashed with his supreme confidence in reading a statute, which could elevate the judiciary over the executive.[55]

On one hand, he professed a great belief that courts should defer to a federal agency's reasonable interpretation of ambiguous statutes, a principle that came to be known as the *Chevron* doctrine. It was a way of reining in judicial discretion and putting issues into the hands of more responsive executive agencies. On the other hand, "*Chevron* deference" kicked in only if a statute was ambiguous, and a justice like Scalia, with so many textualist tools and canons up his sleeve, rarely found ambiguity.[56]

A nice example of this ability to tease out a definite meaning arose in a telecommunications case from 1994, *MCI Communications Corporation v. AT&T*. This case involved efforts by the Federal Communications Commission to deal with the ongoing deregulation of the telephone industry. The administrative law issue was complex, but briefly, the statute at issue imposed government-approved price controls, requiring telephone providers to file their "tariffs" (or prices) for FCC approval. It also provided that the FCC could "modify any requirement" related to the filing of tariffs. In an effort to encourage competition in the telephone industry, the FCC ruled that smaller phone providers competing with AT&T, which then dominated the market, did not have to file their tariffs for approval. The question before the Supreme Court was whether the FCC could eliminate the tariffs under its authority to "modify any requirement" of the statute.

A judge with a strong view in favor of executive power would be expected to show deference to the agency, given the vagueness of the word "modify." But Justice Scalia, in an opinion for the majority of the Court, found no ambiguity. He instead found that a "modification" had to be a minor change, not a major change, and that eliminating any approval of phone company tariffs was a major change.

"'Modify,' in our view, connotes moderate change. It might be good English to say that the French Revolution 'modified' the status of the French nobility—but only because there is a figure of speech called understatement and a literary device known as sarcasm. And it might be unsurprising to discover a 1972 White House press release saying that 'the Administration is modifying its position with regard to prosecution of the war in Vietnam'—but only because press agents tend to impart what is nowadays called 'spin.'" Justice Stevens, for the dissenters, argued that "modify" was ambiguous and that under the *Chevron* doctrine, the FCC's interpretation was reasonable and worthy of deference.[57]

Scalia's professed belief in *Chevron* deference was not shared by all of his fellow conservatives. Years later, he sparred with Chief Justice Roberts over whether deference to administrative decisions under the *Chevron* rule was appropriate when an agency was deciding whether an action was within its jurisdiction. Scalia, for the majority in a 2013 case, *City of Arlington v. FCC*, said the jurisdictional question was no different from any other question, and given the ambiguity in the federal statute setting forth the FCC's jurisdiction, the Court would defer to the agency. Roberts, dissenting, said that the question of jurisdiction was different, and it was the Court's job to figure out if Congress had given an agency power it could wield.[58]

The dispute was again technical, but beneath the surface of Roberts's dissent was a greater skepticism than Scalia expressed about the role of the huge federal bureaucracy and the potential for massive agencies to threaten the separation of powers. The chief justice wrote: "Although modern administrative agencies fit most comfortably within the Executive Branch, as a practical matter they exercise legislative power, by promulgating regulations with the force of law; executive power, by policing compliance with those regulations; and judicial power, by adjudicating enforcement actions and imposing sanctions on those found to have violated their rules. The accumulation of these powers in the same hands is not an occasional or isolated exception to the constitutional plan; it is a central feature of modern American government."[59]

There were some indications that Scalia was having second thoughts about agency deference near the end of his life. Before he left the Court, he expressed doubt on the doctrine of *Auer* (or *Seminole Rock*) deference to an agency's interpretation of its own regulations. He was especially dubious of agencies writing their own interpretations of rules during pending litigation. "Enough is enough" he declared of the practice in a case from 2013. And it went even further, going to *Chevron* itself. In 2016, Justice Alito told a Federalist Society audience that "Before his death, Nino was also rethinking the whole question of *Chevron* deference" out of a belief that agencies "were exploiting *Chevron* to usurp Congress' lawmaking authority."[60]

Future conservative skepticism about the free hand of the executive to interpret laws in the modern administrative state, at least when that power is wielded broadly, seems likely. Not only are Chief Justice Roberts, Justice Alito, and Justice Thomas on record expressing skepticism about *Chevron*, Justice Gorsuch, when still a judge on the Tenth Circuit, wrote an opinion in 2016 attacking *Chevron* deference as incompatible with the Constitution's scheme of separation of powers and with due process and equal protection concerns. In this decision, *Gutierrez-Brizuela v. Lynch*, Judge Gorsuch wrote not just a majority opinion for a three-judge appellate panel but a special concurring opinion just for himself to address the "elephant in the room."

He wrote: "Transferring the job of saying what the law is from the judiciary to the executive unsurprisingly invites the very sort of due process (fair notice) and equal protection concerns the framers knew would arise if the political branches intruded on judicial functions." He believed the

Chevron two-step analysis created great uncertainty, and people relying on agency interpretations "must always remain alert to the possibility that the agency will reverse its current view 180 degrees anytime based merely on the shift of political winds and *still* prevail." He was especially incensed that an agency would apply a new interpretation retroactively. He added that "the founders were wary of [the costs of allowing the executive to declare the law's meaning], knowing that, when unchecked by independent courts exercising the job of declaring the law's meaning, executives throughout history had sought to exploit ambiguous laws as license for their own pre-rogative." One wonders if Scalia might have agreed with Justice Gorsuch on this had he lived longer and revisited the question.[61]

⚖⚖

Scalia was in a majority in many other cases that affected the allocation of political power. He believed in restrictive "standing" doctrines that kept many civil plaintiffs out of court. Even before joining the Court he saw narrow standing doctrines as necessary on separation of powers grounds to avoid "an overjudicialization of the process of self-government." Lax stand-ing rules gave judges too much discretion to hear cases they should not. He set forth a multipart rule-oriented test in *Lujan v. Defenders of Wildlife* from 1992, requiring those who wished to sue to show, among other things, "concrete and particularized" injuries. *Lujan* was influential. Professor Richard M. Re reports that by 2015 courts had cited *Lujan* about 50,000 times (compared with 69,000 cites for *Chevron,* a case that was eight years older). After *Lujan,* Justice Scalia often argued against plaintiffs' assertion of standing, emphasizing in a 2015 dissent that standing is about separa-tion of powers. "It keeps us minding our own business."[62]

He took a narrow view of class actions and a broad view of federal arbitra-tion law—two stances that, in combination, made it very difficult for plain-tiffs' lawyers to use consumer protection law and class-action lawsuits to protect consumers. Here was the anti-regulatory Scalia happy to do his part to keep cases out of court. In the 2011 case *Wal-Mart Stores, Inc. v. Dukes,* for example, Justice Scalia wrote a majority opinion denying class action status to a group of female Wal-Mart workers who alleged that the store violated federal anti-discrimination laws in paying them less than men.

The 5–4 opinion splitting along conservative-liberal lines, consistent with Justice Scalia's general approach, tightened the federal rules for when a class action may be brought.[63]

A year earlier, in *AT&T Mobility v. Concepcion*, Justice Scalia wrote for the Court in killing a consumer class action charging that a cell phone company was illegally charging customers too much sales tax. The contract between the customers and the phone company required arbitration of such claims, keeping them out of court, and barred class actions—the only way it would be economically feasible for lawyers to bring these claims. California courts had held the exclusion of class actions was unconscionable under California law, but Justice Scalia, in another ideological 5–4 decision, held that federal arbitration law blocked the California court ruling, meaning these consumers would have no effective remedy.[64]

In his final term, he appeared ready to reverse his earlier position and hold it unconstitutional for a state to require members of public sector unions to pay "agency fees" when they refused to join a union, a decision that seemed likely to seriously hurt public sector unions. After his death, the Court divided 4–4 on the question, and the Court agreed to hear a new case raising the issue in the 2017–2018 term. That he was generally seen as pro-business was obvious when Dow Chemical settled a price-fixing suit with a group of plaintiffs for $835 million within two weeks after his death. Dow Chemical cited the loss of Scalia from the Court as its reason for settling.[65]

For a populist like Scalia, these cases were odd, and seemed to hurt "the little guy" much more than he ever publicly recognized.

⚖

Had Scalia's jurisprudence on the law of politics and political power gained the Court's full support, it would have threatened some core democratic principles. Individuals, corporations, and other domestic entities would be able to give unlimited contributions directly to candidates for office. Legislatures would be able draw legislative districts for full partisan advantage, ignoring any requirements in Section 2 of the Voting Rights Act, and limited only by a requirement that race not be the predominant factor in redistricting. Politicians would be able to use public employment decisions to reward the loyal and to punish those who belonged to the wrong political party. State legislatures would be allowed to make it much harder for some people to register and vote, so long as the laws did not burden most people. Congress would have only limited power to assure that racial and ethnic minorities have fair representation in legislative bodies. Consumers and labor unions would have much less power against businesses than they now have.

It is a deeply conservative vision of politics, and one that could well come to pass in the years to come.

7

Rescued from the Grave

THE FACTS OF THE "WICHITA MASSACRE" were gruesome, and in his final majority opinion, released just a few weeks before his death, Justice Scalia spared the reader no horrifying detail. He even recounted a few facts not included in the Kansas Supreme Court decision under review. Doing so required Scalia or his clerks to dig through witness testimony from the trial transcript—not a common activity at the Supreme Court.[1]

The case concerned a murderous spree in Wichita, Kansas, in December 2000 by two brothers, Reginald and Jonathan Carr. It began with Reginald and an unknown man engaging in a carjacking. A few days later, "the brothers followed Linda Ann Walenta, a cellist for the Wichita symphony, home from orchestra practice. One of them approached her vehicle and said he needed help. When she rolled down her window, he pointed a gun at her head. When she shifted into reverse to escape, he shot her three times, ran back to his brother's car, and fled the scene. One of the gunshots severed Walenta's spine, and she died one month later as a result of her injuries."

The most gruesome part of the massacre occurred three days later. As Justice Scalia told it:

The brothers burst into a triplex at 12727 Birchwood, where roommates Jason, Brad, and Aaron lived. Jason's girlfriend, Holly, and Heather, a friend of Aaron's, were also in the house. Armed with handguns and a golf club, the brothers forced all five into Jason's bedroom. They demanded that they strip naked and later ordered them into the bedroom closet. They took Holly and Heather from the bedroom, demanded that they perform oral sex and digitally penetrate each other as the Carrs looked on and barked orders. They forced each of the men to have sex with Holly and then with Heather. They yelled that the men would be shot if they could not have sex with the women, so Holly—fearing for Jason's life—performed oral sex on him in the closet before he was ordered out by the brothers.

Jonathan then snatched Holly from the closet. He ordered that she digitally penetrate herself. He set his gun between her knees on the floor. And he raped her. Then he raped Heather.

Reginald took Brad, Jason, Holly, and Aaron one-by-one to various ATMs to withdraw cash. When the victims returned to the house, their torture continued. Holly urinated in the closet because of fright. Jonathan found an engagement ring hidden in the bedroom that Jason was keeping as a surprise for Holly. Pointing his gun at Jason, he had Jason identify the ring while Holly was sitting nearby in the closet. Then Reginald took Holly from the closet, said he was not going to shoot her yet, and raped her on the dining-room floor strewn with boxes of Christmas decorations. He forced her to turn around, ejaculated into her mouth, and forced her to swallow. In a nearby bathroom, Jonathan again raped Heather and then again raped Holly.

At 2 a.m.—three hours after the mayhem began—the brothers decided it was time to leave the house. They attempted to put all five victims in the trunk of Aaron's Honda Civic. Finding that they would not all fit, they jammed the three young men into the trunk. They directed Heather to the front of the car and Holly to Jason's pickup truck, driven by Reginald. Once the vehicles arrived at a snow-covered field, they instructed Jason and Brad, still naked, and Aaron to kneel in the snow. Holly cried, "Oh, my God, they're going to shoot us." Holly and Heather were then ordered to kneel in the snow. Holly went to Jason's side; Heather, to Aaron.

Holly heard the first shot, heard Aaron plead with the brothers not to shoot, heard the second shot, heard the screams, heard the third shot, and the fourth. She felt the blow of the fifth shot to her head, but remained kneeling. They kicked her so she would fall face-first into the snow and ran her over in the pickup truck. But she survived, because a hair clip she had fastened to her hair that night deflected the bullet. She went to Jason, took off her sweater, the only scrap of clothing the brothers had let her wear, and tied it around his head to stop the bleeding from his eye. She rushed to Brad, then Aaron, and then Heather.

Spotting a house with white Christmas lights in the distance, Holly started running toward it for help—naked, skull shattered, and without shoes, through the snow and over barbed-wire fences. Each time a car passed on the nearby road, she feared it was the brothers returning and camouflaged herself by lying down in the snow. She made it to the house, rang the doorbell, knocked. A man opened the door, and she relayed as quickly as she could the events of the night to him, and minutes later to a 911 dispatcher, fearing that she would not live.

Holly lived, and retold this play-by-play of the night's events to the jury. Investigators also testified that the brothers returned to the Birchwood house after leaving the five friends for dead, where they ransacked the place for valuables and (for good measure) beat Holly's dog, Nikki, to death with a golf club.

Kansas eventually charged the brothers with more than fifty counts, including murder, rape, and kidnapping. Both brothers were convicted of numerous crimes and were sentenced to death for the four Birchwood murders, but the Kansas Supreme Court reversed the death sentences on two grounds. First, the trial court failed to instruct the jury that "mitigating factors" against imposing the death penalty did not have to be proven beyond a reasonable doubt. Second, trying the brothers for capital crimes together, rather than giving them each a separate trial, amounted to cruel and unusual punishment in violation of the U.S. Constitution's Eighth Amendment.[2]

Scalia's opinion for the Court's 8–1 majority disposed of both arguments in just five pages, a very short analysis by Supreme Court standards. The question of "mitigating circumstances" in a death penalty case required the jurors not to find facts but to make a judgment that the circumstances did not justify the death penalty. Thus there was no reason to give a burden-of-proof instruction. "In the last analysis, jurors will accord mercy if they deem it appropriate, and withhold mercy if they do not, which is what our case law is designed to achieve." The Court also quickly rejected the argument that the Constitution required separate trials: "Better that two defendants who have together committed the same crimes be placed side-by-side to have their fates determined by a single jury."[3]

Justice Sotomayor dissented for herself alone, arguing that the Supreme

Court never should have taken the case. State courts, she wrote, "as necessary laboratories for experimenting with how best to guarantee defendants
a fair trial," generally should have discretion to "overprotect" federal rights.
She attributed the Supreme Court's reversal of the Kansas court to the hei-
nous nature of the crimes. "The Carr brothers committed acts of 'almost
inconceivable cruelty and depravity,' and the majority is understandably
anxious to ensure they receive their just deserts. . . . But I do not believe that
interest justifies not only 'correcting' the Kansas Supreme Court's error
but also calling into question the procedures of other States. The standard
adage teaches that hard cases make bad law. I fear that these cases suggest a corollary: Shocking cases make too much law." Scalia retorted that
Sotomayor's argument "would enable state courts to blame the unpopular
death-sentence reprieve of the most horrible criminals upon the Federal
Constitution when it is in fact their own doing."[4]

⚖

The result in *Kansas v. Carr* is not surprising, and even Sotomayor in her
dissent did not really argue that the Kansas Supreme Court got the federal
constitutional questions right. What is unusual is the length and detail of
Scalia's narrative account. Why devote so much attention to the facts of the
crime? It hardly seemed necessary, either to garner a majority of votes or to
persuade a reader to reject Sotomayor's dissent: his brief response, that her
position would allow state supreme courts to hide behind federal constitutional arguments in reversing jury determinations, was quite convincing.

Scalia's attention to the gruesome details might have been motivated
by two factors. Most obviously, he was a major supporter of the constitutionality of the death penalty, and he frequently clashed with other justices
who suggested either that the death penalty as a whole or its application in
particular cases was unconstitutional. By highlighting the depravity of the
crimes, he apparently aimed to convince the reader that the death penalty
was justified as retribution, or at least that the people in each state could
decide it was justified. But the extent of the detail exceeded his usual recita-
tion of facts even in death penalty cases.

Less obviously and admittedly more speculatively, Scalia's consumption of conservative media might have motivated him to highlight the facts of the case and dig deeper into the record than is common among justices. Although the Court's opinion makes no mention of it, the Carr brothers were African American, and all of the victims of the Wichita Massacre were white. Conservative commentators argued for years after the murder that the massacre did not get sufficient attention in the mainstream media because the media felt it would be politically incorrect to cover violence perpetrated by African Americans against whites. Writing in 2002, Michelle Malkin compared wall-to-wall mainstream media coverage of Winona Ryder's shoplifting case to lack of coverage of the massacre:

> When such senseless, evil savagery takes place against politically correct victims, the mainstream media is quick to make national news of such crimes. "If this had been two white males accused of killing four black individuals, the media would be on a feeding frenzy and every satellite news organization would be in Wichita doing live reports," wrote Trent Hungate of Wichita in a letter to the Wichita Eagle after the killings two years ago. Indeed. The horrific James Byrd dragging case in Texas and the Matthew Shepard murder in Wyoming, for example, garnered front-page headlines and continuous coverage. But with the exception of local Kansas newspapers, the Associated Press, The Washington Times, Fox News, Court TV and conservative Internet sites, the Carr trial made almost no news. If you read The New York Times or The Washington Post or watched the evening news this week, the Wichita Massacre never happened. Not to worry, though. The latest investigative report on where Winona Ryder got that Hermes handbag is coming up next. Stay tuned.[5]

As David Horowitz put it, "Apparently the sexual torture and brutal executions of four promising youngsters is of no interest to the nation's moral guardians, because the victims happen to be white."[6]

Whether Scalia read those stories (or heard about them on the conservative talk radio shows he said he listened to) and was trying to correct perceived liberal media bias, or was simply motivated by his own moral outrage, he used his prominent position to vividly recount this brutal story of torture, sexual assault, and murder to a national audience. And the story lived on after his death. In 2016 the Supreme Court's reversal of the Kansas Supreme Court in *Carr* became the focus of an effort to defeat in their retention elections four Kansas justices who had voted to reverse the Carr brothers' death sentences. The effort was unsuccessful.[7]

⚖️

No one could accuse Scalia of being "soft on crime," as his decisions in *Carr* and in other death penalty and criminal law cases show. Yet despite his impeccable conservative credentials, in some key areas of constitutional criminal procedure he was remarkably pro-defendant, a fact often pointed to by his supporters as evidence of the justice's fair-mindedness and neutrality.

Consider the case of Michael Crawford, a Washington state resident who was convicted in a 1999 stabbing of a man who had allegedly raped Michael's wife, Sylvia. Sylvia did not testify at Michael's trial because Washington law prevents a married person from being called to testify against a spouse without the accused's permission, but prosecutors played a tape recording of a police interview with Sylvia which seemed to contradict Michael's claim at trial that he was acting in self-defense. Michael claimed that admission of the recording violated his Sixth Amendment right to confront witnesses against him, because Sylvia was not available for cross-examination thanks to marital privilege.

Scalia, in a 2004 opinion in *Crawford v. Washington* joined by six other justices, not only sided with Michael and held that the admission of the tape recording violated the Sixth Amendment's Confrontation Clause. He reversed an earlier precedent on the correct interpretation of the Confrontation Clause and, with the liberal justices' agreement, relied on an originalist understanding of the clause's purpose.[8]

The relevant part of the Sixth Amendment provides that "In all criminal prosecutions, the accused shall enjoy the right . . . to be confronted with the witnesses against him." Before *Crawford*, the Court's test for when testimony violated this clause merged the constitutional question with the law of evidence: testimony from someone not subject to cross-examination could be admitted if it was sufficiently reliable.[9]

Crawford reversed this test and started over from first principles. Scalia wrote, "The Constitution's text does not alone resolve this case," finding the words "witnesses against" to be ambiguous. "We must therefore turn to the historical background of the Clause to understand its meaning."

He then provided a detailed historical examination of a criminal defendant's evolving right to confront witnesses, both in England beginning in the 1600s and in colonial and early America. He traced the development of the Confrontation Clause to historical abuses of the system when witnesses could not be cross-examined, beginning with Sir Walter Raleigh's trial for treason in 1603. "Lord Cobham, Raleigh's alleged accomplice, had implicated him in an examination before the Privy Council and in a letter. At Raleigh's trial, these were read to the jury. Raleigh argued that Cobham had lied to save himself . . . Suspecting that Cobham would recant, Raleigh demanded that the judges call him to appear, arguing that [t]he Proof of the Common Law is by witness and jury: let Cobham be here, let him speak it. Call my accuser before my face . . .' The judges refused, and, despite Raleigh's protestations that he was being tried 'by the Spanish Inquisition,' the jury convicted, and Raleigh was sentenced to death." Scalia explained that after incidents like these, England instituted a series of reforms from which emerged a right to confront accusers.

Relying on the abuses in cases such as Raleigh's, Scalia concluded that under the Confrontation Clause whenever a witness gives "testimonial evidence," there must be an opportunity for cross-examination or else the testimony is inadmissible. Testimonial evidence does not have to be made under oath, but it does have to be serious. He quoted the 1828 edition of Webster's Dictionary: "'Testimony' is typically '[a] solemn declaration or affirmation made for the purpose of establishing or proving some fact . . .' An accuser who makes a formal statement to government officers bears testimony in a sense that a person who makes a casual remark to an acquaintance does not. The constitutional text, like the history underlying the common-law right of confrontation, thus reflects an especially acute concern with a specific type of out-of-court statement." Further, "Where testimonial evidence is at issue . . . the Sixth Amendment demands what the common law required: unavailability and a prior opportunity for cross-examination."

Crawford spawned a line of cases spelling out exactly how the standard works and what counts as "testimonial" evidence. In a 2006 case, for example, Scalia wrote for the Court that a recording of an emergency 911 call was not "testimonial" for purposes of the Confrontation Clause, while a statement made to police after an emergency call about domestic violence was "testimonial" and subject to the rule. If the main purpose of the statement is to help police respond to an emergency, the statement does not fall under the Confrontation Clause, but if the main purpose is to give facts about a potential crime, it does. Scalia pointed to the *Crawford* line of cases with particular pride, telling journalist Joan Biskupic: "When people ask me what opinions I'm most proud of, I say, well, opinions that count the most are majority opinions."[10]

Yet it is not clear that the *Crawford* line will survive in coming decades. In a 2011 case, *Michigan v. Bryant,* Sotomayor, over Scalia's objection, wrote a majority opinion that seemed to reintroduce a "reliability" test for determining whether a witness statement falls under the Confrontation Clause. And in his final Confrontation Clause case on the Court, *Ohio v. Clark,* Scalia strongly objected to a majority opinion by Justice Alito holding that a three-year-old child's statement to a pre-school teacher about possible abuse was not testimonial.[11]

Scalia agreed with the majority on that point, but he saw Alito as laying the groundwork for overturning *Crawford* and reimposing a reliability test. He wrote separately "to protest the Court's shoveling of fresh dirt upon the Sixth Amendment right of confrontation so recently rescued from the grave in *Crawford v. Washington.*" He believed Justice Alito's opinion for the Court was set up to undermine *Crawford.* "*Crawford* remains the law. But when else has the categorical overruling, the thorough repudiation, of an earlier line of cases been described as nothing more than 'adopt[ing] a different approach,'—as though *Crawford* is only a matter of twiddle-dum twiddle-dee [*sic*] preference, and the old, pre-*Crawford* 'approach' remains available? The author unabashedly displays his hostility to *Crawford* and its progeny, perhaps aggravated by inability to muster the votes to overrule them. *Crawford* 'does not rank on the [author of the opinion's] top-ten list of favorite precedents—and . . . the [author] could not restrain [himself] from saying (and saying and saying) so.'"[12]

⚖

The *Crawford* line was hardly the only set of cases in which Scalia's reading of the Constitution led him to embrace rules helping criminal defendants. In a series of cases beginning with *Apprendi v. New Jersey* in 2000, he voted with a Court majority ruling that it violated the Sixth Amendment right to a jury trial for a judge (rather than a jury) to make any factual finding other than the existence of a prior conviction, which could be used to increase a criminal defendant's sentence. The *Apprendi* line has been far-reaching and included a decision in 2005, *United States v. Booker*, striking down the mandatory nature of the U.S. Sentencing Guidelines. The U.S. Sentencing Commission, created by Congress, crafted the guidelines to create more uniformity and fairness in sentencing. *Booker* was a major application of this theory of the Sixth Amendment's jury trial right. By the end of his tenure on the Court, however, Scalia was worried that the *Apprendi* line, like the *Crawford* line, was in danger of being watered down or abandoned by future Courts.[13]

Scalia also sided with criminal defendants when he found criminal statutes to be unconstitutionally vague in violation of the Constitution's Due Process Clause. For example, in a 2015 case, *Johnson v. U.S.*, he wrote a majority opinion striking down a part of the Armed Career Criminal Act that increased the penalties for committing a "violent felony" while in possession of an illegal firearm. Under the law, violent felonies included "burglary, arson, or extortion, [or any felony that] involves use of explosives, *or otherwise involves conduct that presents a serious potential risk of physical injury to another.*" The Court found the last part of the definition, which I have highlighted above (the "residual clause"), too vague to be enforced. It ruled that a court could not increase the sentence of a criminal who had unlawfully possessed a short-barrel shotgun, because it would be unclear whether that gun possession involved "conduct that presents a serious potential risk of physical injury to another." Scalia wrote: "We are convinced that the indeterminacy of the wide-ranging inquiry required by the residual clause both denies fair notice to defendants and invites arbitrary enforcement by judges. Increasing a defendant's sentence under the clause denies due process of law."[14]

Perhaps most important, Scalia also wrote some pro-defendant opinions related to the Fourth Amendment's right to be free of unreasonable searches and seizures. Few criminal cases actually go to trial, so these cases no doubt affect the rights of many more people than his Confrontation Clause jurisprudence, a right that only comes into play at a criminal trial.

In *United States v. Jones*, Scalia wrote a majority opinion holding that attaching a GPS device to track a vehicle's movements was a "search" for Fourth Amendment purposes. The opinion relied upon a very old doctrinal idea—that a "trespass to chattels" (or personal property) constituted a search for Fourth Amendment purposes. But the opinion had a very modern application: it was a "search" for the police to put a tracking device on your car or otherwise touch your things, meaning that generally the government would require a warrant before being able to do such things. This changed earlier thinking about when such conduct could be considered an unreasonable search violating the Fourth Amendment. (The opinion also featured a back-and-forth on originalism with Justice Alito, who mockingly wrote of a "very tiny constable" hidden in a stagecoach in 1791 listening to conversation as a way of understanding the scope of the Fourth Amendment.)[15]

In 2013, he wrote a dissent, joined by Justices Ginsburg, Kagan, and Sotomayor, objecting to a Maryland law that required the routine collection of DNA samples, for use by law enforcement, from criminals arrested for serious offenses but not yet convicted. He wrote that it "taxes the credulity of the credulous" to accept the majority's "assertion that DNA is being taken, not to solve crimes, but to *identify* those in the State's custody." And there were other Fourth Amendment cases too, such as the *Kyllo* case in 2001, in which Justice Scalia wrote for a five-justice majority, with Justice Stevens dissenting, that the police's use of thermal imaging technology during an investigation could constitute a "search" under the amendment.[16]

Justice Scalia's views here might be seen as pro-defendant, but perhaps it is more accurate to say they reflected a distrust of government and his strong belief in personal privacy. For whatever reason, these concerns were not well reflected in many of the justice's other criminal procedure decisions, in areas from the privilege against self-incrimination to ineffective assistance of counsel claims to habeas corpus.

⚖️

These decisions—most notably, but not only, in the Confrontation Clause area—do indeed suggest that Scalia was not motivated solely by conservative "law and order" values and was sometimes willing to follow his jurisprudential commitments to places where, ideologically, he might have preferred not to go. But it is easy to exaggerate the extent to which he favored criminal defendants' rights. Outside of the areas just discussed, he was a reliable conservative vote on core criminal law issues, from the death penalty to the right of habeas corpus to *Miranda* warnings. It is important not to exaggerate when he voted against type.

He was an enthusiastic supporter of the death penalty from the time he arrived on the Court. In his final term he both wrote *Kansas v. Carr* and gave an unusual oral concurrence in *Glossip v. Gross,* harshly criticizing Justices Breyer's and Ginsburg's call to abolish the death penalty. He agreed with Justice Alito's opinion for the Court (over the liberal justices' dissent) that Oklahoma's drugs used for lethal injections did not violate the Eighth Amendment's prohibition on cruel and unusual punishment. In his written concurrence, he attacked Breyer, stating that "it is impossible to hold unconstitutional that which the Constitution explicitly contemplates" in the Fifth Amendment's requirement of due process in capital cases.[17]

Early in his tenure on the Court, Scalia rejected an equal protection challenge to the constitutionality of the death penalty based upon what plaintiffs presented as a racial disparity in capital sentencing. According to statistical evidence presented by challengers to Georgia's death penalty in *McCleskey v. Kemp,* decided in 1987, "defendants charged with killing white persons received the death penalty in 11% of the cases, but defendants charged with killing blacks received the death penalty in only 1% of the cases." Scalia sided with four other justices in rejecting the equal protection argument, signing on to Justice Powell's opinion that a statistical study demonstrating racial bias was insufficient to justify the challenge.[18]

Yet in a private memorandum to the other justices written during the *McCleskey* drafting process, Scalia wrote that even proven racial disparities in implementing the death penalty did not bother him, because these disparities were inevitable and "ineradicable" given unconscious juror prejudice. "I do not share the view, implicit in the opinion, that an effect of racial factors upon sentencing, if it could be shown by sufficiently strong statistical evidence, would require reversal. Since it is my view that the unconscious operation of irrational sympathies and antipathies, including racial, upon jury decisions and (hence) prosecutorial decisions is real, acknowledged in the decisions of this court, and ineradicable, I cannot honestly say that all I need is more proof." He said he would write separately on this issue but never did.[19]

In 1990, he found that mandatory imposition of the death penalty (without any discretion in sentencing) for certain crimes would not constitute "cruel and unusual" punishment in violation of the Eighth Amendment: "The mandatory imposition of death—without sentencing discretion—for a crime which States have traditionally punished with death cannot possibly violate the Eighth Amendment, because it will not be 'cruel' (neither absolutely nor for the particular crime) and it will not be 'unusual' (neither in the sense of being a type of penalty that is not traditional nor in the sense of being rarely or 'freakishly' imposed). It is quite immaterial that most States have abandoned the practice of automatically sentencing to death all offenders guilty of a capital crime, in favor of a separate procedure in which the sentencer is given the opportunity to consider the appropriateness of death in the individual case; still less is it relevant that mandatory capital sentencing is (or is alleged to be) out of touch with 'contemporary community values' regarding the administration of justice."[20]

Scalia believed it was not cruel and unusual punishment to execute those who committed crimes as minors, or to execute the cognitively disabled. He wrote a majority opinion for the Court in the 1989 case *Stanford v. Kentucky* rejecting the Eighth Amendment attack on imposing the death penalty on minors. He concluded that there was not sufficient objective evidence of a national consensus to label such executions cruel and unusual.[21]

In 2005, when the Court overruled *Stanford* in *Roper v. Simmons,* Scalia issued a bitter dissent. He disagreed with the Court's finding of a national consensus, believing that the Court should examine only states that employ the death penalty when determining a national consensus: "consulting States that bar the death penalty concerning the necessity of making an exception to the penalty for offenders under 18 is rather like including old-order Amishmen in a consumer-preference poll on the electric car. Of *course* they don't like it, but that sheds no light whatever on the point at issue." He rejected the Court's use of practices in other countries to help define "cruel and unusual," lamenting that "the views of our own citizens are essentially irrelevant to the Court's decision today," while "the views of other countries and the so-called international community take center stage." Even worse, he wrote, was that the Court used international evidence selectively: "to invoke alien law when it agrees with one's own thinking, and ignore it otherwise, is not reasoned decisionmaking, but sophistry."[22]

He dissented again in 2012, when the Court in *Miller v. Louisiana* ruled, 5–4, that mandatory life imprisonment without the possibility of parole for those who committed their crimes before the age of eighteen violated the Eighth Amendment. And in his last published dissent, in *Montgomery v. Louisiana* in 2016, he strongly objected to the Court's decision to extend *Miller* retroactively to anyone who had been sentenced as a juvenile before *Miller* was decided. *Montgomery* allowed a sixty-nine-year-old prisoner to raise a *Miller* claim in federal court via a writ of habeas corpus. Scalia wrote that the Court, "in Godfather fashion," had essentially made state legislatures "an offer they can't refuse" to allow those convicted of life imprisonment without the possibility of parole while juveniles to become eligible for parole.[23]

The Court traveled a similar path in prohibiting the execution of the cognitively disabled. In 1989, in *Penry v. Lynaugh,* it rejected a categorical Eighth Amendment argument against such executions, but it remanded the case to allow a jury to consider certain mitigating evidence in deciding the defendant's penalty. Scalia dissented on the latter part of the holding.[24] The Court then overruled *Penry* in the *Adkins v. Virginia* case of 2002, which concluded that the execution of individuals with cognitive disabilities constitutes cruel and unusual punishment.[25]

Beginning with what he considered "faulty assumptions" that the Eighth Amendment prohibited excessive punishments and that sentencing juries could not properly account for "the 'diminished capacities' of the retarded," Scalia explained why he saw no constitutional problem with executing the cognitively impaired.[26]

He rejected the majority's argument that imposing the death penalty on the cognitively impaired likely did not serve the purposes of retribution or deterrence. "Retribution is not advanced, the argument goes, because the mentally retarded are *no more culpable* than the average murderer, whom we have already held lacks sufficient culpability to warrant the death penalty. Who says so? Is there an established correlation between mental acuity and the ability to conform one's conduct to the law in such a rudimentary matter as murder? Are the mentally retarded really more disposed (and hence more likely) to commit willfully cruel and serious crime than others? In my experience, the opposite is true: being childlike generally suggests innocence rather than brutality."

He wrote that there was no scientific evidence showing that "a mildly retarded individual who commits an exquisite torture-killing is 'no more culpable' than the 'average' murderer in a holdup-gone-wrong or a domestic dispute." "The fact that juries continue to sentence mentally retarded offenders to death for extreme crimes shows that society's moral outrage sometimes demands execution of retarded offenders. By what principle of law, science, or logic can the Court pronounce that this is wrong?" He also questioned the majority's view that no "mentally retarded" individuals could be deterred by the death penalty.[27]

Scalia also rejected the argument that a criminal defendant who could prove his innocence should be entitled to raise such a claim after conviction through federal habeas corpus review. Concurring in the decision of *Herrera v. Collins* in 1993, he wrote: "There is no basis in text, tradition, or even in contemporary practice (if that were enough) for finding in the Constitution a right to demand judicial consideration of newly discovered evidence of innocence brought forward after conviction. In saying that such a right exists, the dissenters apply nothing but their personal opinions to invalidate the rules of more than two-thirds of the States, and a Federal Rule of Criminal Procedure for which this Court itself is responsible. If the system that has been in place for 200 years (and remains widely approved) 'shock[s]' the dissenters' consciences, perhaps they should doubt the calibration of their consciences, or, better still, the usefulness of 'conscience shocking' as a legal test." He continued to reject many actual-innocence habeas corpus claims in his years on the Court.[28]

Scalia was no friend of *Miranda* warnings (requiring police to remind those arrested of their right to remain silent and to an attorney) or of the exclusionary rule, which the Court created to exclude illegally collected evidence from trial. As Professor Barry Friedman explained about *Miranda*, Scalia was part of 5–4 conservative majorities watering down the rule. "They decided that police can in some circumstances repair the failure to issue

Miranda warnings by telling the suspect about his rights after he already has confessed, then simply getting a new statement. They held that even if the statement itself is kept out because no *Miranda* warnings were read, any physical evidence (like guns and drugs) that the suspect led them to can be admitted at trial, creating incentives for police not to read the warnings. They have said that you waive your right to remain silent if you say as much as one word, even after the police question you for long stretches of time. In fact, there isn't really even a 'right to remain silent' anymore, because if you're questioned without *Miranda* warnings, but clam up because you know your rights, the prosecutor can use your silence against you anyway."[29]

On the exclusionary rule, Scalia rejected the argument that illegally obtained evidence must always be excluded at trial to deter the police from breaking the law. In the 2006 case *Michigan v. Hudson,* writing for the Court over the objection of the four liberal justices, he rejected an argument to exclude evidence police obtained after violating the "knock and announce" rule. That rule requires the police to wait a reasonable time before entering a home after knocking and announcing their presence. The state of Michigan conceded that the entry into the defendant's home, where the police found drugs and guns, was unconstitutional, but argued that the appropriate remedy was not to exclude the evidence it obtained. Scalia agreed, finding the suppression at trial of illegally obtained evidence a "rule of last resort" given its "substantial social costs." Justice Breyer, for the dissenters, complained that a rule without a remedy would not deter illegal conduct: "the Court destroys the strongest legal incentive to comply with the Constitution's knock-and-announce requirement. And the Court does so without significant support in precedent."[30]

⚖️

The "war on terror" brought out perhaps the greatest tension between Scalia's commitment to enforcing the original understanding of the Constitution and his belief that the United States faced grave danger from "radical Islamists." In a 2004 case, *Hamdi v. Rumsfeld,* the Supreme Court considered whether an American citizen, Yaser Hamdi, was entitled to a writ of habeas corpus. Hamdi had been captured in Afghanistan shortly after the attacks of September 11, 2001, in New York and Washington and was being held in the brig of a ship off the coast of Virginia.

The Bush administration claimed he was an enemy combatant who could lawfully be held without a trial under a congressional act authorizing such detentions. The Court could not produce a majority opinion, but a plurality of justices held that "due process demands that a citizen held in the United States as an enemy combatant be given a meaningful opportunity to contest the factual basis for that detention before a neutral decisionmaker."[31]

Justice Scalia, joined by Justice Stevens, dissented, writing that as an American citizen on U.S. soil, Hamdi was not being given enough protection from government action. In such an instance, Scalia argued, the government had only two choices: either it had to charge the citizen with a crime, or Congress had to pass a resolution suspending the writ of habeas corpus in wartime. If neither was done, Hamdi had to be set free. This was a surprising position for Scalia to take, given his antipathy toward people labeled enemy combatants, and he expressed some doubt about his position: "I frankly do not know whether these tools are sufficient to meet the Government's security needs, including the need to obtain intelligence through interrogation. It is far beyond my competence, or the Court's competence, to determine that. But it is not beyond Congress's. If the situation demands it, the Executive can ask Congress to authorize suspension of the writ—which can be made subject to whatever conditions Congress deems appropriate, including even the procedural novelties invented by the plurality today."[32]

The opinion must have been tough for Scalia to write, given that his son Matthew served as an army officer in Iraq. He told a Swiss audience in March 2006, while another of the war on terror cases, *Hamdan v. Rumsfeld*, was pending before the Court: "War is war, and it has never been the case that when you captured a combatant you have to give them a jury trial in your civil courts. Give me a break. . . . If [a combatant] was captured by my army on a battlefield, that is where he belongs. I had a son on that battlefield and they were shooting at my son and I'm not about to give this man who was captured in a war a full jury trial. I mean it's crazy."[33]

In *Hamdan*, Justice Scalia dissented from the Court's holding that under the Detainee Treatment Act of 2005, certain non-citizen detainees held in military prison at the U.S. naval base at Guantánamo Bay, Cuba, had the right to bring habeas corpus cases before a judge. He thought the majority deliberately mangled the meaning of the act by misreading its unreliable legislative history, including statements made on the floor by senators. It was, he wrote, a "fantasy that Senate floor speeches are attended (like the Philippics of Demosthenes) by throngs of eager listeners, instead of being delivered (like Demosthenes' practice sessions on the beach) alone into a vast emptiness. . . . With regard to the floor statements, at least the Court shows some semblance of seemly shame, tucking away its reference to them in a halfhearted footnote. Not so for its reliance on the DTA's drafting history, which is displayed prominently. I have explained elsewhere that such drafting history is no more legitimate or reliable an indicator of the objective meaning of a statute than any other form of legislative history."[34]

Two years after *Hamdan,* and four years after *Hamdi,* a hardened tone surfaced again in a case involving non-citizen enemy combatants held at the Guantánamo prison. The naval base is under American control but on Cuban soil. In the *Boumediene v. Bush* case of 2008, a 5–4 majority in an opinion by Justice Kennedy held that the procedures spelled out in the Detainee Treatment Act of 2005 were inadequate, and that the prisoners "may invoke the fundamental procedural protections of habeas corpus. The laws and Constitution are designed to survive, and remain in force, in extraordinary times. Liberty and security can be reconciled; and in our system they are reconciled within the framework of the law. The Framers decided that habeas corpus, a right of first importance, must be a part of that framework, a part of that law."[35]

In his dissent, Scalia wrote that contrary to his "usual practice," he believed it "appropriate to begin with a description of the disastrous consequences of what the Court has done today." He minced no words in pushing his nationalism: "America is at war with radical Islamists. The enemy began by killing Americans and American allies abroad: 241 at the Marine barracks in Lebanon, 19 at the Khobar Towers in Dhahran, 224 at our embassies in Dar es Salaam and Nairobi, and 17 on the USS Cole in Yemen. On September 11, 2001, the enemy brought the battle to American soil, killing 2,749 at the Twin Towers in New York City, 184 at the Pentagon in Washington, D. C., and 40 in Pennsylvania. It has threatened further attacks against our homeland; one need only walk about buttressed and barricaded Washington, or board a plane anywhere in the country, to know that the threat is a serious one. Our Armed Forces are now in the field against the enemy, in Afghanistan and Iraq. Last week, 13 of our country-men in arms were killed."

He lamented that the *Boumediene* decision "will make the war harder on us. It will almost certainly cause more Americans to be killed. That con-sequence would be tolerable if necessary to preserve a time-honored legal principle vital to our constitutional Republic. But it is this Court's blatant *abandonment* of such a principle that produces the decision today. . . . In the long term, then, the Court's decision today accomplishes little, except perhaps to reduce the well-being of enemy combatants that the Court os-tensibly seeks to protect. In the short term, however, the decision is devas-tating."[36]

Justice Scalia agreed with Chief Justice Roberts's separate dissent in *Bou-mediene* that the Detainee Treatment Act provided enough procedural pro-tections to satisfy the "essential protections that habeas corpus guarantees." But more fundamentally, he believed the right to habeas corpus did not extend to aliens abroad at all, considering Guantánamo to be under Cuban sovereignty. He concluded his opinion with the ominous warning, "The Nation will live to regret what the Court has done today. I dissent."[37]

It is uncertain that the nation has lived to regret the decisions in *Hamdi, Hamdan,* or *Boumediene.* Soon after the *Hamdi* ruling, the government de-cided to free Hamdi and send him to Saudi Arabia, provided he renounced his U.S. citizenship and followed some other conditions. "It's quite some-thing for the government to declare this person one of the worst of the worst, hold him for almost three years and then, when they're told by the Supreme Court to give him a fair hearing, turn around and give up," law professor David Cole told the *New York Times* in 2004.[38]

Hamdan, who was Osama bin Laden's personal driver, was convicted by a military jury of the war crime of providing military support for terrorism and sentenced to sixty-six months in prison. After the Supreme Court's ruling, a panel of judges for the United States Court of Appeals for the D.C. Circuit, in an opinion by Judge Brett Kavanaugh, overturned the conviction on the ground that international law at the time of Hamdan's activities did not define them as war crimes. He returned to Yemen, where, as of 2014, he was living with his wife and children.[39]

Boumediene, too, was released, after a trial court found no credible evidence against him. Interrogated on and off for seven years at Guantánamo and released in 2009, Boumediene "likened himself to a caged cat, toyed and tormented by fate and circumstance. 'I learned patience. . . . There is no other choice but patience.'" According to a *New York Times* article, in 2012 he was living in France and looking for work.[40]

8

The Justice of Contradictions

THE CONSPIRACY THEORIES BEGAN SOON after the sudden death of Antonin Scalia at a remote Texas ranch near the Mexican border on February 13, 2016, in the middle of that year's heated presidential election campaign.

In a video posted to Facebook, the conspiracy theorist behind the website *Infowars,* Alex Jones, called for a murder investigation: "I was the first to come out and say this should be a murder investigation, and they better not *not* do an autopsy . . . Then he's found with a pillow over his face." The presidential candidate Donald Trump, in an interview with radio host Michael Savage a few days later, agreed: "It's a horrible topic, but they say they found a pillow on his face, which is a pretty unusual place to find a pillow." Savage called for an assassination investigation: "This is going to be bigger and bigger and bigger. We need the equivalent of a Warren Commission; we need an immediate autopsy before the body is disposed of."[1]

It turned out Scalia did not die with a pillow on his face, and there was every reason to believe the seventy-nine-year-old justice, who did not share information about his declining health with the public, died in his sleep of natural causes. But he died as he lived, on his own terms, giving the public little insight into his private life, and with his family supplying minimal information to the public. Given his reticence and today's hyper-polarized atmosphere fueled by false rumors and "fake news," especially in the middle of a presidential election that could determine the balance of power on the Supreme Court for a generation, the conspiracy theories were unsurprising.

⚖️

Scalia arrived at Cibolo Creek Ranch, a luxurious hunting lodge in Presidio County, Texas, on February 12, 2016. Businessman John Poindexter, who owned the ranch, did not charge Scalia (or anyone else) for the lodging or hunting. Having declined protection from U.S. marshals, Scalia arrived on a private plane, paid for by an unknown person, with C. Allen Foster, a prominent Washington lawyer who had argued before the Supreme Court in 1993. The Court had turned down consideration of an age discrimination lawsuit from one of Poindexter's companies a year before the visit.[2]

Both Poindexter and Foster are officers in the International Order of St. Hubertus, an exclusive hunting society with origins in seventeenth-century Austria. Although several other individuals at the ranch were members, Scalia had no known ties to the order. According to the *Washington Post*, "Members of the worldwide, male-only society wear dark-green robes emblazoned with a large cross and the motto 'Deum Diligite Animalia Diligentes,' which means 'Honoring God by honoring His creatures,' according to the group's website. Some hold titles, such as Grand Master, Prior, and Knight Grand Officer. The order's name is in honor of Hubert, the patron saint of hunters and fishermen."[3]

After having dinner with Poindexter and Foster, Scalia said he was tired and went to his room before 10:00 p.m. His body was found the next day. Poindexter originally told the *San Antonio Express-News*, "We discovered the judge in bed, a pillow over his head." In response to the conspiracy claims, he quickly clarified that the pillow was between the headboard and the justice's head. He told the *Los Angeles Times* that Scalia looked peaceful, "almost as if a model had been put in the bed." Justice Scalia likely would have appreciated the unintentional ambiguity of the phrase "a pillow over his head."[4]

A little after noon on February 13, Poindexter called the Presidio County Sheriff's Office to obtain the phone number of the local U.S. Marshal Service office. Sheriff Danny Dominguez contacted the U.S. Marshals and proceeded to Cibolo Creek Ranch. He also tried to reach the two local justices of the peace for an inquest, but both were out of town. Sheriff Dominguez contacted county judge Cinderela Guevara and asked if she could conduct the inquest. Judge Guevara, following standard operating procedure in west Texas, agreed to do it via a phone call. Texas state law gives local officials discretion regarding inquests and autopsies out of necessity, given the large distances and the fact that many west Texas counties do not have the resources or the population to sustain medical examiners.[5]

After arriving at the ranch, Sheriff Dominguez entered Scalia's room with Poindexter, Foster, and George Vanetten, the ranch manager. According to the sheriff's report, Justice Scalia was found in bed with the covers pulled up to his chin and three pillows elevating his head. The top pillow had shifted in the night and covered his eyes but did not reach his mouth. A CPAP breathing machine was on a bedside table but was not turned on or attached. There was no sign of struggle, and Scalia's luggage was neatly folded and organized.[6]

Dominguez called Judge Guevara, who pronounced Antonin Scalia dead at 1:52 p.m. Shortly thereafter, U.S. Marshals arrived and began an investigation. A spokesperson for the Marshal Service stated that no evidence existed to suggest Scalia's death was due to anything but natural causes, although the service released no public report.[7]

Following the Scalia family's wishes, Judge Guevara did not order an autopsy. This decision came after the judge received information about the justice's poor health from Rear Admiral Brian P. Monahan, the attending physician for members of Congress and the Court. Monahan's letter, which was not released to the public but portions of which were read to the Associated Press, stated that Scalia suffered from coronary artery disease, obesity, diabetes, sleep apnea, degenerative joint disease, chronic obstructive pulmonary disease, and high blood pressure. The letter also identified him as a smoker and revealed that he had seen his doctor three days before his death for a rotator cuff injury but was considered too weak to undergo surgery. Given his age and numerous medical conditions, many experts have concluded that Scalia's death was not abnormal, but without an autopsy, it was impossible to determine the exact cause of death.[8]

The family accepted that Scalia died of natural causes and pushed back against the conspiracy theories. Speaking on *The Laura Ingraham Show* a few days after the justice's death, his son Eugene Scalia said: "Honestly, I think it's a distraction from a great man and his legacy at a time when there's so much to be said about that and to help people even more fully appreciate that. And, on a personal level, I think it's a bit of a hurtful distraction for a family that's mourning."[9]

Unlike Ruth Bader Ginsburg, who routinely had the Supreme Court release public information about her health issues (including a battle with cancer), Scalia had made almost none of his health problems public. He authorized only one health-related press release in his twenty-nine years on the Court, pertaining to a shoulder surgery in 2003. The family and government officials declined to release his death certificate or any other information.[10]

Justice Scalia died as he lived. When the Supreme Court released its annual financial disclosure forms in 2016, it did not release a report for Justice Scalia, which could have revealed more information about the trip to the ranch and whether anyone with business before the Court was paying for any part of it. Adam Liptak reported for the *New York Times* that the Poindexter trip was not the only one for which there would be no public information: "Justice Scalia was an enthusiastic traveler, taking more than 250 privately funded trips from 2004 to 2014. A few weeks before he died, he visited Singapore and Hong Kong. A court spokeswoman said there would be no disclosure form detailing Justice Scalia's travels in 2015."[11]

⚖

Despite his advanced age and evident obesity, Scalia's death came as a shock to many people. Some observers had whispered that in recent years that he was getting crankier on the bench, and they pointed to some odd episodes, such as the oral concurrence in the *Glossip* death penalty case in which he went back to discuss the already-issued decision in the *Obergefell* case. But if he was beginning to miss a step mentally, it was not evident in his most important work product. Until the end, his opinions reflected not only deep legal reasoning but his distinctive, caustic, and humorous voice. When the Court convened for oral arguments in March 2016, that voice was obviously missing. In place of the gregarious Scalia stood an empty seat covered with a black wool crepe.[12]

Scalia's death prompted a torrent of tributes, services, speeches, panel discussions, and writings reflecting on the larger-than-life justice and his influence on the Court and American life. President Obama, whose policies and programs Justice Scalia had often rejected, called him "a brilliant legal mind with an energetic style, incisive wit, and colorful opinions."[13]

In a tribute given on the day of the justice's death, the president added that he planned to fulfill his "constitutional responsibilities to nominate a successor in due time. There will be plenty of time for me to do so, and for the Senate to fulfill its responsibility to give that person a fair hearing and a timely vote. These are responsibilities that I take seriously, as should everyone. They're bigger than any one party. They are about our democracy. They're about the institution to which Justice Scalia dedicated his professional life, and making sure it continues to function as the beacon of justice that our Founders envisioned."[14]

But Obama did not get to replace Scalia on the Court. Senate majority leader Mitch McConnell, a Republican from Kentucky, announced within an hour after Scalia's death became public that the Senate would consider no replacement named by President Obama. "The American people should have a voice in the selection of their new Supreme Court Justice. Therefore, this vacancy should not be filled until we have a new president." Other Republicans in the Senate fell in line, including all of the candidates in the Republican presidential primary campaign, as well as the chairman of the Senate Judiciary Committee, Chuck Grassley, an Iowa Republican up for reelection.[15]

A month later, President Obama nonetheless nominated Merrick Garland, a well-respected and well-liked moderate liberal who served as chief judge of the United States Court of Appeals for the District of Columbia Circuit, the court where Justice Scalia had served, that was often called the second most important judicial body in the country. A judge of impeccable credentials and little controversy, whose record in criminal law cases was in some respects to the right of Scalia's, Garland was the kind of judge Republicans ordinarily would have loved for a Democratic president to nominate. But these were not ordinary times.[16]

Republican obstructionism was a gamble, but it paid off. Although Democrats loudly protested that Garland deserved a hearing, and that the people already *had* a voice in the selection of the next Supreme Court justice when they reelected President Obama in 2012, Republicans paid no price: to the contrary, their obstruction played well with Republican voters. Senator Grassley handily won reelection in Iowa, and the Supreme Court issue seemed to resonate more with Republicans than with Democrats in the 2016 presidential election. According to exit polls, of the one in five voters who said Supreme Court appointments were their "most important issue," 56 percent supported Trump and 41 percent supported Clinton. Of the 28 percent of voters who said Supreme Court appointments were not important to their vote, 52 percent supported Clinton while 39 percent supported Trump.[17]

During the campaign, Democratic nominee Hillary Clinton pledged to nominate a justice who would overturn the Supreme Court's 2010 decision in *Citizens United v. Federal Election Commission,* the case that helped free up money in political campaigns consistent with Justice Scalia's long-term vision. Republican nominee Donald Trump promised to nominate an originalist like Scalia, and he released a list of twenty-one judges from whom he promised to pick Scalia's replacement. He thanked the Federalist Society and the Heritage Foundation for helping him compile the list. All of his potential nominees were strongly conservative. One academic study looked at their use of originalism and reliance on Scalia's non-judicial writings to create a "Scalia-ness" score.[18]

⚖️

Beyond some platitudes, Trump did not say what he found so appealing about Scalia, and it seems unlikely that the new president, who apparently paid little attention to the details of jurisprudence, knew much of Scalia's methodologies or specific positions in cases. Indeed, during the presidential transition, Trump tweeted a statement condemning people who burned American flags, threatening them with serious punishment: "Nobody should be allowed to burn the American flag—if they do, there must be consequences—perhaps loss of citizenship or year in jail!" He posted this tweet right after a segment on *Fox & Friends* about a flag-burning controversy at Hampshire College connected to Trump's victory.[19]

Critics were quick to point out that Scalia had voted in *Texas v. Johnson* that flag burning was protected by the First Amendment. On social media, links spread to a 2012 CNN interview in which Piers Morgan asked Scalia about throwing flag burners in jail. Scalia responded: "If I were king, I would not allow people to go about burning the American flag. However, we have a First Amendment which says that the right of free speech shall not be abridged, and it is addressed in particular to speech critical of the government. I mean, that was the main kind of speech that tyrants would seek to suppress. Burning the flag is a form of expression. 'Speech' doesn't just mean written words or oral words. It could be semaphore. Burning a flag is a symbol that expresses an idea. 'I hate the government. The government is unjust. Whatever.'"[20]

Trump surely did not support appointing more justices like Scalia because of the late justice's position on flag burning. More likely he did so because that is what the conservative Republican base supporting Trump's election really wanted. The Supreme Court was a key issue for those voters essential to Trump's victory.

Many of those supporters, too, likely knew little about the nuances of Scalia's jurisprudence, but they knew of his reputation as a disruptor. Scalia was anti-elitist, conservative, brilliant, and loud, calling out living constitutionalists like the Reagan-appointed Anthony Kennedy as "pretentious" and "egotistical" for betraying the conservative cause. The right-leaning populist Scalia opposed (at least as a constitutional matter) abortion and gay rights, fought hard for states to be able to carry out the death penalty and for the rights of the white working class against affirmative action programs in education and employment. He was against extending habeas corpus rights to foreign detainees at Guantánamo, for state power over federal power, for America over foreign powers and influence, for freeing up political money as free speech, and for killing excessive regulation and litigation that he said would hurt small businesses and the little guy. He gave voice and logic to conservatives who at the end of the twentieth century and the beginning of the twenty-first were still railing against the Warren Court of the 1960s and the social change the Court helped usher into the American scene.

He was a man ahead of, and later a creature of, polarized America in the late twentieth and early twenty-first centuries. An enemy of political correctness, he was not quite the "Fox News justice" that the legal commentator Jeffrey Toobin made him out to be, but Scalia the disruptor surely seemed like the kind of justice Trump could get behind, even if they did not agree on every position.

This picture of Scalia, while full of truth, was not the whole story, and his failure to fully follow the Republican party line went well beyond the flag-burning cases and others showing his conservative libertarianism. In some (but by no means all) of his constitutional criminal procedure decisions, he was surprisingly in favor of criminal defendants. Although this position followed Scalia's distrust of the government, it did not always put him on the side of law-and-order conservatives.

And there were other examples, such as the cases in which a majority of Supreme Court justices held that when juries awarded very large punitive damages in tort cases, the amounts were sometimes unconstitutional under the Due Process Clause. In the 1996 case *BMW v. Gore,* Scalia wrote in dissent, arguing that the courts should not police the sizes of damage awards: "I do not regard the Fourteenth Amendment's Due Process Clause as a secret repository of substantive guarantees against 'unfairness'—neither the unfairness of an excessive civil compensatory award, nor the unfairness of an 'unreasonable' punitive award. What the Fourteenth Amendment's procedural guarantee assures is an opportunity to contest the reasonableness of a damages judgment in state court; but there is no federal guarantee a damages award actually *be* reasonable." It was a decision that favored tort plaintiffs and trial lawyers, not what you'd expect from what liberals caricatured as a relentlessly result-oriented right-wing justice.[21]

⚖

Scalia was a justice of contradictions. As much as he could rightly point to cases like *BMW v. Gore* as evidence of neutrality, there were many more counter-examples of him ignoring his methodology to reach conservative results. He claimed to be an originalist in constitutional interpretation, but he did not consistently apply this principle. He never explained why historical practice at the time of the founding or the ratification of amendments was irrelevant in those cases where he chose to ignore it. Sometimes his originalism was purely textual. At other times he relied more on historical practice or tradition. We do not know precisely why he sometimes found that one trumped the other, and he was inconsistent in his practice.

Sometimes, out of what he said was respect for settled precedent, he agreed to be bound by substantive due process ideas, such as the incorporation of the Bill of Rights against the states, but at other times he refused to do so, as in the abortion cases, where *stare decisis* carried no weight with him. Sometimes he ignored clear words, as on questions of the scope of state immunity under the Eleventh Amendment.

He used a wooden textualist analysis of statutes that often led to deeply conservative results, but sometimes, to reach results more to his liking, he resorted to pulling rabbits out of his hat, such as a canon of interpretation that he himself acknowledged acted like a thumb on the scale and did not depend on pure linguistic analysis. For an anti-elitist he certainly could unleash the fancy words, causing readers to scramble for their dictionaries.

He allowed his views of good politics to affect his judgment on the appropriate balance between First Amendment rights and the ability to police legislative self-interest, where he voted consistently to strike reasonable campaign money limits but to allow unlimited partisan gerrymandering and cutbacks in voting rights by self-interested legislatures. He rarely rejected a death penalty sentence and saw no constitutional problem with states executing those convicted of crimes as juveniles or those who were cognitively impaired. He almost always sided with governments engaging in prayer and religious activities.

He asserted his positions in all of these cases, even when contradictory, with unassailable conviction and sharpness. The other side was not only wrong but grievously so. The Court's decision in *Boumediene,* the enemy combatant case, would get Americans killed, he claimed. He portrayed the other side as offering irrational analysis, illogic, or—increasingly often in his later years—displaying questionable motives. The other justices were there to impose their values on society, to put the Court's views over the views of the people or Congress or the states, and only *he* could be counted on to be neutral and never impose *his* values.

As nasty as he could be in a dissenting opinion, he was also a charmer and a comedian, friends with the liberal Justice Ginsburg, who joked that she sometimes wanted to strangle him. Scalia could dish it out like no one else, but he did not always take it well, sometimes coming off as remarkably thin-skinned. Whether it was the student in 2009 who asked him about the inconsistency between his public appearances and his opposition to cameras in the courtroom, or the questioner at the Federalist Society event in 2008 who saw contradictions in his federalism jurisprudence in the *Gonzalez v. Raich* marijuana case of 2005, or Professor Alan Dershowitz asking him about his decision to ignore originalist evidence in a Fifth Amendment case, or the *University of Chicago Law Review* reaching out to ask the justice to respond to Yale professor Jack Balkin's book, *Living Originalism,* Scalia's mode was to deflect, demur, or decline comment when pushed on his inconsistencies. He left it to others to defend him, and most of the charges of inconsistency remained unanswered. He followed the second half of Disraeli's maxim to "never complain, never explain."

Scalia let his values affect his jurisprudence. Within two days at the end of the term in June 2013, he both loudly decried the Court's failure to defer to Congress's judgment in passing the Defense of Marriage Act (refusing federal recognition to same-sex marriages) in *United States v. Windsor* and joined in a majority opinion in *Shelby County v. Holder* refusing to defer to Congress's bipartisan judgment that states with a history of racial discrimination in voting still needed to be subject to federal oversight of their voting rules. In *Windsor,* he lamented "a Supreme Court standing (or rather enthroned) at the apex of government, empowered to decide all constitutional questions, always and everywhere 'primary' in its role." In *Shelby County,* he looked down from the Court's same apex and determined that the national will had to yield to his view of federalism.[22]

His greatest contradiction came in his approach to the legitimacy of the Supreme Court. The *raison d'etre* for his language-based tools of interpretation was to legitimize the Supreme Court's decisionmaking process. He saw himself remaking legal analysis to serve the greater good. But his attacks on fellow justices for not using his methodology served to delegitimize their decisions, and the Court's by extension. Worse, his doctrines were so flexible that he could reach a range of interpretations and still claim fidelity to his ostensibly neutral methodology. Part of what must have subconsciously attracted him to his theories and methodologies is that they mostly led him where he wanted to go, and at other times constrained him in ways he could live with.

That is not to say that Scalia was more driven by ideology than other justices. He proclaimed himself as following a higher standard, and did not live up to it. Who could do so when given so much power? The gap between Scalia's stated approach and his practice in deciding real cases revealed the difficulty of using any methodology, even a strict rule-based one, to limit judicial discretion.

What's worse, he used his incredible gift of language to relentlessly attack his opponents, often through dissenting opinions. His talent as a writer made these opinions entertaining, but they were scathing, too, and they increased the coarseness of legal discourse, making it more acceptable to not only disagree but to pummel one's opponents with hurtful and unnecessary stridency.

His patriotism was unquestionable, as was his brilliance as a legal thinker. He gave the courts a standard way of reviewing statutes, with a methodology even Scalia's ideological opponents regularly relied upon. He convinced his followers that there indeed were neutral tools, tools which usually favored conservative results. And he showed how to further an agenda with pugnaciousness, attacking the legitimacy, and not merely the correctness, of his ideological opponents.

⚖️

Now, just a few years after Justice Scalia's death, his legacy will be put to the test. It will begin with consideration of his cases, and extend to his judicial methodology. He wrote few blockbuster opinions. His Second Amendment opinion in *Heller* seems unlikely to be overruled, but gun rights could be limited or expanded under that decision depending upon who sits on the Court. A more conservative Court might not preserve some of his decisions that went against type. Conservatives like Justice Alito questioned his approach to the Confrontation Clause beginning in *Crawford* and to the *Apprendi* sentencing cases. Neither Alito nor Chief Justice Roberts seems committed to Scalia's strong textualism in statutory interpretation, and the Court, with Justice Gorsuch taking the lead, could well limit or abandon the deference to agency interpretations begun in the *Chevron* case which Scalia defended.

In constitutional cases, the doctrine of originalism has proven to be malleable in the hands of those who wish to reach varying results. The Court may include many self-styled originalist justices over the next few decades, but they could well reach conclusions that would have raised Justice Scalia's ire. One day there may be an originalist defense of the argument that the Constitution contains a right of same-sex couples to marry. Originalism seems likely to continue to be wielded as a delegitimization tool against ideological opponents.

Trump's surprising victory in the 2016 election gave him a chance to shape the Supreme Court. Given the ages of the justices, it appeared likely he could fill multiple seats for the Court during his presidency. His first appointment of Judge Neil Gorsuch, from the United States Court of Appeals for the Tenth Circuit, put another strong judicial writer on the Court. Before joining the Court, Gorsuch described himself as a Scalia fan and a textualist and originalist in Scalia's mode. Like Scalia, he believed other methodologies would unconstitutionally turn judges into legislators.

In his first few months on the Court, Gorsuch revealed he had much in common with Justice Scalia: he strongly endorsed textualist analysis of opinions, sided with a criminal defendant against Chief Justice Roberts and Justice Thomas, and exhibited a kind of aggressiveness on the bench that showed he would not hold back in immediately sharing his vision of the Constitution and the law. And it was a Scalian vision. He admonished his colleagues in a statutory interpretation case that "If a statute needs repair, there's a constitutionally prescribed way to do it. It's called legislation." And at oral argument in the 2017 Wisconsin partisan gerrymandering case, he dismissively interjected that "maybe we can just for a second talk about the arcane matter, the Constitution." Think Scalia, but without the spontaneous wit and charm. Without Scalia, Gorsuch would have been just as conservative but he would not have been packaging his jurisprudence in Scalian terms and he would perhaps not have been as aggressive out of the box. [23]

Gorsuch's appointment means that Scalia's language-based interpretive approaches are likely to live on in the judiciary at least in the near term, and meanwhile the originalism industry is thriving among (mostly conservative) scholars in the legal academy. Whether or not the jurisprudence gains further traction will depend in part on future appointments to the Court.

Regardless of how many originalists and textualists join the Court, a different and more significant pattern is likely to continue: in the most contentious cases, originalist conservative justices (like Gorsuch and Thomas) joining with non-originalist conservative justices (like Alito and Roberts) will use different methodologies to reach similar results, and liberal justices (like Kagan and Sotomayor) will use eclectic methodologies to reach the opposite results. It will be ideology and party, not interpretive methodology, that will define the Court's fault lines.

There is no reason to think that Trump's appointments to the Court—or any future president's appointments—will lessen the primary divide on the Supreme Court between conservatives appointed by Republican presidents and liberals appointed by Democratic presidents. Indeed, in these polarized times, ideological and party divides will probably be more common on the Court, with originalism and textualism unlikely to be a good predictor of results in the most divided cases.

Scalia's most certain legacy is a continuation of the Court's conservative voting pattern. Despite his occasional steps out of line, Scalia was part of a conservative majority that had strong views of states' rights, was skeptical of affirmative action, campaign finance laws, and laws protecting voting rights, and favored businesses over consumers, unions, and workers. Those trends are likely to continue, barring significant Court vacancies during Democratic administrations. On issues such as gun rights, abortion rights, administrative law, and immigration, the Court is likely to move in a more conservative direction.

Speaking before a meeting of the Philadelphia Bar Association in 2004, Justice Scalia remarked: "As long as judges tinker with the Constitution to 'do what the people want,' instead of what the document actually commands, politicians who pick and confirm new federal judges will naturally want only those who agree with them politically."[24]

The comment was vintage Scalia, railing against liberal constitutional theory and the jurists embracing it. Part of his critique was exactly right. Justices who approached the Constitution as a living document were likely to be swayed by many factors, including public opinion and their own values, in deciding difficult cases. Presidents were increasingly likely to nominate, and senators to confirm or reject, nominees who would reach predictable conclusions in the most important cases.

But Scalia's blind spot was his belief that it is possible to objectively and neutrally determine what the Constitution "actually commands." In his twenty-nine years on the Court, he always said he did so. But it wasn't so. It is a lesson Americans need to know: neutrality so far has proven impossible, and it appears there will be no methodology created to answer all questions. Uncertainty in interpretation is inevitable, despite what Scalia was trying to sell.

The president and the Senate that would vote to confirm more Justice Scalias for the bench might talk the language of "originalism" and "judicial restraint," but what they really wanted were more judges who voted like him, and sometimes even showing what might pejoratively be called "judicial activism," because at the end of the day the Supreme Court has always been a political institution, deciding the most difficult cases by considering text, history, practice, and, yes, each justice's values. Even Justice Scalia's.

NOTES

Preface

1. *United States v. Windsor,* 133 S. Ct. 2675, 2697–98 (2013); *Shelby County v. Holder,* 133 S. Ct. 2612 (2013).
2. *King v. Burwell,* 135 S. Ct. 2480, 2500 (Scalia, J., dissenting) (2015) ("The Court's next bit of interpretive jiggery-pokery involves other parts of the Act that purportedly presuppose the availability of tax credits on both federal and state Exchanges."); Adam Liptak, *Sidebar: Scalia Lands at Top of Sarcasm Index. Shocking,* N.Y. Times, Jan. 19, 2015, http://www.nytimes.com/2015/01/20/us/scalia-lands-at-top-of-sarcasm-index-of-justices-shocking.html ("Justice Scalia might have a different objection. 'I'm a snoot,' he once said.").
3. Joan Biskupic, American Original: The Life and Constitution of Supreme Court Justice Antonin Scalia 23 (2009); Kannon K. Shanmugam, *Justice Scalia: A Personal Remembrance,* 41 J. Sup. Ct. History 252 (2016), http://onlinelibrary.wiley.com/doi/10.1111/jsch.12117/full.

Chapter 1. The Disruptor

1. For details on the opinion writing process, see *The Opinion-Writing Process,* The Supreme Court Opinion Writing Database (Washington University), http://supremecourtopinions.wustl.edu/ (last visited July 8, 2016). On the number of petitions received and cases heard by the Supreme Court, see *Frequently Asked Questions,* Supreme Court of the United States, http://www.supremecourt.gov/faq.aspx#faqgi9 (last visited July 8, 2016) (answering question: "How many cases are appealed to the Court each year and how many cases does the Court hear?").
2. On why the end of the term generally brings the most drama, see Lee Epstein, William M. Landes, & Richard A. Posner, *The Best for Last: The Timing of U.S. Supreme Court Decisions,* 64 Duke L.J. 991 (2015).

3. *King v. Burwell*, 135 S. Ct. 2480 (2015); *Obergefell v. Hodges*, 135 S. Ct. 2584 (2015).

4. The 2012 case was *National Federal of Independent Business v. Sebelius*, 132 S. Ct. 2566 (2012). On Chief Justice Roberts upholding Congress's power to mandate insurance or paying a penalty under its tax powers, see *id.* at 2583–2601. For a fuller textual defense of the position of the majority in *King*, see Abbe Gluck, *Symposium: The Grant in* King: *Obamacare subsidies as textualism's big test*, SCOTUSBlog, Nov. 7, 2014, http://www.scotusblog.com/2014/11/symposium-the-grant -in-king-obamacare-subsidies-as-textualisms-big-test/.

5. *King*, 135 S. Ct. at 2492–93 ("Here, the statutory scheme compels us to reject petitioners' interpretation because it would destabilize the individual insurance market in any State with a Federal Exchange, and likely create the very 'death spirals' that Congress designed the Act to avoid.").

6. *King*, 135 S. Ct. at 2507 (Scalia, J., dissenting). You can listen to Justice Scalia's oral dissent in the *King v. Burwell* case on the Oyez website, at https://www.oyez .org/cases/2014/14-114, by clicking on "Opinion Announcement—June 25, 2015 (Part 2) (last visited June 8, 2016).

7. *Obergefell*, 135 S. Ct. at 2604 ("These considerations lead to the conclusion that the right to marry is a fundamental right inherent in the liberty of the person, and under the Due Process and Equal Protection Clauses of the Fourteenth Amendment couples of the same-sex may not be deprived of that right and that liberty.").

8. *Id.* at 2630 n. 22 (Scalia, J., dissenting).

9. *Id.* at 2630 (Scalia, J., dissenting).

10. *Bush v. Gore*, 531 U.S. 98, 128–29 (Stevens, J., dissenting).

11. Lesley Stahl, *Justice Scalia on the Record*, CBS News, 60 Minutes, Apr. 24, 2008, http://www.cbsnews.com/news/justice-scalia-on-the-record/.

12. Jimmy Hoover, *Scalia Sears Supreme Court for Foreign Law References*, Law 360, May 25, 2015, https://www.law360.com/articles/661690/scalia-sears-supreme -court-for-foreign-law-references. George Mason originally changed its name to the "Antonin S. Scalia School of Law," but that caused some trouble: "George Mason University recently renamed its law school after the late Supreme Court Justice Antonin Scalia—and then quickly realized the acronym that name created was problematic. The school first announced it would change the name to The Antonin Scalia School of Law, or ASSoL, after receiving an anonymous $30 million donation on March 31. Observers took to Twitter to comment on the acronym's similarity to a vulgarity, with many of those tweeting not a fan of the conservative justice." Daniella Diaz, *GMU law school naming after Antonin Scalia Hits Snag*, CNN, Apr. 5, 2016, http://www.cnn.com/2016/04/05/politics/george -mason-university-antonin-scalia-law-school-name-change/.

13. Antonin Scalia, *The Rule of Law as a Law of Rules*, 56 U. Chi. L. Rev. 1175, 1179 (1989).

14. On conservative libertarianism generally, see Steven J. Heyman, *The Conservative-Libertarian Turn in First Amendment Jurisprudence*, 117 W. Va. L. Rev. 231 (2014). For a perceptive analysis tying Scalia's ideas to those of philosopher Friedrich

Hayek, see Gautam Bhatia, *The Politics of Statutory Interpretation: The Hayekian Foundations of Justice Antonin Scalia's Jurisprudence*, 42 Hastings Const. L.Q. 525 (2015).

15. Mark Berman & Jerry Markon, *Why Justice Scalia Was Staying for Free at Texas Resort*, Wash. Post, Feb. 17, 2016, https://www.washingtonpost.com/news/post-nation/wp/2016/02/17/justice-scalias-death-and-questions-about-who-pays-for-supreme-court-justices-to-visit-remote-resorts/; Amy Brittain & Sari Horwitz, *Justice Scalia Spent His Last Hours with Members of This Secretive Society of Elite Hunters*, Wash. Post, Feb. 25, 2016, https://www.washingtonpost.com/world/national-security/justice-scalia-spent-his-last-hours-with-members-of-this-secretive-society-of-elite-hunters/2016/02/24/1d77af38-db20-11e5-891a-4ed04f4213e8_story.html; Adam Liptak, *Justices Disclose Privately Paid Trips and Gifts*, N.Y. Times, Jun. 22, 2016, http://www.nytimes.com/2016/06/23/us/politics/justices-disclose-privately-paid-trips-and-gifts.html.

16. *Cheney v. U.S. Dist. Court*, 541 U.S. 913, 928 (2004) (Scalia, J., mem.).

17. Adam Liptak, *Antonin Scalia, Justice on the Supreme Court, Dies at 79*, N.Y. Times, Feb. 13, 2016; http://www.nytimes.com/2016/02/14/us/antonin-scalia-death.html; Joan Biskupic, American Original: The Life and Constitution of Supreme Court Justice Antonin Scalia 23, 74 (2009).

18. Frank B. Cross, *Determinants of Citations to Supreme Court Opinions (And the Remarkable Influence of Justice Scalia)*, 18 Sup. Ct. Econ Rev. 177 (2010).

19. I calculated these figures for Stone, Seidman et al., Constitutional Law (7th ed. 2013) and Eskridge, Frickey et al., Cases and Materials on Legislation and Regulation (5th ed. 2014) using electronic versions of the books. In the constitutional law casebook, I counted only solely-written majority, concurring, and dissenting opinions featured as a principal opinion as indicated by the use of large and small caps with the Justice's name. Data available upon request from the author.

For an earlier look at Justice Scalia's dominance in the constitutional law casebooks, see Ralph A. Rossum, Antonin Scalia's Jurisprudence: Text and Tradition 205–6 (2006). Rossum also calculated the number of law review articles containing the name of a (then-) current Supreme Court justice in the title. Scalia has 120, followed by Rehnquist (then the chief justice) at 57, O'Connor at 48, and the remaining justices between 2 and 16.

20. Jennifer Senior, *In Conversation: Antonin Scalia*, New York, Oct. 6, 2013, http://nymag.com/news/features/antonin-scalia-2013-10/#.

21. Andrew D. Martin & Kevin M. Quinn, *Scalia Was Almost Never the Most Conservative Justice on the Supreme Court*, FiveThirtyEight, Feb. 15, 2016, http://fivethirtyeight.com/features/scalia-was-almost-never-the-most-conservative-justice-on-the-supreme-court/; *see also* Lee Epstein, William M. Landes, & Richard A. Posner, *Revisiting the Ideology Rankings of Supreme Court Justices*, 44 J. Legal Stud. S295 (2015), tbl. 1 (ranking Scalia behind Rehnquist and Thomas in conservatism, among the justices with whom he served).

22. These figures are calculated using the Supreme Court database tool (http://Su

premeCourtDatabase.org) hosted by Washington University. These data only go through the 2014 term. Using the Supreme Court website (http://supremecourt .gov), I found two more majority opinions and two more dissents Justice Scalia wrote in the October 2015 term before passing away.

23. Richard M. Re, *Justice Kagan on Textualism's Success,* PrawfsBlawg, Dec. 7, 2015, http://prawfsblawg.blogs.com/prawfsblawg/2015/12/justice-kagan-on-textual isms-victory.html (quoting Justice Kagan's remarks at Harvard Law School "Scalia Lecture," posted at https://www.youtube.com/watch?v=dpEtszFToTg, at the 8:25 minute mark); see also Jeffrey Rosen, *What Made Antonin Scalia Great,* The Atlantic, Feb. 15, 2016, http://www.theatlantic.com/politics/archive/2016/02/ what-made-antonin-scalia-great/462837/ ("Perhaps the greatest sign of Scalia's influence is that liberal justices and scholars now make arguments about constitutional text and history, insisting that the conservative justices are ignoring the text and original understanding of the Constitution that Scalia insisted should be their guide. More than any justice since the liberal lion William Brennan, Scalia changed the way Americans debate the Constitution, and for that he deserves great respect.").

24. Martin & Quinn, *supra* note 21.

25. *Fisher v. University of Texas at Austin,* 136 S. Ct. 2198 (2016); *Whole Woman's Health v. Hellerstedt,* 136 S. Ct. 2292 (2016).

26. David Cole, *Scalia: The Most Influential Justice Without Influence in Supreme Court History,* The Nation, Feb. 18, 2016, https://www.thenation.com/article/scalia-the-most-in fluential-justice-without-influence-in-supreme-court-history/ ("There is no question that Justice Scalia made originalism respectable. His tireless advocacy on behalf of this interpretive method almost single-handedly transformed it from a widely rejected straw man in the 1980s into a serious subject of legal theory today. . . . But to be an originalist means always to be looking backward. As a result, unless an originalist justice is so persuasive that the Court as a whole adopts his or her method, that justice is unlikely to be very good at predicting or influencing future legal developments. As constitutional law evolves over the course of history to respond to new challenges, originalists are likely to be left behind, gazing back at a more and more remote (and less and less relevant) history.").

Chapter 2. Word Games

1. AP, *Ruling Limits Judges' Power to Exclude Evidence,* Observer-Reporter (Wash., Pa), May 23, 1989, https://goo.gl/H5QC5w; *Green v. Bock Laundry Machine Co.,* 490 U.S. 504 (1989).

2. *Diggs v. Lyons,* 741 F. 2d 577, 582 (3d Cir. 1984); *id.* at 583 (Gibbons, J., dissenting).

3. The quotes in the next few paragraphs come from Justice Stevens's majority opinion in *Green,* 490 U.S. 504 (1989).

4. Antonin Scalia, A Matter of Interpretation: Federal Courts and the Law 23–24 (1997); William N. Eskridge, Jr., *The New Textualism,* 37 UCLA L. Rev. 621 (1990).

5. Antonin Scalia & Bryan A. Garner, Reading Law: The Interpretation of Legal Texts 199 (2012).
6. *Conroy v. Aniskoff*, 507 U.S. 511, 519 (1993) (Scalia, J., concurring in the judgment) (quoting Judge Leventhal).
7. Kenneth A. Shepsle, *Congress Is a "They," Not an "It": Legislative Intent as Oxymoron*, 12 Int'l Rev. L. & Econ. 239 (1992).
8. *Hirschey v. F.E.R.C.*, 777 F. 2d 1, 7 n.1 (D.C. Cir. 1985) (concurring opn.).
9. *Conroy*, 507 U.S. at 519.
10. The quotes in the next few paragraphs come from Justice Scalia's concurring opinion in *Green*, 490 U.S. at 527 (Scalia, J., concurring in the judgment).
11. William N. Eskridge, Jr., Dynamic Statutory Interpretation 46–47 (1994).
12. *Id.*
13. *Green*, 490 U.S. at 530–35 (Blackmun, J., dissenting).
14. Edward P. Lazarus, *The Case of the Severed Arm: A Tribute to Associate Justice Harry A. Blackmun*, 43 Am. U. L. Rev. 725, 728–29 (1994). Federal Rule of Evidence 609(a) now reads:

   (a) In General. The following rules apply to attacking a witness's character for truthfulness by evidence of a criminal conviction:
      (1) for a crime that, in the convicting jurisdiction, was punishable by death or by imprisonment for more than one year, the evidence:
      (A) must be admitted, subject to Rule 403, in a civil case or in a criminal case in which the witness is not a defendant; and
      (B) must be admitted in a criminal case in which the witness is a defendant, if the probative value of the evidence outweighs its prejudicial effect to that defendant; and
      (2) for any crime regardless of the punishment, the evidence must be admitted if the court can readily determine that establishing the elements of the crime required proving—or the witness's admitting—a dishonest act or false statement.

15. Nina Totenberg, *Justice Scalia, the Great Dissenter, Opens Up*, NPR, Apr. 28, 2008, http://www.npr.org/templates/story/story.php?storyId=89986017.
16. Scalia, *supra* note 4, at 27–29. These next few paragraphs draw from Richard L. Hasen, *The Democracy Canon*, 62 Stan. L. Rev. 69 (2009).
17. *Id.* at 20, 28–29.
18. Antonin Scalia, *Assorted Canards of Contemporary Legal Analysis*, 40 Case W. Res. L. Rev. 581, 581–86 (1990).
19. Lawrence M. Solan, *Learning Our Limits: The Decline of Textualism in Statutory Cases*, 1997 Wis. L. Rev. 235, 236–37 (1997). He gives this example of the game:

   Imagine a Wittgensteinian parlor game, in which a participant begins by uttering a sentence that contains only commonly used words. Another player then must create the most bizarre story she can that is loyal to the language in the first player's sentence. When each person, has had a chance to make up a story, the player who told the most imaginative one wins. The trick is to imagine real, but unconventional uses of the words in the sentence. For example, if the sentence is, "Bill threw the ball over the tree," a winning story might be one in which "throw" means "corruptly cause the loss of a competitive event," as in, "the quarterback, who had accepted a bribe from organized crime, threw the game." "Ball" might mean a formal dance. "Over" is interpreted nonprototypically to mean "about" rather than "above." The story might involve some kind of inter-family competition among high society members over which family organizes the best ball. One member of one of the families, Bill, was angry over his sibling's unilateral decision to have his favorite tree cut down, and he decided to get his revenge by undermining the family's chances of winning the competition. Perhaps the reader can come up with an even wilder response. What makes the game fun is that it forces us to suspend whatever conventional notions we have about how words are likely to be used. In understanding language, we ordinarily take advantage of contextual cues and of knowledge of how words are used prototypically. The game, in contrast, requires us to take all words out of context, to ignore our knowledge of the prototypical uses of words, and to create arbitrary new contexts. Thus, the game depends on the notion that we ordinarily use context and our knowledge of prototypical instances of a concept when we understand language. Otherwise, there would be nothing different between the game on the one hand, and ordinary language understanding on the other.

For the past ten years, the Supreme Court has been interpreting statutes according to a set of rules that very much resemble the rules of this parlor game. Developed largely by Justice Scalia, the methodology, which has been called the "new textualism," intentionally eschews many of the contextual and cognitive cues that make language meaningful. Of course, the Court's textualism is not exactly like our parlor game. But the similarities are clear enough. Instead of insisting that the interpreter assume no context whatsoever, as does the parlor game, the Court has selected a few categories of contextual information as the only ones that the interpreter may consider. These include the language of related provisions of the statute being examined, and perhaps more remote sections of the United States Code, in the case of federal statutes. They also include the prior interpretive decisions of the Court. To the extent that other information, such as legislative history, is allowed into the picture at all (a move that Justice Scalia rejects but others accept), its role is limited to potentially disconfirming the plain language analysis in especially egregious cases. As in our game, the Court has rejected reliance on prototypical understandings of words, and has substituted the outer bounds of dictionary definitions for our everyday knowledge of how words are ordinarily used. Perhaps most significantly, neither the game nor the Court permits prior consideration of the broader ramifications of the proffered interpretation.

20. *United States v. Marshall,* 908 F. 2d 1312 (7th Cir. 1990) (en banc).

21. *Lamie v. United States Trustee*, 540 U.S. 526, 538 (2004); *King v. Burwell*, 135 S. Ct. at 2504, 2505 (2015) (Scalia, J., dissenting).

22. *U.S. v. Agyemano*, 2015 WL 1321887, *6 (E.D. Ky. 2015).

23. *United States v. Detroit Medical Center*, 833 F. 3d 671, 679 (6th Cir. 2016).

24. *U.S. ex rel. Totten v. Bombardier Corp.*, 380 F. 3d 488, 491 (D.C. Cir. 2004); *id.* at 503, 515–16 (Garland, J., dissenting).

25. On dictionary shopping, see James J. Brudney & Lawrence Baum, *Oasis or Mirage: The Supreme Court's Thirst for Dictionaries in the Rehnquist and Roberts Eras*, 55 Wm. & Mary L. Rev. 483 (2013); Ellen P. Aprill, *The Law of the Word: Dictionary Shopping in the Supreme Court*, 30 Ariz. St. L.J. 275 (1998).

26. *Muscarello v. U.S.*, 524 U.S. 125, 142 (1998) (Ginsburg, J., dissenting).

27. Abbe R. Gluck & Lisa Schultz Bressman, *Statutory Interpretation from the Inside— An Empirical Study of Congressional Drafting, Delegation, and the Canons: Part I*, 65 Stan. L. Rev. 901, 907 (2013).

28. Lisa Schultz Bressman & Abbe R. Gluck, *Statutory Interpretation from the Inside— An Empirical Study of Congressional Drafting, Delegation, and the Canons: Part II*, 66 Stan. L. Rev. 725, 728–29 (2014).

29. Robert A. Katzmann, Judging Statutes 48 (2014).

30. *Yates v. U.S.*, 135 S. Ct. 1074 (2015). The quotes in the next few paragraphs come from the opinions in *Yates*.

31. *Exxon Mobil Corp. v. Allapattah Servs., Inc.*, 545 U.S. 546, 568 (2005) (Kennedy, J.) ("As we have repeatedly held, the authoritative statement is the statutory text, not the legislative history or any other extrinsic material. Extrinsic materials have a role in statutory interpretation only to the extent they shed a reliable light on the enacting Legislature's understanding of otherwise ambiguous terms. Not all extrinsic materials are reliable sources of insight into legislative understandings, however, and legislative history in particular is vulnerable to two serious criticisms. First, legislative history is itself often murky, ambiguous, and contradictory. Judicial investigation of legislative history has a tendency to become, to borrow Judge Leventhal's memorable phrase, an exercise in 'looking over a crowd and picking out your friends.' See Wald, Some Observations on the Use of Legislative History in the 1981 Supreme Court Term, 68 Iowa L. Rev. 195, 214 (1983). Second, judicial reliance on legislative materials like committee reports, which are not themselves subject to the requirements of Article I, may give unrepresentative committee members—or, worse yet, unelected staffers and lobbyists— both the power and the incentive to attempt strategic manipulations of legislative history to secure results they were unable to achieve through the statutory text. We need not comment here on whether these problems are sufficiently prevalent to render legislative history inherently unreliable in all circumstances, a point on which Members of this Court have disagreed. It is clear, however, that in this instance both criticisms are right on the mark.").

32. *Zedner v. U.S.*, 547 U.S. 489, 509–11 (2006) (Scalia, J. concurring in part and concurring in the judgment).

33. This statistic is based on a Westlaw search in March 2017 for citations to the book in a database of state and federal court decisions (scalia /4 garner /4 "reading law").

34. *U.S. v. Rentz,* 777 F. 3d 1105, 1107 (10th Cir. 2015) (en banc).

35. *Transam Trucking v. Administrative Review Board,* 833 F. 3d 1206 (10th Cir. 2016); *see also* Jed Handelsman Shugerman, *Neil Gorsuch and the "Frozen Trucker,"* Slate, Mar. 21, 2017, http://www.slate.com/articles/news_and_politics/jurispru dence/2017/03/neil_gorsuch_s_arrogant_frozen_trucker_opinion_shows_he _wants_to_be_like.html.

36. Senate Committee on the Judiciary, Hearing on the Nomination of Neil Gor- such to Be An Associate Justice of the U.S. Supreme Court, Afternoon Session, March 21, 2017, *available at:* http://congressional.proquest.com/congressional/ docview/t65.d40.03210003.t19?accountid=14509. A video of the exchange is available on YouTube beginning around the 6:40-minute mark at: https://www .youtube.com/watch?v=E7E3Bb98uKw. At the same hearing, Gorsuch offered this defense of his decision to Senator Durbin:

> Senator, all I can tell you is my job is to apply the law you write. The law, as written, said that he would be protected if he refused to operate. And I think by any plain understanding, he operated the vehicle. And if Congress wishes to revise the law, I wrote this—I said it was an unkind decision. I said it may have been a wrong decision, a bad decision.
>
> My job isn't to write the law, Senator, it's to apply the law. And if Congress passes a law saying a trucker in those circumstances gets to choose how to operate his vehicle, I will be the first one in line to enforce it. I've been stuck on the highway in Wyoming in a snow storm. I know what's involved. I don't make light of it, I take it seriously.

37. *Henson v. Santander Consumer, U.S.A., Ltd,* 137 S. Ct. 1718 (2017); *Perry v. Merit Systems Protection Bd.,* 137 S. Ct. 1975, 1990 (2017) (Gorsuch, J., dissenting); Adam Liptak, *Sidebar: Confident and Assertive, Gorsuch Hurries to Make His Mark,* N.Y. Times, Jul. 3, 2017, https://www.nytimes.com/2017/07/03/us/politics/neil -gorsuch-supreme-court.html (quoting Justice Alito).

38. The remarks are described by Professor John McGinnis in John O. McGinnis, *Our Two Supreme Courts,* Library of Law and Liberty, May 6, 2015, http://www .libertylawsite.org/2015/05/06/our-two-supreme-courts/. The discussion here draws a bit from Richard L. Hasen, *Why the Most Urgent Civil Rights Cause of Our Time Is the Supreme Court Itself,* TPM Café, Sept. 28, 2015, http://talkingpoints memo.com/cafe/supreme-court-greatest-civil-rights-cause.

39. Brett M. Kavanaugh, *Fixing Statutory Interpretation,* 129 Harv. L. Rev. 2118 (2016).

40. *Id.* at 2121. For a thoughtful response from Judge Katzmann, see Robert A. Katz- mann, *Response to Judge Kavanaugh's Review of* Judging Statutes, 129 Harv. L. Rev. F. 388 (2016), http://harvardlawreview.org/2016/06/response-to-judge-kavanaughs -review-of-judging-statutes/.

41. Kavanaugh, *supra* note 39, at 2157, 2159 ("It's not my place here to say whether *King v. Burwell* was right or wrong in its outcome. That's not relevant for present purposes and beyond the scope of this Book Review. But I think the question of whether it was right or wrong depends on what one thinks about a mistake canon . . . that does not allow resort to legislative history but does allow courts to look at the overall Act and adopt what they conclude Congress *meant* rather than what Congress *said*.").

42. John F. Manning, *The Absurdity Doctrine*, 116 Harv. L. Rev. 2387, 2392, 2479–80 (2003).

Chapter 3. From Faint-Hearted to Full-Throated

1. The audio of the oral argument in *Brown v. Entertainment Merchants Association* is posted at: https://www.oyez.org/cases/2010/08-1448. A transcript of the oral argument in the case, when it was then known as *Schwarzenegger v. Entertainment Merchants Association* is posted at: https://www.supremecourt.gov/oral_argu ments/argument_transcripts/08-1448.pdf. The case opinions are available 564 U.S. 786 (2011). Further quotations from the case in this chapter come from the oral argument or opinions.

2. SCOTUSBlog Stat Pack, Justice Agreement, All Cases, October Term 2010, June 28, 2011, http://www.scotusblog.com/2011/06/final-october-term-2010-stat-pack -available/. The 2011 term statistics are at: http://sblog.s3.amazonaws.com/wp -content/uploads/2012/06/SB_agreement_OT11_final.pdf. The 2012 term statis- tics are at: http://scotusblog.com/wp-content/uploads/2013/06/agreement_OT12 .pdf. The 2013 term statistics are at: http://sblog.s3.amazonaws.com/wp-content /uploads/2014/07/SCOTUSblog_tables_OT13.pdf. The 2014 term statistics are at: http://sblog.s3.amazonaws.com/wp-content/uploads/2015/07/SB_agreement -tables_OT14.pdf.

3. Editorial, *Maybe Not Scalito*, Wash. Post, Jun. 6, 2006, http://www.washington post.com/wp-dyn/content/article/2006/06/06/AR2006060600052.html ("Justice Alito's critics tagged him 'Scalito,' suggesting that he is a clone of Jus- tice Antonin Scalia. Yet in his opinion for the court [in *Zedner v. United States*], Justice Alito committed one of the cardinal sins of Scaliaesque judging: He cited the act's legislative history.").

4. On the history of originalism see Johnathan O'Neill, Originalism in American Law and Politics 3 (2005). Eric Segall, a noted critic of originalism, has traced the idea as far back as a 1900 article in the *Harvard Law Review*. Eric J. Segall, *A Cen- tury Lost: The End of the Originalism Debate*, 15 Constitutional Commentary 411 (1998) (discussing Arthur W. Machen, *The Elasticity of the Constitution*, 14 Harv. L. Rev. 200 (1900)). Chapter 3 of O'Neill's book traces the return of originalism in the Warren Court, and the role of Hugo Black.

5. Steven G. Calabresi, *A Critical Introduction to the Originalism Debate*, 1, 23, in Orig- inalism: A Quarter-Century of Debate (Steven G. Calabresi ed. 2007) (discussing

role of Meese and Bork in putting forth originalist ideas). Classic early works in the modern originalist tradition, earlier known as "interpretivism," include Robert H. Bork, *Neutral Principles and Some First Amendment Problems,* 47 Indiana L.J. 1 (1971–72) and Raoul Berger, Government by Judiciary (1971). On the history of the Federalist Society and its role in the conservative legal movement, see Amanda Hollis-Brusky, Ideas with Consequences: The Federalist Society and the Conservative Counterrevolution 182 n.3 (2015); Ann Southworth, Lawyers of the Right 27–28, 130–41, pp. 198–99 n.24 (2008); Steven M. Teles, The Rise of the Conservative Legal Movement 158–59 (2008) (discussing how Republican presidents relied upon the Federalist Society to screen judicial nominees and other appointees); Gary Lawson, *Dedication: On Getting It Right: Remembering Justice Antonin Scalia,* 96 Boston U. L. Rev. 299, 300–301 (2016); *id.,* at 141 ("Perhaps [the Federalist Society's] most important elite sponsor of the society in its early years was then-professor Antonin Scalia, who first helped connect the Yale and Chicago contingents with the conservative law group at Stanford, helped them with fund-raising, spoke at their first conference, hosted visiting Harvard Law Federalist Society members at his home, when the Society had its first conference at the University of Chicago law School, and facilitated the Society's early move into an office at the American Enterprise Institute."). On the emergence of modern originalism, see *Panel on Originalism and Pragmatism,* in Originalism, *supra,* at 151–59 (comments of Dean Larry Kramer).

6. Antonin Scalia, A Matter of Interpretation 38 (1997); see also Antonin Scalia & Bryan A. Garner, Reading Law 435 (2012) (defining "original meaning" as "The understanding of a text, esp. an important text such as the Constitution, reflecting what an informed, reasonable member of the community would have understood at the time of adoption according to then-prevailing linguistic meanings and interpretive principles").

7. Calabresi, *supra* note 5, at 12 ("The point is that the original meaning of the constitutional text and not the intentions of the framers, that is law was made by Justice Scalia in an important speech to the Justice Department in June 1986, just days before his nomination to the Supreme Court . . ."); *see also Panel on Originalism and Pragmatism,* in Calabresi, *supra* note 5, at 151–55 (comments of Dean Larry Kramer, tracing the different formulations of originalism from the 1970s through its current Justice Scalia-inspired public-meaning originalism).

8. Katie Glueck, *Scalia: The Constitution Is Dead,* Politico, Jan. 29, 2013, http://www .politico.com/story/2013/01/scalia-the-constitution-is-dead-086853 (quoting Justice Scalia from talk at Southern Methodist University).

9. Antonin Scalia, *Originalism: The Lesser Evil,* 57 U. Cinn. L. Rev. 849, 864 (1989) ("Having made that endorsement, I hasten to confess that in a crunch I may prove a faint-hearted originalist. I cannot imagine myself, any more than any other federal judge, upholding a statute that imposes the punishment of flogging."). On Justice Scalia's lack of consistency across cases, see Michael W. McConnell, *Textualism and the Dead Hand of the Past,* 66 Geo. Wash. L. Rev. 1127, 1137 n.45 (1998):

Justice Scalia may fairly be criticized for failing to address the relation between the various aspects of his constitutional jurisprudence. At times, he writes as if "plain meaning" were the alpha and omega of constitutional interpretation. At other times, he stresses history in the form of original meaning. See *Antonin Scalia, Originalism: The Lesser Evil,* 57 U. Cinn. L. Rev. 849, 852 (1989). At still other times, he advocates interpretation of the Constitution in light of the long-standing traditions and experience of the nation. See Rutan v. Republican Party, 497 U.S. 62, 95–97 (1990) (Scalia, J., dissenting); *Michael H. v. Gerald D.,* 491 U.S. 110, 122–24 (1989) (Scalia, J.). Finally, at still other times, he trumpets the need for judicial deference to the present-day decisions of "the people, through their elected representatives." *City of Boerne v. Flores,* 117 S. Ct. 2157, 2176 (1997) (Scalia, J., concurring). As explained in the text, these various methods have something very important in common: they all respect the will of the people, as expressed at various points in time. But by failing to articulate the connection between these methods, or to explain how to decide cases when they are in conflict, Justice Scalia leaves himself open to the charge of inconsistency.

For a catalog of major cases in which Justice Scalia avoided application of originalism, see Eric J. Segall, *Will the Real Justice Scalia Please Stand Up?,* 50 Wake Forest L. Rev. 101 (2015).

10. *Ginsberg v. N.Y.,* 390 U.S. 629 (1968).
11. *U.S. v. Stevens,* 559 U.S. 460 (2010).
12. *Brown,* 564 U.S. at 817–18 (Alito, J., concurring in the judgment).
13. Chapter 6 discusses these justices' competing views on campaign finance disclosure.
14. SCOTUSBlog Stat Pack, Justice Agreement, All Cases, October Term 2010, June 28, 2011, http://www.scotusblog.com/2011/06/final-october-term-2010-stat-pack -available/. The 2011 term statistics are at: http://sblog.s3.amazonaws.com/ wp-content/uploads/2012/06/SB_agreement_OT11_final.pdf. The 2012 term statistics are at: http://scotusblog.com/wp-content/uploads/2013/06/agreement _OT12.pdf. The 2013 term statistics are at: http://sblog.s3.amazonaws.com/wp -content/uploads/2014/07/SCOTUSblog_tables_OT13.pdf. The 2014 term statistics are at: http://sblog.s3.amazonaws.com/wp-content/uploads/2015/07/SB_ agreement-tables_OT14.pdf.
15. *Brown v. Entertainment Merchants Ass'n,* 564 U.S. at 822 (Thomas, J., dissenting) ("In my view, the 'practices and beliefs held by the Founders' reveal another category of excluded speech: speech to minor children bypassing their parents."). See Brief Amicus Curiae Common Sense Media Supporting Petitioner at 12 http:// www.abanet.org/publiced/preview/briefs/pdfs/09-10/08-1448_PetitionerAm CuCommonSenseMedia.pdf ("The Framers clearly understood that children's rights as an audience for entertainment could be limited, including in terms of violence"); Adam Liptak, *Justice Thomas Breaks Ten Years of Silence at Supreme Court,* N.Y. Times, Feb. 29, 2016, http://www.nytimes.com/2016/03/01/us/politics/su preme-court-clarence-thomas.html.

16. *Brown,* 540 U.S. at 835 (Thomas, J., dissenting).
17. *Erznoznik v. Jacksonville,* 422 U.S. 205 (1975).
18. *Brown,* 564 U.S. 795 n.3.
19. On linguistics, see Professor Solan's work cited in the last chapter. On critiques by historians, a good representative statement is that of Gordon Wood, commenting in Scalia, A Matter of Interpretation, *supra* note 6, at 49. Scalia and Garner respond to what they call "the false notion that lawyers and judges, not being historians, are unqualified to do the historical research that originalism requires" in Scalia & Garner, *supra* note 6, at 399.
20. Justice Breyer, one of the Court's liberals, also dissented in *Brown,* but from a very different angle. *Brown,* 564 U.S. at 840 (Breyer, J., dissenting). He offered a detailed look at the social science evidence (much included in an appendix) on the effect of violent video games on the brains of minors. While one might accuse Justices Scalia and Thomas of being armchair linguists and historians, one might also accuse Justice Breyer of being an armchair social scientist.
21. *Texas v. Johnson,* 491 U.S. 397 (1989); Steven J. Heyman, *The Conservative-Libertarian Turn in First Amendment Jurisprudence,* 117 W. Va. L. Rev. 231, 298 (2014).
22. *Snyder v. Phelps,* 562 U.S. 443, 448 (2011).
23. *Id.* at 463 (Alito, J., dissenting).
24. Justice Thomas wrote:

> My understanding of "the freedom of speech" is also consistent with this Court's precedents. To be sure, the Court has held that children are entitled to the protection of the First Amendment, see, *e.g., Erznoznik v. Jacksonville,* 422 U.S. 205, 212–213 (1975), and the government may not unilaterally dictate what children can say or hear, see *id; Tinker v. Des Moines Independent Community School Dist.,* 393 U.S. 503, 511 (1969). But this Court has never held, until today, that "the freedom of speech" includes a right to speak to minors (or a right of minors to access speech) without going through the minors' parents.

> *Brown,* 564 U.S. at 837 (Thomas, J., dissenting).
25. *Gitlow v. New York,* 268 U.S. 652 (1925). For an introduction to the dispute about substantive due process, see Erwin Chemerinsky, Constitutional Law: Principles and Policies 569–73 (5th ed. 2015).
26. On selective incorporation, see Chemerinsky, *supra* note 25, at 524–32.
27. *Zelman v. Simmons-Harris,* 536 U.S. 639, 677 (2002) (Thomas, J., concurring); Chemerinsky, *supra* note 25, at 528. A state religion in New Jersey could be otherwise unconstitutional, Thomas suggests, such as if it impeded the free exercise of religion, separately protected in the First Amendment.
28. *McDonald v. City of Chicago,* 561 U.S. 742 (2010).
29. *District of Columbia v. Heller,* 554 U.S. 570 (2008).
30. *McDonald,* 561 U.S. at 791 (Scalia, J., concurring).
31. *Slaughter-House Cases,* 86 U.S. (16 Wall.) 36 (1872).
32. The transcript of the oral argument in the *McDonald* case is posted at https://

www.supremecourt.gov/oral_arguments/argument_transcripts/08-1521.pdf and the relevant discussion appears at pages 5–7.

33. *McDonald*, 561 U.S. at 805–57 (Thomas, J., concurring in part and concurring in the judgment).

34. Randy Barnett, *"Judicial engagement" is not the same as "judicial activism,"* Volokh Conspiracy, Jan. 28, 2014, https://www.washingtonpost.com/news/volokh-con spiracy/wp/2014/01/28/judicial-engagement-is-not-the-same-as-judicial-activ ism/?utm_term=.b9fd45303eb8.

35. Scalia, *supra* note 6, at 138–39; *see also* Scalia & Garner, *supra* note 6, at 411–13 (defending application of *stare decisis* in some non-originalist cases).

36. *See* Scalia, *supra* note 9, at 864.

37. Marcia Coyle, the Roberts Court: The Struggle for the Constitution 165 (2013). *See also* Jennifer Senior, *In Conversation: Antonin Scalia*, New York, Oct. 6, 2013, http://nymag.com/news/features/antonin-scalia-2013-10/:

> **You've described yourself as a fainthearted originalist. But really, how faint-hearted?**
> I described myself as that a long time ago. I repudiate that.
> **So you're a stouthearted one.**
> I try to be. I try to be an honest originalist! I will take the bitter with the sweet! What I used "fainthearted" in reference to was—
> **Flogging, right?**
> Flogging. And what I would say now is, yes, if a state enacted a law permitting flogging, it is immensely stupid, but it is not unconstitutional. A lot of stuff that's stupid is not unconstitutional. I gave a talk once where I said they ought to pass out to all federal judges a stamp, and the stamp says—*Whack!* [*Pounds his fist.*]—STUPID BUT CONSTITUTIONAL. *Whack!* [*Pounds again.*] STUPID BUT CONSTITUTIONAL! *Whack!* STUPID BUT CONSTITUTIONAL . . . [*Laughs.*] And then somebody sent me one.

38. Coyle, *supra* note 37, at 165.

39. Ilya Somin, *Scalia and Constitutional Property Rights,* Wash. Post, Volokh Conspir-acy, Feb. 15, 2016, https://www.washingtonpost.com/news/volokh-conspiracy/ wp/2016/02/15/justice-scalia-and-constitutional-property-rights/?utm_term= .ca017c1f55b7; *Kelo v. City of New London,* 545 U.S. 469 (2005).

40. Segall, *supra* note 9; Randy E. Barnett, *Scalia's Infidelity: A Critique of "Faint-Hearted" Originalism,* 75 U. Cinn. L. Rev. 7, 13 (2006). Barnett writes:

> On his account of the proper approach to interpreting the Constitution, then, Justice Scalia proves unfaithful to the original meaning of the text in three distinct ways. First, he is willing to ignore the original meaning of those por-tions of the Constitution that do not meet his criteria of the rule of law as the law of rules. Second, he is willing to avoid objectionable outcomes that would result from originalism by invoking the precedents established by the dead hand of nonoriginalist justices. Third, where precedent is unavailing as an es-

cape route, he is willing simply to abandon originalist results that he and most others would find too onerous by some unstated criteria.

41. *Chavez v. Martinez,* 538 U.S. 760 (2003). The exchange with Dershowitz is quoted in Bruce Allen Murphy, Scalia: A Court of One 396 (2014). Letter from Justice Antonin Scalia to Ms. Tara Levens and Mr. Michael Kenstowicz, University of Chicago Law Review, dated June 25, 2015, Special Collections Research Center, University of Chicago Law Review, Records, Addenda, Accession no. 2017-072, Box 287. Another example of Justice Scalia deflecting such a question appears in Chapter Six's discussion of *Gonzales v. Raich.*

42. *Michael H. v. Gerald D.,* 491 U.S. 110, 124 (1989).

43. *Troxel v. Granville,* 530 U.S. 57, 92 (2000) (Scalia, J., dissenting).

44. *Plessy v. Ferguson,* 163 U.S. 537 (1896); *Brown v. Board of Educ.,* 347 U.S. 483 (1954); Michael J. Klarman, Brown, *Originalism, and Constitutional Theory: A Response to Professor McConnell,* 81 Va. L. Rev. 1881 (1995) (responding to Michael W. McConnell, *Originalism and the Desegregation Decisions,* 81 Va. L. Rev. 947 (1995)); Stephen A. Siegel, *The Federal Government's Power to Enact Color-Conscious Laws: An Originalist Inquiry,* 92 Nw. U. L. Rev. 477 (1998).

45. Scalia & Garner, *supra* note 6, at 88. *See also Rutan v. Republican Party of Ill.,* 497 U.S. 62, 95–96 n.1 (1990) (Scalia, J., dissenting):

> In my view the Fourteenth Amendment's requirement of "equal protection of the laws," combined with the Thirteenth Amendment's abolition of the institution of black slavery, leaves no room for doubt that laws treating people differently because of their race are invalid. Moreover, even if one does not regard the Fourteenth Amendment as crystal clear on this point, a tradition of *unchallenged* validity did not exist with respect to the practice in *Brown.* To the contrary, in the 19th century the principle of "separate-but-equal" had been vigorously opposed on constitutional grounds, litigated up to this Court, and upheld only over the dissent of one of our most historically respected Justices.

> For a critique of Justice Scalia's defense of Brown as originalist, see Ronald Turner, *A Critique of Antonin Scalia's Originalist Defense of* Brown v. Board of Education, 62 UCLA L. Rev. Disc. 170 (2014), http://www.uclalawreview.org/pdf/discourse/62-9.pdf. On the Rosen conversation, see Jeffrey Rosen, *What Made Antonin Scalia Great,* The Atlantic, Feb. 15, 2016, https://www.theatlantic.com/politics/archive/2016/02/what-made-antonin-scalia-great/462837/.

46. Richard A. Posner, *The Incoherence of Antonin Scalia,* The New Republic, Aug. 23, 2012, https://newrepublic.com/article/106441/scalia-garner-reading-the-law-textual-originalism (reviewing Scalia & Garner, *supra* note 6); see also *Debate on Radicals in Robes,* in Originalism, *supra* note 5, at 293 (comments of Professor Cass Sunstein) (calling the originalist case against separate but equal "no longer preposterous after Judge McConnell's argument, but Michael Klarman and other historians find that he has made a plausible argument, but not a convincing

one"). The McConnell article is Michael W. McConnell, *Originalism and the Desegregation Decisions,* 81 Va. L. Rev. 947 (1995).

47. *See Regents of the Univ. of Cal. v. Bakke,* 438 U.S. 265, 397 (1978) (plurality opinion) (Marshall, J., concurring) ("The Congress that passed the Fourteenth Amendment is the same Congress that passed the 1866 Freedmen's Bureau Act, an Act that provided many of its benefits only to Negroes."); *id.* at 398 ("Since the Congress that considered and rejected the objections to the 1866 Freedmen's Bureau Act concerning special relief to Negroes also proposed the Fourteenth Amendment, it is inconceivable that the Fourteenth Amendment was intended to prohibit all race-conscious relief measures.").

48. *Legally Speaking: The Originalist,* Cal. Lawyer, Jan. 2011, http://ww2.callawyer.com/story.cfm?eid=913358&evid=1 (emphasis added).

49. Antonin Scalia, *Forward,* In Originalism: A Quarter-Century of Debate 43, 44–45 (Steven G. Calabresi ed 2007).

50. I computed these data with date-restricted searches in Westlaw's "Journals and Law Reviews" database, searching for the term "originalism." As noted above, an earlier term used for "originalism" is "interpretivism," and across this time period its use rose in the early 1990s and then declined. The figures are 1980–84, 128 articles; 1984–89, 246 articles; 1990–94, 289 articles; 1995–99, 270 articles; 2000–2004, 206 articles; 2005–9, 167 articles; 2010–14, 133 articles.

51. Hollis-Brusky, *supra* note 5, at 2. The $18 million figure comes from the Federalist Society's "990" tax form from 2015, available from Guidestar, and on file with the author.

52. *Id.* at 20, 54–57 (showing how Justice Thomas crafted his *McDonald* concurrence based upon ideas put forward by Federalist Society scholars).

53. Calabresi, *supra* note 5, at 33 ("The real anti-discrimination issue before the Supreme Court today is discrimination on the basis of sexual orientation. Are laws that discriminate on that basis 'necessary and proper'? I think the answer is plainly yes."); *id.* at 36; Steven G. Calabresi & Hannah M. Begley, *Originalism and Same Sex Marriage,* 70 U. Miami L. Rev. 648 (2016); William Baude, *Is Originalism Our Law?,* 115 Colum. L. Rev. 2349, 2482 (2015) (making originalist case for originalist reading of Fourteenth Amendment to include right to same-sex marriage); Orin Kerr, *Is There an Originalist Case for a Right to Same-Sex Marriage?,* Volokh Conspiracy, Wash. Post, Jan. 28, 2015, https://www.washingtonpost.com/news/volokh-conspiracy/wp/2015/01/28/is-there-an-originalist-case-for-a-right-to-same-sex-marriage/?utm_term=.8b93220a50e6 ("I fear that what are being described as originalist arguments may just be products of the Level of Generality Game with the word 'originalist' tacked on"). For a critique of Baude's originalism, see Eric Segall, *Originalism as Faith,* 38 Cornell L. Rev. Online 102 (2016), http://cornelllawreview.org/files/2016/12/Segallfinal.pdf.

54. *Panel on Originalism and Pragmatism, supra* note 5, at 155, 193 (comments of Dean Larry Kramer); *see also Panel on Originalism and Precedent,* in Originalism, *supra* note 5, at 218 (comments of Professor David Strauss) ("even if you have . . . figured

out what the understandings were, the original understandings might not resolve the issue you are trying to resolve. . . . Even if you have figured out what the understandings were . . . it is often not going to be clear—I think routinely it is not going to be clear—what those understandings say about today's issues.").

55. Jack Balkin, Living Originalism (2014).

56. *Citizens United v. Fed. Elec. Comm'n,* 558 U.S. 310, 385 (Scalia, J., concurring); *id.* at 425 (Stevens, J., concurring in part and dissenting in part); Hollis-Brusky, *supra* note 5, at 86 ("Scalia and Stevens both mobilized numerous sources from the Originalist canon, as well as scholarship on the early founding period and the role of corporations, in their attempts to persuade their audience that history and Originalism were on their side"). In a follow-on case to *Citizens United, McCutcheon v. FEC,* 134 S. Ct. 1434 (2014), the Constitutional Accountability Center submitted an *amicus* brief by Professor Lawrence Lessig, putting forward an originalist argument for the Supreme Court to sustain campaign contribution and spending limits. The brief is available at: http://theusconstitution.org/sites/de fault/files/briefs/CAC-McCutcheon-v-FEC-Amicus-Brief.pdf. Professor Solum's testimony in support of Gorsuch before the Senate Judiciary Committee is posted at: https://www.judiciary.senate.gov/download/03-23-17-solum-testimony.

57. Honorable Neil M. Gorsuch, *Of Lions and Bears, Judges and Legislators, and the Legacy of Justice Scalia,* 66 Case Western Res. L. Rev. 905, 906 (2016).

58. *Id.* at 916–17.

59. *Bush v. Gore,* 531 U.S. 98 (2000). On the role reversal of the justices on the scope of the equal protection clause, see Richard L. Hasen, Bush v. Gore *and the Future of Equal Protection Law in Elections,* 29 Fla. St. U. L. Rev. 377 (2001).

Chapter 4. Mr. Justice Scalia, the Fish

1. Federalist Society, Keynote Address by Paul Clement—Event Audio/Video, 2016 National Student Symposium, Mar. 4, 2016. Video of the 2016 event is posted at https://www.fed-soc.org/multimedia/detail/keynote-address-by-paul-clement -event-audiovideo and the fish tale begins around the 28-minute mark. My transcription of Clement's remarks slightly edits his prose for clarity.

2. A short version of the story appears in Joan Biskupic, *No Shades of Gray for Justice Scalia,* USA Today, Sept. 18, 2002 (accessed from Lexis USA Today database Sept. 19, 2016). On Judge Bybee and torture, see Karl Vick, *Friends Say Judge Bybee Regrets Interrogation Memo He Signed,* Wash. Post, Apr. 25, 2009, http://www.wash ingtonpost.com/wp-dyn/content/article/2009/04/24/AR2009042403888.html.

3. NPR Staff, *Scalia and Ginsburg: Best Buddies,* Feb. 15, 2016, http://www.npr.org /2016/02/15/466848775/scalia-ginsburg-opera-commemorates-sparring-su preme-court-friendship; Richard Wolf, *Scalia and Ginsburg: Buddies Beyond the Bench,* USA Today, Feb. 23, 2015, http://www.usatoday.com/story/news/politics /2015/02/13/supreme-court-scalia-ginsburg/23301095/; Bill Mears, *Kagan Hunts with Buddy Scalia, Bags Deer,* CNN, July 2, 2013; Nina Totenberg, *Scalia v. Ginsburg: Supreme Court Sparring, Put to Music,* NPR, July 10, 2013, http://www.npr.org

/2013/07/10/200137481/scalia-v-ginsburg-supreme-court-sparring-put-to-mu
sic. On the elephant picture, Scalia said that Ginsburg's feminist friends gave
her a hard time about him being in front on the elephant. Justice Ginsburg interrupted to clarify: "The driver explained it was a matter of distribution of weight."
Ariane de Vogue, *Ginsburg and Scalia on Parasailing, Elephants and Not Being
'100% Sober,'* CNN, Feb. 13, 2015, http://www.cnn.com/2015/02/13/politics/gins
burg-scalia-parasailing-sotu-wine/.

4. Josh Verges, *At UMN, Sotomayor Addresses Scalia, Perry Mason—and Trump, Sort of,*
Twin Cities Pioneer Press, Oct. 18, 2016, http://www.twincities.com/2016/10/17/
umn-sotomayor-speech/.

5. Jay Wexler, *Laugh Tracks,* 59 Green Bag 2d 59, 60 (2005). For a later study
reaching similar conclusions, see Ryan Malphurs, *"People Did Sometimes Stick
Things in My Underwear": The Function of Laughter at the U.S. Supreme Court,* 10
Comm. L. Rev. 63 (2011). *See also* Adam Liptak, *Sidebar: A Taxonomy of Supreme
Court Humor,* N.Y. Times, Jan. 24, 2011, http://www.nytimes.com/2011/01/25/
us/25bar.html ("Mr. Malphurs said his goal was to remedy these flaws [in the
Wexler study], noting that the Wexler study 'lacked the methodological rigor and
insight normally attributable to social scientific studies.' Asked about the Malphurs study, Professor Wexler said, 'I'm not sure what to think about it, but I'm
pretty sure it makes me want to die.'").

6. *U.S. v. Windsor,* 133 S. Ct. 2675, 2709 (Scalia, J., dissenting) (2013) ("As I have
said, the real rationale of today's opinion, whatever disappearing trail of its legal-
istic argle-bargle one chooses to follow, is that DOMA is motivated by bare desire
to harm couples in same-sex marriages."); *King v. Burwell,* 135 S. Ct. 2480, 2500
(Scalia, J., dissenting) (2015) ("The Court's next bit of interpretive jiggery-pokery
involves other parts of the Act that purportedly presuppose the availability of tax
credits on both federal and state Exchanges."). On the "hot bench" at oral argument, see Adam Liptak, *Sidebar: A Most Inquisitive Court? No Argument There,*
N.Y. Times, Oct. 7, 2013, http://www.nytimes.com/2013/10/08/us/inquisitive
-justices-no-argument-there.html.

7. The Honorable Antonin G. Scalia, *A Look Back: 1994 William O. Douglas Lecture
Series Transcript,* 51 Gonzaga L. Rev. 583, 598 (2016) (quoting transcript of answer
Justice Scalia gave to a questioner at a 1994 law school event).

8. Jennifer Senior, *In Conversation: Antonin Scalia,* New York, Oct. 6, 2013, http://
nymag.com/news/features/antonin-scalia-2013-10/; Kevin Merida & Michael A.
Fletcher, Supreme Discomfort: The Divided Soul of Clarence Thomas 325 (2007);
"Rather Read" (music video), https://vimeo.com/122237720.

9. *Obergefell v. Hodges,* 135 S. Ct. 2584, 2630, & n. 22 (2015) (Scalia, J., dissenting).
The next few paragraphs and study in the following section draw from Richard L.
Hasen, *The Most Sarcastic Justice,* 18 Green Bag 2d 215 (2015).

10. *Atkins v. Virginia,* 536 U.S. 304, 338 (2002) (Scalia, J., dissenting); *Johnson v.
Transp. Agency, Santa Clara Cnty.,* 480 U.S. 616, 677 (1987) (Scalia, J., dissenting); *J.E.B. v. Alabama,* 511 U.S. 127, 156 (1994) (Scalia, J., dissenting).

11. *Planned Parenthood v. Casey,* 505 U.S. 833, 983 (1992) (Scalia, J., dissenting); *Cnty.*

of Sacramento v. Lewis, 523 U.S. 833, 860 (1998) (Scalia, J., concurring in the judgment).

12. Erwin Chemerinsky, The Case Against the Supreme Court 323–24 (2014) (quoting numerous cases).

13. *Mitchell v. U.S.,* 526 U.S. 314, 338 (1999) (Scalia, J., dissenting); *District of Columbia v. Heller,* 554 U.S. 570, 587 (2008); *Lee v. Weisman,* 505 U.S. 577, 636 (1992) (Scalia, J., dissenting) ("The Court's argument that state officials have 'coerced' students to take part in the invocation and benediction at graduation ceremonies is, not to put too fine a point on it, incoherent.")

14. Panel Discussion, *The Supreme Court and the 2016 Elections,* UC Irvine School of Law, Feb. 22, 2016, http://www.law.uci.edu/events/election-law/scotus-elections -2016feb22.html (comments of Ed Whelan). The particular comment from Whelan may be viewed at this link on YouTube at the 33:40 mark: https://www .youtube.com/watch?v=J5abuGNhdno.

15. Justice Scalia made the comment about being a snoot in an interview with his later co-author Bryan Garner. The Scribes Journal of Legal Writing 61 (2010) (interview with Justice Scalia); Adam Liptak, *Sidebar: Scalia Lands at Top of Sarcasm Index. Shocking,* N.Y. Times, Jan. 19, 2015, http://www.nytimes.com/2015/01/20/ us/scalia-lands-at-top-of-sarcasm-index-of-justices-shocking.html ("Justice Scalia might have a different objection. 'I'm a snoot,' he once said."). Liptak also reports that Justice Scalia in his opinions appeared to define sarcasm in a narrower way, of "saying one thing to mean another." *Id.* On being "sharp," see Senior, *supra* note 8.

16. *Id.* According to a partial transcript of the Pottinger interview with Justice Scalia, he said: "I guess what concerns an—an awful is—is the coarsening of our culture. It—it's become—It has become a much—a much less uh . . . decent, respectful culture. All you have to do is turn on the tube any night and it's coarse."). The partial transcript is posted at: https://web.archive.org/web/20080724105102/ http://www.plumtv.com/html/transcript_BP_AScalia2.html. The show was on Season 1, Episode 5 of "Beyond Politics," first airing May 28, 2006. http://www .tv.com/shows/beyond-politics/justice-antonin-scalia-2113763/.

17. Gina Pace, *Justice Scalia Gives Obscene Hand Gesture?,* CBS News, Mar. 27, 2006, http://www.cbsnews.com/news/justice-scalia-gives-obscene-gesture/; Adam Winkler, *Justice Scalia & the Coarsening of American Culture,* Huffington Post, July 1, 2006 (updated May 25, 2011), http://www.huffingtonpost.com/adam-winkler/ justice-scalia-the-coarse_b_24203.html/.

18. Senior, *supra* note 8.

19. *Planned Parenthood v. Casey,* 505 U.S. 833 (1992); Jeffrey Rosen, The Supreme Court: The Personalities and Rivalries that Defined America 199 (2006). In support of his statement, Rosen cited to Christopher E. Smith, Justice Antonin Scalia and the Supreme Court's Conservative Moment 99–100 (1993) ("By forcing the issue [in *Casey*] in a strident and personal way, Scalia pushed his colleagues away by offending them."). But Smith's book cites a *Wall Street Journal* article which

does not support the claim, and instead makes a different claim about how the different justices responded to criticism from Justice Scalia. Paul M. Barrett, *Independent Justice: David Souter Emerges as a Reflective Moderate on the Supreme Court*, Wall St. J. Feb. 2, 1993, at A1 ("'There is no question that [Justice Souter] doesn't take criticism from Justice Scalia as personally as Kennedy and O'Connor,' says a lawyer who clerked last term for another Justice."). See also Kathleen M. Sullivan, *Foreword: The Justices of Rules and Standards*, 106 Harv. L. Rev. 22, 122 n. 602 (1992) ("observers have speculated that Justice Scalia's blistering sarcasm toward Justice O'Connor's and Justice Kennedy's opinions may indicate some personal animosity that has driven them toward the center.").

Accounts of *Casey* do not give any hint that Justices O'Connor, Kennedy, and Souter were in play in *Casey* or that Justice Scalia pushed them away. *See* Linda Greenhouse, Becoming Justice Blackmun 203–6 (2006) (describing deliberations and drafting history of *Casey*); Joan Biskupic, American Original: The Life and Constitution of Supreme Court Justice Antonin Scalia 196–98 (2009); Bruce Allen Murphy, Scalia: A Court of One 206–15 (2014); *see also* Edward Lazarus: Closed Chambers: The Rise, Fall, and Future of the Modern Supreme Court 46–47 (1999) ("Scalia reportedly visited Kennedy at his home to plead with him to change his mind, again. As liberals gathered secondhand, Scalia initially appealed to his and Kennedy's shared anti-abortion Catholic beliefs and, failing in that, warned Kennedy that he was destined to become another Blackmun—a sentimentalist scorned by both conservatives and serious thinkers generally.").

20. Mark Tushnet, A Court Divided: The Rehnquist Court and the Future of Constitutional Law 63, 149 (2005); John Paul Stevens, Five Chiefs: A Supreme Court Memoir 118 (2011); Biskupic, *supra* note 19, at 281 (2005).

21. Irin Carmon & Shana Knizhnik, Notorious RBG: The Life and Times of Ruth Bader Ginsburg 116 (2015); Biskupic, *supra* note 19, at 279, 290; John C. Jeffries, Jr., Justice Lewis F. Powell, Jr. 534 (1994).

22. Jeffrey Toobin, The Nine: Inside the Secret World of the Supreme Court 120 (2007); Biskupic *supra* note 19, at 289.

23. Lazarus, *supra* note 19, at 42.

24. Chemerinsky, *supra* note 12.

25. *Obergefell v. Hodges*, 135 S. Ct. 2584, 2628–29 (2015) (Scalia, J., dissenting) (original emphases).

26. Ed Whelan, *Justice Scalia and Diversity on the Supreme Court*, NRO Bench Memos, Sept. 7, 2016, http://www.nationalreview.com/bench-memos/439770/liptak-scalia-diversity.

27. Gallup, Supreme Court poll, http://www.gallup.com/poll/4732/supreme-court.aspx (last visited September 29, 2016).

28. Michael Smith & Frank Newport, *Most Republicans Continue to Disapprove of Supreme Court*, Gallup, Sept. 29, 2016, http://www.gallup.com/poll/195902/republicans-continue-disapprove-supreme-court.aspx?g_source=supreme%20court&g_medium=search&g_campaign=tiles; Andrea Louise Campbell & Nath-

aniel Persily, *The* Health Care Case *in the Public's Mind: Opinion on the Supreme Court and Health Reform in a Polarized Era,* in The Health Care Case: The Supreme Court's Decision and Its Implications 245 (Nathaniel Persily, Gillian E. Metzger & Trevor W. Morrison, eds., 2013).

29. Justin McCarthy, *U.S. Support for Gay Marriage Stable After High Court Ruling,* Gallup, July 17, 2015, http://www.gallup.com/poll/184217/support-gay-marriage-stable-high-court-ruling.aspx. Dan Eggen, *Poll: Large Majority Opposes Supreme Court Decision on Campaign Financing,* Wash. Post, Feb. 17, 2010, http://www.washingtonpost.com/wp-dyn/content/article/2010/02/17/AR2010021701151.html; Greg Stohr, *Bloomberg Poll: Americans Want Supreme Court to Turn Off Political Spending Spigot,* Bloomberg Politics, Sept. 28, 2015, http://www.bloomberg.com/politics/articles/2015-09-28/bloomberg-poll-americans-want-supreme-court-to-turn-off-political-spending-spigot.

30. *Q & A with Antonin Scalia,* C-SPAN, May 2, 2008, https://www.c-span.org/video/?205000-1/qa-antonin-scalia; Tony Mauro, *Justice Scalia, Out of the Closet,* The BLT: Blog of Legal Times, May 7, 2008, http://legaltimes.typepad.com/blt/2008/05/justice-scalia.html. Justice Scalia made a similar point in his interview with Stan Pottinger on a television program, "Beyond Politics:"

I've just sort of given up. I mean, I, you know, I stayed out of uhm . . . interviews like this, for example, uhm . . . not because I'm—I'm any more secretive and private a person. Uh . . . It wasn't a Greta Garbo uh . . . phenomenon. Uh . . . Rather, it was my—my belief in accord with a tradition of—of Anglo-Saxon judges, that judges should not make public spectacles of themselves, that they should not be on the front pages, that courts in a democracy should—should be in the background. I mean, you're gonna be on the front page whether you like it or not and uh . . . if you do not appear personally, uh . . . you can be demonized a lot more readily uh . . . than—than if you uh . . . if you appear occasionally and so on.

Beyond Politics, *supra* note 16.
31. C-SPAN, *supra* note 30.
32. The next few paragraphs and data are drawn from Richard L. Hasen, *Celebrity Justice: Supreme Court Edition,* 19 Green Bag 2d 157 (2016).
33. Christopher W. Schmidt & Carolyn Shapiro, *Oral Dissenting in the Supreme Court,* 19 Wm. & Mary Bill of Rts. J. 75, 108 (2010).
34. Michael D. Shear, *Ruth Bader Ginsburg Expresses Regret for Criticizing Donald Trump,* N.Y. Times, July 14, 2016, http://www.nytimes.com/2016/07/15/us/politics/ruth-bader-ginsburg-donald-trump.html:

Justice Ruth Bader Ginsburg's indignant dissents from the bench have turned her into a heroine of the left, beloved for methodically skewering her conservative colleagues. On the internet, she has become the Notorious R.B.G.

But after being roundly criticized for a remarkable series of interviews in which she mocked Donald J. Trump, the presumptive Republican nominee for president, Justice Ginsburg on Thursday did something highly unusual for a member of the nation's highest court: She admitted making a mistake.

"Judges should avoid commenting on a candidate for public office," she wrote in a brief statement issued by the court, admitting her remarks were "ill advised" and expressing regret. "In the future I will be more circumspect."

35. Biskupic, *supra* note 19, at 356.
36. Lee Epstein, William M. Landes & Richard A. Posner, The Behavior of Federal Judges: A Theoretical and Empirical Study of Rational Choice 313 (2013); Biskupic, *supra* note 19, at 301.
37. The audio of Justice Scalia's remark is posted at http://www.cnn.com/videos/ politics/2015/12/11/supreme-court-audio-protesters-origwx-js.cnn. The next few paragraphs draw from Richard L. Hasen, *Why the Most Urgent Civil Rights Issue of Our Time Is the Supreme Court Itself*, Talking Points Memo, Sept. 28, 2015, http:// talkingpointsmemo.com/cafe/supreme-court-greatest-civil-rights-cause.
38. The oral argument audio is posted at: https://www.supremecourt.gov/oral_argu ments/audio/2014/14-556-q1. The outburst begins around the 27-minute mark and is difficult to decipher.
39. Jeffrey Toobin, *Justice Scalia's Shameful Joke*, Daily Comment, The New Yorker, Apr. 28, 2015, http://www.newyorker.com/news/daily-comment/on-gay-marriage-its -not-scalias-court. Dahlia Lithwick & Mark Joseph Stern, *Not All Must Rise: Many of the People Who Will Witness Supreme Court History Paid a Ton for the Privilege*, Slate, Apr. 27, 2015, http://www.slate.com/articles/news_and_politics/jurispru dence/2015/04/standing_in_line_for_supreme_court_gay_marriage_argu ments_draw_crowd_days.html.
40. *Glossip v. Gross*, 135 S. Ct. 2726 (2016).
41. Dahlia Lithwick, *Supreme Court Breakfast Table, Scalia Goes Off Script*, Slate, June 29, 2015, http://www.slate.com/articles/news_and_politics/the_breakfast_table/ features/2015/scotus_roundup/scalia_in_glossip_v_gross_supreme_court_deci sion_oklahoma_may_kill_using.html. The audio of Justice Scalia's announced concurrence in *Glossip* may be listened to at the Oyez website by going to https:// www.oyez.org/cases/2014/14-7955 and choosing "Opinion Announcement— June 29, 2015 (Part 4)."
42. The 2007 Seattle schools case is *Parents Involved in Community Schools v. Seattle School Dist. No. 1*, 551 U.S. 701 (2007). Justice Breyer's statement in his oral dissent is at the 32:54 mark in the audio of the opinion announcement posted at the Oyez website, https://www.oyez.org/cases/2006/05-908.
43. *Arizona Free Enterprise Club's Freedom Club PAC v. Bennett*, 564 U.S. 721, 780 (Kagan, J., dissenting) ("As against all this, the majority claims to have found three smoking guns that reveal the State's true (and nefarious) intention to level the playing field. But the only smoke here is the majority's, and it is the kind that goes with mirrors.").

44. *United States v. Windsor,* 133 S. Ct. 2675, 2718 (2013) (Alito, J., dissenting).
45. *Schuette v. Coalition to Defend Affirmative Action,* 134 S. Ct. 1623, 1675–76 (2014) (Sotomayor, J., dissenting); *id.* at 1638–39 (Roberts, C.J., concurring).

Chapter 5. *Kulturkampf*

1. Ian Samuel, *The Counter-Clerks of Justice Scalia,* 10 NYU J. L. & Lib. 1 (2016); *United States v. Windsor,* 133 S. Ct. 2675 (2013). The quotes from Samuel in this chapter appear in the cited law review article.
2. Jennifer Senior, *In Conversation: Antonin Scalia,* New York, Oct. 6, 2013, http:// nymag.com/news/features/antonin-scalia-2013-10/;
3. Bruce Hay, *I Thought I Could Reason with Antonin Scalia: A More Naïve Young Fool Never Drew Breath,* Salon, Feb. 27, 2016, http://www.salon.com/2016/02/27/i _thought_i_could_reason_with_antonin_scalia_a_more_naive_young_fool _never_drew_breath/.
4. *In Memoriam: Justice Antonin Scalia,* 130 Harv. L. Rev. 1, 14 (2016) (comments of Rachel E. Barkow), http://cdn.harvardlawreview.org/wp-content/uploads/2016 /11/1-30_Compiled-Tributes_Online.pdf.
5. Gil Seinfeld, *The Good, The Bad, and The Ugly: Reflections of a Counter-Clerk,* 114 Mich. L. Rev. First Impressions 111 (2016), http://michiganlawreview.org/ wp-content/uploads/2016/04/114MichLRevFI111_Seinfeld.pdf.
6. *Lawrence v. Texas,* 539 U.S. 558, 602 (2003) (Scalia, J., dissenting).
7. Samuel, *supra* note 1 (citations omitted).
8. *Hollingsworth v. Perry,* 133 S. Ct. 2652 (2013); David Savage, *Scalia Defends Comparing Laws Against Homosexuality to Murder,* L.A. Times, Dec. 11, 2012, http://ar ticles.latimes.com/2012/dec/11/nation/la-na-nn-scalia-laws-homosexuality-mur der-20121211.
9. Senior, *supra* note 2.
10. *Roe v. Wade,* 410 U.S. 113 (1973).
11. *Skinner v. Oklahoma,* 316 U.S. 535 (1942).
12. *Griswold v. Conn.,* 381 U.S. 479, 484–85 (1965) ("The foregoing cases suggest that specific guarantees in the Bill of Rights have penumbras, formed by emanations from those guarantees that help give them life and substance. Various guarantees create zones of privacy. . . . These cases bear witness that the right of privacy which presses for recognition here is a legitimate one."). For a general overview of these "reproductive" autonomy cases and their connections to *Roe,* see Erwin Chemerinsky, Constitutional Law: Principles and Policies sec. 10.3 (5th ed. 2015).
13. *Eisenstadt v. Baird,* 405 U.S. 438 (1972); *Carey v. Population Servs. Int'l,* 431 U.S. 678 (1977).
14. *Roe v. Wade,* 410 U.S. 113, 153, 155–64 (1973).
15. John Hart Ely, *The Wages of Crying Wolf: A Comment on* Roe v. Wade, 82 Yale L.J. 920 (1973); Chemerinsky, *supra* note 12, at 856–57.
16. Ruth Bader Ginsburg, *Some Thoughts on Autonomy and Equality in Relation to* Roe

v. Wade, 63 N.C. L. Rev. 375, 383 (1985). For an argument that *Roe* did not create a backlash against abortion rights, see Linda Greenhouse and Reva B. Siegel, *Before (and After)* Roe v. Wade: *New Questions About Backlash*, 120 Yale L.J. 2028 (2011).

17. Even so, the authoring justices in the majority did not say *Roe* was necessarily correct when initially decided. *Planned Parenthood v. Casey*, 505 U.S. 833, 871 (1992) ("We do not need to say whether each of us, had we been Members of the Court when the valuation of the state interest came before it as an original matter, would have concluded, as the *Roe* Court did, that its weight is insufficient to justify a ban on abortions prior to viability even when it is subject to certain exceptions."). *Webster v. Reproductive Health Services*, 492 U.S. 490 (1989).

18. *Stenberg v. Carhart*, 530 U.S. 914 (2000) (striking down Nebraska "partial birth" abortion law under undue burden test); *Gonzales v. Carhart*, 550 U.S. 124, 159 (2007) (upholding the federal Partial Birth Abortion Act under undue burden test).

19. *Whole Woman's Health v. Hellerstedt*, 136 S. Ct. 2292, 2300 (2016).

20. *Webster*, 492 U.S. at 532–33 (Scalia, J., concurring in part and concurring in the judgment). He added:

> Ordinarily, speaking no more broadly than is absolutely required avoids throwing settled law into confusion; doing so today preserves a chaos that is evident to anyone who can read and count. Alone sufficient to justify a broad holding is the fact that our retaining control, through *Roe*, of what I believe to be, and many of our citizens recognize to be, a political issue, continuously distorts the public perception of the role of this Court. We can now look forward to at least another Term with carts full of mail from the public, and streets full of demonstrators, urging us—their unelected and life-tenured judges who have been awarded those extraordinary, undemocratic characteristics precisely in order that we might follow the law despite the popular will—to follow the popular will. Indeed, I expect we can look forward to even more of that than before, given our indecisive decision today.

> *Id.* at 535.

21. *Casey*, 505 U.S. at 980–81 (Scalia, J., concurring in the judgment in part and dissenting in part).

22. *Ohio v. Akron Center for Reproductive Health*, 497 U.S. 502, 523 (1990) (Scalia, J., concurring).

23. *Casey*, 505 U.S. at 980 n.1; *see also Michael H. v. Gerald D.*, 491 U.S. 110, 127–28, n. 6 (1989) (opinion of Scalia, J.) (defending tradition as the basis for determining the scope of some constitutional rights); *Loving v. Virginia*, 388 U.S. 1 (1967).

24. *Stenberg*, 530 U.S. at 953 (Scalia, J., dissenting).

25. Steve Benen, *Scalia Rejects Privacy Rights*, The Rachel Maddow Show/Maddow Blog, July 30, 2012, http://www.msnbc.com/rachel-maddow-show/scalia-rejects-privacy-rights (quoting *Fox News Sunday* interview).

26. *Bowers v. Hardwick*, 478 U.S. 186 (1986).

27. The Court wrote:

> Striving to assure itself and the public that announcing rights not readily identifiable in the Constitution's text involves much more than the imposition of the Justices' own choice of values on the States and the Federal Government, the Court has sought to identify the nature of the rights qualifying for heightened judicial protection. In *Palko v. Connecticut*, 302 U.S. 319, 325, 326, 288 (1937), it was said that this category includes those fundamental liberties that are "implicit in the concept of ordered liberty," such that "neither liberty nor justice would exist if [they] were sacrificed." A different description of fundamental liberties appeared in *Moore v. East Cleveland*, 431 U.S. 494, 503 (1977) (opinion of Powell, J.), where they are characterized as those liberties that are "deeply rooted in this Nation's history and tradition." See also *Griswold v. Connecticut*, 381 U.S., at 506.
>
> It is obvious to us that neither of these formulations would extend a fundamental right to homosexuals to engage in acts of consensual sodomy. Proscriptions against that conduct have ancient roots. Sodomy was a criminal offense at common law and was forbidden by the laws of the original thirteen States when they ratified the Bill of Rights. In 1868, when the Fourteenth Amendment was ratified, all but 5 of the 37 States in the Union had criminal sodomy laws. In fact, until 1961, all 50 States outlawed sodomy, and today, 24 States and the District of Columbia continue to provide criminal penalties for sodomy performed in private and between consenting adults. Against this background, to claim that a right to engage in such conduct is "deeply rooted in this Nation's history and tradition" or "implicit in the concept of ordered liberty" is, at best, facetious.
>
> Nor are we inclined to take a more expansive view of our authority to discover new fundamental rights imbedded in the Due Process Clause. The Court is most vulnerable and comes nearest to illegitimacy when it deals with judge-made constitutional law having little or no cognizable roots in the language or design of the Constitution. That this is so was painfully demonstrated by the face-off between the Executive and the Court in the 1930's, which resulted in the repudiation of much of the substantive gloss that the Court had placed on the Due Process Clauses of the Fifth and Fourteenth Amendments. There should be, therefore, great resistance to expand the substantive reach of those Clauses, particularly if it requires redefining the category of rights deemed to be fundamental. Otherwise, the Judiciary necessarily takes to itself further authority to govern the country without express constitutional authority. The claimed right pressed on us today falls far short of overcoming this resistance.

Bowers, 478 U.S. at 191–94 (footnotes and some citations omitted).

28. *Romer v. Evans*, 517 U.S. 620, 627 (1996) ("Homosexuals, by state decree, are put in a solitary class with respect to transactions and relations in both the private and governmental spheres. The amendment withdraws from homosexuals, but no

others, specific legal protection from the injuries caused by discrimination, and it forbids reinstatement of these laws and policies."); *id.* at 632 (The amendment's "sheer breadth is so discontinuous with the reasons offered for it that the amendment seems inexplicable by anything but animus toward the class it affects; it lacks a rational relationship to legitimate state interests.").

29. *Id.* at 636 (Scalia, J., dissenting).
30. *Id.* at 645–46.
31. He continued:

> The interviewer may refuse to offer a job because the applicant is a Republican; because he is an adulterer; because he went to the wrong prep school or belongs to the wrong country club; because he eats snails; because he is a womanizer; because she wears real-animal fur; or even because he hates the Chicago Cubs. But if the interviewer should wish not to be an associate or partner of an applicant because he disapproves of the applicant's homosexuality, *then* he will have violated the pledge which the Association of American Law Schools requires all its member schools to exact from job interviewers: "assurance of the employer's willingness" to hire homosexuals. This law-school view of what "prejudices" must be stamped out may be contrasted with the more plebeian attitudes that apparently still prevail in the United States Congress, which has been unresponsive to repeated attempts to extend to homosexuals the protections of federal civil rights laws.

> *Id.* at 652.

32. *Lawrence v. Texas,* 539 U.S. 558 (2003). Justice O'Connor, who had signed on to *Bowers,* did not vote to overturn it, but concluded that the Texas law, by banning "deviate sexual intercourse" between people of the same sex but not those of opposite sexes, violated the Equal Protection Clause. *Id.* at 579–85 (O'Connor, J., concurring in the judgment).
33. *Id.* at 586–605 (Scalia, J., dissenting).

> At the end of its opinion—after having laid waste the foundations of our rational-basis jurisprudence—the Court says that the present case "does not involve whether the government must give formal recognition to any relationship that homosexual persons seek to enter." Do not believe it. More illuminating than this bald, unreasoned disclaimer is the progression of thought displayed by an earlier passage in the Court's opinion, which notes the constitutional protections afforded to "personal decisions relating to *marriage,* procreation, contraception, family relationships, child rearing, and education," and then declares that "[p]ersons in a homosexual relationship may seek autonomy for these purposes, just as heterosexual persons do." (emphasis added). Today's opinion dismantles the structure of constitutional law that has permitted a distinction to be made between heterosexual and homosexual unions, insofar as formal recognition in marriage is concerned. If moral disapprobation of homosexual conduct is "no legitimate state interest" for purposes of proscribing

that conduct; and if, as the Court coos (casting aside all pretense of neutrality), "[w]hen sexuality finds overt expression in intimate conduct with another person, the conduct can be but one element in a personal bond that is more enduring"; what justification could there possibly be for denying the benefits of marriage to homosexual couples exercising "[t]he liberty protected by the Constitution"? Surely not the encouragement of procreation, since the sterile and the elderly are allowed to marry. This case "does not involve" the issue of homosexual marriage only if one entertains the belief that principle and logic have nothing to do with the decisions of this Court. Many will hope that, as the Court comfortingly assures us, this is so.

Id. at 604 (Scalia, J., dissenting).

34. *United States v. Windsor*, 133 S. Ct. 2675, 2693 (2016).
35. *Obergefell v. Hodges*, 135 S. Ct. 2584, 2597–98 (2015).
36. *Id.* at 2598, 2608.
37. *Id.* at 2626, 2630 (Scalia, J., dissenting):

The opinion is couched in a style that is as pretentious as its content is egotistic. It is one thing for separate concurring or dissenting opinions to contain extravagances, even silly extravagances, of thought and expression; it is something else for the official opinion of the Court to do so. Of course the opinion's showy profundities are often profoundly incoherent. "The nature of marriage is that, through its enduring bond, two persons together can find other freedoms, such as expression, intimacy, and spirituality." (Really? Who ever thought that intimacy and spirituality [whatever that means] were freedoms? And if intimacy is, one would think Freedom of Intimacy is abridged rather than expanded by marriage. Ask the nearest hippie. Expression, sure enough, *is* a freedom, but anyone in a long-lasting marriage will attest that that happy state constricts, rather than expands, what one can prudently say.) Rights, we are told, can "rise . . . from a better-informed understanding of how constitutional imperatives define a liberty that remains urgent in our own era." (Huh? How can a better-informed understanding of how constitutional imperatives [whatever that means] define [whatever that means] an urgent liberty [never mind], give birth to a right?) And we are told that, "[i]n any particular case," either the Equal Protection or Due Process Clause "may be thought to capture the essence of [a] right in a more accurate and comprehensive way," than the other, "even as the two Clauses may converge in the identification and definition of the right." (What say? What possible "essence" does substantive due process "capture" in an "accurate and comprehensive way"? It stands for nothing whatever, except those freedoms and entitlements that this Court *really* likes. And the Equal Protection Clause, as employed today, identifies nothing except a difference in treatment that this Court *really* dislikes. Hardly a distillation of essence. If the opinion is correct that the two clauses "converge in the identification and definition of [a] right," that is only because the majority's

likes and dislikes are predictably compatible.) I could go on. The world does
not expect logic and precision in poetry or inspirational pop-philosophy; it demands them in the law. The stuff contained in today's opinion has to diminish
this Court's reputation for clear thinking and sober analysis.

38. *Id.* at 2628–30.
39. *Burwell v. Hobby Lobby Stores*, 134 S. Ct. 1751 (2014); *Masterpiece Cakeshop, Ltd. v. Colorado Civil Rights Comm'n*, No. 16-111, *cert. granted* Jun. 26, 2017.
40. Justice Scalia took the same position on sex discrimination. He explained in an interview in 2011:

> **In 1868, when the 39th Congress was debating and ultimately proposing the 14th Amendment, I don't think anybody would have thought that equal protection applied to sex discrimination, or certainly not to sexual orientation. So does that mean that we've gone off in error by applying the 14th Amendment to both?**
> Yes, yes. Sorry, to tell you that. . . . But, you know, if indeed the current society has come to different views, that's fine. You do not need the Constitution to reflect the wishes of the current society. Certainly the Constitution does not require discrimination on the basis of sex. The only issue is whether it prohibits it. It doesn't. Nobody ever thought that that's what it meant. Nobody ever voted for that. If the current society wants to outlaw discrimination by sex, hey we have things called legislatures, and they enact things called laws. You don't need a constitution to keep things up-to-date. All you need is a legislature and a ballot box. You don't like the death penalty anymore, that's fine. You want a right to abortion? There's nothing in the Constitution about that. But that doesn't mean you cannot prohibit it. Persuade your fellow citizens it's a good idea and pass a law. That's what democracy is all about. It's not about nine superannuated judges who have been there too long, imposing these demands on society.

> *Legally Speaking: The Originalist,* Cal. Lawyer, Jan. 2011, http://ww2.callawyer.com /story.cfm?eid=913358&evid=1 (emphasis added).

Justice Scalia backed off just a bit in his interview with Jennifer Senior in 2013:

> **What about sex discrimination? Do you think the Fourteenth Amendment covers it?**
> Of course it covers it! No, you can't treat women differently, give them higher criminal sentences. Of course not.
> **A couple of years ago, I think you told** *California Lawyer* **something different.**
> What I was referring to is: The issue is not whether it prohibits discrimination on the basis of sex. Of course it does. The issue is, "What is discrimination?"
> If there's a reasonable basis for not letting women do something—like going into combat or whatnot . . .

Let's put it this way: Do you think the same level of scrutiny that applies to race should apply to sex?
I am not a fan of different levels of scrutiny. Strict scrutiny, intermediate scrutiny, *blah blah blah blah*. That's just a thumb on the scales.

But there are some intelligent reasons to treat women differently. I don't think anybody would deny that. And there really is no, virtually no, intelligent reason to treat people differently on the basis of their skin.

Senior, *supra* note 2.

41. *Fisher v. Univ. of Texas*, 133 S. Ct. 2411, 2418 (2013) (quoting *Regents of University of California v. Bakke*, 438 U.S. 265, 305 (1978) (opinion of Powell, J.).

42. *Grutter v. Bollinger*, 539 U.S. 306, 346 (Scalia, J., concurring in part and dissenting in part).

43. *Id.* at 343 (O'Connor, J., for the Court).

44. *Fisher v. Univ. of Texas*, 136 S. Ct. 2198, 2210 (2016).

45. Transcript of Oral Argument at 67–68, *Fisher v. Univ. of Texas*, 136 S. Ct. 2198 (2016) (No. 14-981), 2015 WL 8482483.

46. Joan Biskupic, American Original: The Life and Constitution of Supreme Court Justice Antonin Scalia 160 (2009).

47. Seinfeld, *supra* note 5, at 118–19.

48. A mostly clean slate but not a fully clean slate. In *United States v. Miller*, 307 U.S. 174 (1939), the Supreme Court rejected a Second Amendment challenge by persons convicted of possessing sawed-off shotguns. Many read the case as limiting the scope of the Second Amendment to the possession of firearms for military service, not personal use. Justice Stevens, in his dissent in *District of Columbia v. Heller*, 554 U.S. 570, 636 (2008) (Stevens, J., dissenting) argued that *Miller* controlled the outcome of the case.

Justice Scalia, however, argued that *Miller* did not so hold or limit the Court's ability to recognize a personal right to bear arms:

Justice STEVENS places overwhelming reliance upon this Court's decision in *Miller*. "[H]undreds of judges," we are told, "have relied on the view of the Amendment we endorsed there," and "[e]ven if the textual and historical arguments on both sides of the issue were evenly balanced, respect for the well-settled views of all of our predecessors on this Court, and for the rule of law itself . . . would prevent most jurists from endorsing such a dramatic upheaval in the law." And what is, according to Justice STEVENS, the holding of *Miller* that demands such obeisance? That the Second Amendment "protects the right to keep and bear arms for certain military purposes, but that it does not curtail the Legislature's power to regulate the nonmilitary use and ownership of weapons."

Nothing so clearly demonstrates the weakness of Justice STEVENS' case. *Miller* did not hold that and cannot possibly be read to have held that. The judgment in the case upheld against a Second Amendment challenge two men's federal indictment for transporting an unregistered short-barreled shotgun in interstate commerce, in violation of the National Firearms Act. It is entirely clear that the Court's basis for saying that the Second Amendment did not apply was *not* that the defendants were "bear [ing] arms" not "for . . . military purposes" but for "nonmilitary use." Rather, it was that the *type of weapon at issue* was not eligible for Second Amendment protection: "In the absence of any evidence tending to show that the possession or use of a [short-barreled shotgun] at this time has some reasonable relationship to the preservation or efficiency of a well-regulated militia, we cannot say that the Second Amendment guarantees the right to keep and bear *such an instrument.*" (emphasis added). "Certainly," the Court continued, "it is not within judicial notice that this weapon is any part of the ordinary military equipment or that its use could contribute to the common defense." Beyond that, the opinion provided no explanation of the content of the right.

This holding is not only consistent with, but positively suggests, that the Second Amendment confers an individual right to keep and bear arms (though only arms that "have some reasonable relationship to the preservation or efficiency of a well regulated militia"). Had the Court believed that the Second Amendment protects only those serving in the militia, it would have been odd to examine the character of the weapon rather than simply note that the two crooks were not militiamen. Justice STEVENS can say again and again that *Miller* did not "turn on the difference between muskets and sawed-off shotguns; it turned, rather, on the basic difference between the military and nonmilitary use and possession of guns," but the words of the opinion prove otherwise. The most Justice STEVENS can plausibly claim for *Miller* is that it declined to decide the nature of the Second Amendment right, despite the Solicitor General's argument (made in the alternative) that the right was collective. *Miller* stands only for the proposition that the Second Amendment right, whatever its nature, extends only to certain types of weapons.

Heller, 554 U.S. at 621–22.
49. *Id.* at 636.
50. Nina Totenberg interview with Justice Scalia, February 12, 2013, quoted in Bruce Allen Murphy, Scalia: A Court of One 390 & n. 41 (2014). For more on the evolution of gun rights in the United States culminating in the *Heller* decision, see Adam Winkler, Gun Fight: The Battle over the Right to Bear Arms in America (2011).
51. Sara Aronchick Solow & Barry Friedman, *How to Talk About the Constitution,* 25 Yale J. L. & Humanities 69, 76 (2013); Laurence Tribe & Joshua Matz, Uncertain Justice: The Roberts Court and the Constitution 172 (2009); see also Reva B. Siegel, *Dead or Alive: Originalism as Popular Constitutionalism in* Heller, 122 Harv. L. Rev. 191 (2008).
52. Nelson Lund, *The Second Amendment,* Heller, *and Originalist Jurisprudence,* 56 UCLA L. Rev. 1343, 1345, 1356 (2009).

53. *McDonald v. City of Chicago*, 561 U.S. 742 (2010). See the extensive discussion of *McDonald* in Chapter 4.

54. *Salazar v. Buono*, 559 U.S. 700 (2010).

55. Transcript of Oral Argument at 38–39, *Salazar v. Buono*, 559 U.S. 700 (2010) (No. 08-472), 2009 WL 3197881.

56. Erwin Chemerinsky, *The Jurisprudence of Justice Scalia: A Critical Appraisal*, 22 U. Haw. L. Rev. 385, 386–89 (2000).

57. *Employment Division of Oregon v. Smith*, 494 U.S. 872, 888–89 (1990) (internal quotation marks and citations omitted).

58. *City of Boerne v. Flores*, 521 U.S. 507, 544 (1997) (Scalia, J., concurring in part).

59. *Lemon v. Kurtzman*, 403 U.S. 602 (1971); *Edwards v. Aguillard*, 482 U.S. 578, 615 (1987) (Scalia, J., dissenting); *Lamb's Chapel v. Center Moriches Union Free School Dist.*, 508 U.S. 384, 398 (1993) (Scalia, J., concurring).

60. *Aguillard*, 482 U.S. at 610; *Lee v. Weisman*, 505 U.S. 577, 632 (1992) (Scalia, J., dissenting); *McCreary Cty., Ky. v. Am. Civil Liberties Union of Ky*, 545 U.S. 844, 894 (2005) (Scalia, J., dissenting); *Van Orden v. Perry*, 545 U.S. 677 (2005) (Scalia, J., concurring); *Town of Greece v. Galloway*, 134 S. Ct. 1811, 1837 (2014) (Thomas, J., concurring).

   The one exception to this pattern is *Hernandez v. Commissioner of Internal Revenue*, 490 U.S. 680 (1989). There, Scalia joined O'Connor's dissent concluding that the federal government violated the clause by denying charitable deductions for "auditing" services paid by members of the Church of Scientology but allowing members of other religious groups to deduct payments for religious services. *Id.* at 713 (O'Connor, J., joined by Scalia, J., dissenting) ("In my view, the IRS has misapplied its longstanding practice of allowing charitable contributions under § 170 in a way that violates the Establishment Clause. It has unconstitutionally refused to allow payments for the religious service of auditing to be deducted as charitable contributions in the same way it has allowed fixed payments to other religions to be deducted.").

   On all of Justice Scalia's Establishment Clause votes, see Christopher Valentino, "Memorandum on Establishment Clause Votes of Justice Scalia" to Professor Richard L. Hasen dated December 5, 2016 (on file with the author).

61. Professor Massaro's comments can be found on You Tube at https://www.you tube.com/watch?v=TPanio8ybR4&feature=youtu.be&t=44m20s at around the 44-minute mark. The comments were part of a Federalist Society panel titled "How Justice Scalia's Writing Style Affected American Jurisprudence," held on November 17, 2016, during the National Lawyers Convention of 2016 in Washington, D.C. She expanded on her thoughts in a Q & A with journalist Tony Mauro. Tony Mauro, *At Federalist Society, Scholar Casts Scalia's Sharp Rhetoric in Negative Light*, Nat'l L.J., Sup. Ct. Brief, Nov. 22, 2016, http://www.national lawjournal.com/supremecourtbrief/id=1202773027992/At-Federalist-Society -Scholar-Casts-Scalias-Sharp-Rhetoric-in-Negative-Light.

62. Senior, *supra* note 2.

Chapter 6. Home of the Brave

1. Portions of this chapter draw from Richard L. Hasen, *After Scalia: The Future of United States Election Law,* America-ho (Biannual journal of Japanese American Society for Legal Studies) (2017) (in Japanese). The trailer and advertisements for *Hillary: The Movie* are posted at http://www.hillarythemovie.com/trailer.html (last visited November 25, 2016). For more on the film and its role in the campaign finance reform debate, see Richard L. Hasen, Plutocrats United ch. 4 (2016).

2. *Citizens United v. FEC,* 558 U.S. 310 (2010). For a description of the legal changes to U.S. campaign laws since *Citizens United,* see Hasen, *supra* note 1, ch. 1.

3. *Austin v. Michigan Chamber of Commerce,* 494 U.S. 652 (1990).

4. *Buckley v. Valeo,* 424 U.S. 1 (1976).

5. *Id.* at 48–49.

6. *Austin,* 494 U.S. at 660.

7. *Id.* at 679 (Scalia, J., dissenting).

8. *Id.* at 691.

9. *McConnell v. Federal Election Commission,* 540 U.S. 93 (2003).

10. *Federal Elec. Comm'n v. Wisc. Right to Life,* 551 U.S. 449 (2007) (opinion of Roberts, C.J., for the Court in part and joined by Alito, J., in part); *Id.* at 498 n.7 (Scalia, J., concurring in part and concurring in the judgment).

11. Scalia's concurrence in response to the dissent by Stevens summed up his agreement with the outcome in *Citizens United:*

> The [First] Amendment is written in terms of "speech," not speakers. Its text offers no foothold for excluding any category of speaker, from single individuals to partnerships of individuals, to unincorporated associations of individuals, to incorporated associations of individuals—and the dissent offers no evidence about the original meaning of the text to support any such exclusion. We are therefore simply left with the question whether the speech at issue in this case is "speech" covered by the First Amendment. No one says otherwise. A documentary film critical of a potential Presidential candidate is core political speech, and its nature as such does not change simply because it was funded by a corporation. Nor does the character of that funding produce any reduction whatever in the "inherent worth of the speech" and "its capacity for informing the public." Indeed, to exclude or impede corporate speech is to muzzle the principal agents of the modern free economy. We should celebrate rather than condemn the addition of this speech to the public debate.

> *Citizens United,* 558 U.S. at 393 (Scalia, J., concurring).

12. *Bluman v. F.E.C.,* 132 S. Ct. 1087 (2012). *Bluman* was a summary affirmance of the lower court—that is, a ruling without providing any reasoning for agreeing with the lower court decision. For a critique, see Hasen, *supra* note 1, ch. 4.

13. The Center for Responsive Politics tallies the 2012 spending at: http://www.open secrets.org/outsidespending/fes_summ.php?cycle=2012. The 2016 spending is summarized at: https://www.opensecrets.org/outsidespending/fes_summ.php?

cycle=2016. The list of individual donors to Super PACs in 2016 is posted at: https://www.opensecrets.org/outsidespending/summ.php?disp=D. On Adelson in 2012, see Theodoric Meyer, *How Much Did Sheldon Adelson Really Spend on Election 2012?*, ProPublica, Dec. 20, 2012, https://www.propublica.org/article/ how-much-did-sheldon-adelson-really-spend-on-campaign-2012. On Steyer in 2014, see Jason Plautz, *Tom Steyer Spent $74 Million on the Election. He Didn't Get Much to Show for It,* The Atlantic, Nov. 5, 2014, http://www.theatlantic.com/pol itics/archive/2014/11/tom-steyer-spent-74-million-on-the-election-he-didnt-get -much-to-show-for-it/452727/.

14. *McIntyre v. Ohio Elections Com'n,* 514 U.S. 334, 385 (1995) (Scalia, J., dissenting).

15. *Doe v. Reed,* 561 U.S. 186, 228 (2010) (Scalia, J., concurring in the judgment).

16. *Id.* (Thomas, J., dissenting); *Citizens United,* 558 U.S. at 480 (Thomas, J., concurring in part and dissenting in part). In *McIntyre,* Justice Scalia explained why he believed an originalist understanding of the First Amendment did not require a government to allow anonymous campaign speech:

> What we have, then, is the most difficult case for determining the meaning of the Constitution. No accepted existence of governmental restrictions of the sort at issue here demonstrates their constitutionality, but neither can their nonexistence clearly be attributed to constitutional objections. In such a case, constitutional adjudication necessarily involves not just history but judgment: judgment as to whether the government action under challenge is consonant with the concept of the protected freedom (in this case, the freedom of speech and of the press) that existed when the constitutional protection was accorded. In the present case, *absent other indication,* I would be inclined to agree with the concurrence that a society which used anonymous political debate so regularly would not regard as constitutional even moderate restrictions made to improve the election process. (I would, however, want further evidence of common practice in 1868, since I doubt that the Fourteenth Amendment time-warped the post-Civil War States back to the Revolution.)
>
> But there *is* other indication, of the most weighty sort: the widespread and longstanding traditions of our people. Principles of liberty fundamental enough to have been embodied within constitutional guarantees are not readily erased from the Nation's consciousness. A governmental practice that has become general throughout the United States, and particularly one that has the validation of long, accepted usage, bears a strong presumption of constitutionality. And that is what we have before us here.

McIntyre, 514 U.S. at 375 (Scalia, J., dissenting).

17. *See Vieth v. Jubelirer,* 541 U.S. 267, 274 (2004).

18. 2 U.S.C. § 2c (1967); *Colegrove v. Green,* 328 U.S. 549 (1946).

19. *Baker v. Carr,* 369 U.S. 186 (1962); *Reynolds v. Sims,* 377 U.S. 533 (1964); Voting Rights Act, 52 U.S.C. § 10101 et seq.; *Miller v. Johnson,* 515 U.S. 900 (1995).

20. *Davis v. Bandemer,* 478 U.S. 109 (1986).

21. *Vieth*, 541 U.S. 267 (2004).

22. *Id.* at 293 (Scalia, J., plurality opinion).

23. Gill v. Whitford, No. 16-1161, *jurisdiction postponed* Jun. 19, 2017.

24. *Ariz. Legislature v. Arizona Indep. Redistricting Comm'n*, 135 S. Ct. 2652 (2015). Article I, Section 4 of the Constitution provides in part that: "The times, places and manner of holding elections for Senators and Representatives, shall be prescribed in each state by the legislature thereof; but the Congress may at any time by law make or alter such regulations, except as to the places of choosing Senators."

25. *Rutan v. Republican Party of Ill.*, 497 U.S. 62, 93 (1990) (Scalia, J., dissenting).

26. *Thornburg v. Gingles*, 478 U.S. 30 (1986).

27. *Holder v. Hall*, 512 U.S. 874, 891 (1994) (Thomas, J., joined by Scalia, J., dissenting); *Reno v. Bossier Parish Sch. Bd.*, 528 U.S. 320 (2000); *Shaw v. Reno*, 509 U.S. 630 (1993); *Miller v. Johnson*, 515 U.S. 900 (1994); *Bartlett v. Strickland*, 556 U.S. 1, 26 (2009) (Thomas, J., joined by Scalia, J., dissenting).; *League of United Latin Am. Citizens (LULAC) v. Perry*, 548 U.S. 399, 512 (2006) (Scalia, J., concurring in part and dissenting in part).

28. *Shelby County v. Holder*, 133 S. Ct. 2612 (2013); *id.* at 2650 (Ginsburg, J., dissenting).

29. Transcript of Oral Argument at 46–47, *Shelby County v. Holder*, 133 S. Ct. 2612 (2013) (No. 12-96), 2013 WL 6908203.

30. Adam Liptak, *Sidebar: On and Off the Bench, the Eminently Quotable Justice Scalia*, N.Y. Times, May 11, 2009, http://www.nytimes.com/2009/05/12/us/12bar.html.

31. See Richard L. Hasen, *Race or Party? How Courts Should Think About Republican Efforts to Make It Harder to Vote in North Carolina and Elsewhere*, 127 Harv. L. Rev. F. 58 (2014).

32. *Crawford v. Marion County Election Board*, 553 U.S. 181 (2008); *see generally* Richard L. Hasen, The Voting Wars (2012).

33. *Crawford*, 553 U.S. at 205–6 (Scalia, J., concurring in the judgment).

34. On the effort of courts to soften the harshness of these voter identification laws, see Richard L. Hasen, *Softening Voter ID Laws Through Litigation: Is It Enough?*, 2016 Wis. L. Rev. Forward 100 (2016).

35. *Crawford*, 553 U.S. at 208.

36. *Id.* at 209 (Souter, J., dissenting); *id.* at 236 (Breyer, J., dissenting).

37. *Id.*

38. *Bush v. Gore*, 531 U.S. 98 (2000).

39. *See* Hasen, *supra* note 31, ch. 1. For a general overview, see Howard Gillman, The Votes That Counted: How the Court Decided the 2000 Presidential Election (2001).

40. *Bush*, 531 U.S. at 104–5.

41. *Id.* at 133 (Souter, J., dissenting); *id.* at 144–45 (Breyer, J., dissenting); *id.* at 123 (Stevens, J., dissenting); *id.* at 135 (Ginsburg, J., dissenting).

42. Lesley Stahl, *Justice Scalia on the Record*, CBS News, 60 Minutes, Apr. 24, 2008,

http://www.cbsnews.com/news/justice-scalia-on-the-record/; *Arizona v. Inter-Tribal Council of Arizona*, 133 S. Ct. 2247, 2268 n.2 (2013) (Thomas, J., dissenting) ("This Court has recognized, however, that 'the state legislature's power to select the manner for appointing [presidential] electors is plenary; it may, if it chooses, select the electors itself.' *Bush v. Gore*, 531 U.S. 98, 104 (2000) (*per curiam*)"); *Ariz. Legislature v. Arizona Indep. Redistricting Comm'n*, 135 S. Ct. 2652 (2015). Article II of the Constitution provides in part that "Each state shall appoint, in such manner as the Legislature thereof may direct, a number of electors, equal to the whole number of Senators and Representatives to which the State may be entitled in the Congress."

43. *City of Boerne v. Flores*, 521 U.S. 507 (1997); *Printz v. United States*, 521 U.S. 898, 905, 935 (1997).

44. *Comptroller of Treasury of Maryland v. Wynne*, 135 S. Ct. 1787, 1807 (2015) (Scalia, J., dissenting); *id.* at 1811 (Thomas, J., dissenting).

45. *Arizona v. U.S.*, 132 S. Ct. 2492, 2521–22 (2012) (Scalia, J., dissenting).

46. Eric J. Segall, *The Constitution According to Justices Scalia and Thomas: Alive and Kickin'*, 91 Wash U. L. Rev. 1663, 1670 (2014); *Hans v. Louisiana*, 134 U.S. 1 (1890); *Alden v. Maine*, 527 U.S. 706 (1999).

47. *Gonzales v. Raich*, 545 U.S. 1 (2005); Bruce Allen Murphy, Scalia: A Court of One 323 (2015); Joan Biskupic, American Original: The Life and Constitution of Supreme Court Justice Antonin Scalia 9 (2009).

48. *Printz*, 521 U.S. at 922. On the significance of this paragraph, see Jay S. Bybee, Printz, *the Unitary Executive, and the Fire in the Trash Can: Has Justice Scalia Picked the Court's Pocket?*, 77 Notre Dame L. Rev. 269 (2001).

49. *Morrison v. Olson*, 487 U.S. 654 (1988).

50. *Id.* at 699 (Scalia, J., dissenting).

51. The text of the 1998 Starr report is posted at the *Washington Post* website at: http://www.washingtonpost.com/wp-srv/politics/special/clinton/icreport/icreport.htm.

52. *Morrison*, 487 U.S. at 710–13.

53. Jennifer Senior, *In Conversation: Antonin Scalia*, New York, Oct. 6, 2013, http://nymag.com/news/features/antonin-scalia-2013-10/.

54. *N.L.R.B. v. Noel Canning*, 134 S. Ct. 2550, 2592 (2014) (Scalia, J., concurring in the judgment).

55. Robin Bravender, *Scalia and* Chevron: *It's Complicated,* Greenwire, Feb. 19, 2016, http://www.eenews.net/stories/1060032640. For one of Justice Scalia's last important separation of powers decisions, see his dissent in *Zivotofsky v. Kerry,* 135 S. Ct. 2076, 2116 (2015) (Scalia, J., dissenting). In *Zivotofsky,* Justice Scalia dissented from a decision rejecting a congressional directive requiring the State Department to issue passports recognizing Jerusalem as the capital of Israel.

56. *Chevron U.S.A., Inc. v. Natural Resources Defense Council*, 467 U.S. 837 (1984).

57. *MCI Comm. Corp. v. AT&T Inc.*, 512 U.S. 218, 228 (1994); *id.* at 245 (Stevens, J., dissenting).

58. *City of Arlington v. FCC*, 133 S. Ct. 1863 (2013).

59. *Id.* at 1877–78 (Roberts, C.J., dissenting).
60. *Decker v. Northwest Environment Law Ctr.*, 133 S. Ct. 1326, 1339 (2013) (Scalia, J., concurring in part and dissenting in part) ("I join Parts I and II of the Court's opinion; I agree that these cases are not moot and that the District Court had jurisdiction. I do not join Part III. The Court there gives effect to a reading of EPA's regulations that is not the most natural one, simply because EPA says that it believes the unnatural reading is right. It does this, moreover, even though the agency has vividly illustrated that it can write a rule saying precisely what it means—by doing *just that* while these cases were being briefed. Enough is enough."); Robin Bravender, Alito snubs *Chevron*, Obama EPA's 'eraser,' Greenwire, Nov. 17, 2016, http://www.eenews.net/stories/1060045952/ (quoting Justice Alito).
61. *Gutierrez-Brizuela v. Lynch*, 834 F. 3d 1142, 1152 (10th Cir. 2016) (Gorsuch, J., concurring).
62. Antonin Scalia, *The Doctrine of Standing as an Essential Element of the Separation of Powers*, 17 Suffolk U. L. Rev. 881 (1983); *Lujan v. Defenders of Wildlife*, 504 U.S. 555 (1992); *' Ariz. Legislature v. Arizona Indep. Redistricting Comm'n*, 135 S. Ct. 2652, 2695 (Scalia, J., dissenting) (2015); Richard Re, *Standing's Lujan-ification*, Prawfs-Blawg, Jan. 31, 2015, http://prawfsblawg.blogs.com/prawfsblawg/2015/01/standings-lujan-ification.html. On Scalia's narrow approach to standing generally, see Erwin Chemerinsky, Closing the Court-House Door: How Your Constitutional Rights Became Unenforceable 17–18 (2016).
63. *Wal-Mart Stores, Inc. v. Dukes*, 564 U.S. 338 (2011).
64. *AT&T Mobility, LLC. v. Concepcion*, 563 U.S. 333 (2011).
65. The union case in which the Court divided 4–4 was *Friedrichs v. Calif. Teachers Ass'n*, 136 S. Ct. 1083 (2016) (judgment affirmed by vote of equally divided Court). On the hope that Justice Scalia would have sided against the unions based on remarks he made at the *Friedrichs* oral argument, see Charlotte Garden, *What Will Become of Public-Sector Unions Now?*, The Atlantic, Feb. 16, 2016, http://www.theatlantic.com/business/archive/2016/02/scalia-friedrichs/462936/ ("On the day *Friedrichs* was argued, those hoping for signs of a union-friendly Scalia left the Court severely disappointed. With his trademark gusto, Scalia tore into core arguments made by the union and government attorneys."). The new case raising this issue is *Janus v. AFSCME Council 31*, No. 16-1466 (cert. granted Sept. 28, 2017). On the Dow settlement, see Brian Cyran, *Justice Scalia's Death Prompts Dow Chemical to Settle Lawsuit*, Dealbook, Breaking Views, N.Y. Times, Feb. 26, 2016, http://www.nytimes.com/2016/02/27/business/dealbook/justice-scalias-death-prompts-dow-chemical-to-settle-lawsuit.html.

Chapter 7. Rescued from the Grave

1. *Kansas v. Carr*, 136 S. Ct. 633 (2016). Justice Scalia cited two facts not included in the briefs filed by the parties or the Kansas Supreme Court opinion. One is that

the only surviving victim, Holly, urinated in the closet out of fear. The other is that Holly performed oral sex on another victim, out of fear for his life, because the two defendants stated that they would shoot the male victims if they could not have sex with the female victims. The footnote which begins the reciting of these facts reads: "The facts for this portion of the opinion come from the Kansas Supreme Court, 300 Kan. 1, 18–38, 331 P.3d 544, 575–586 (2014), and witness testimony. See 21–A Tr. 59–75 (Oct. 7, 2002), 22–B Tr. 39–124 (Oct. 8, 2002), 23–A Tr. 4–118 (Oct. 9, 2002), 23–B Tr. 5–133 (Oct. 9, 2002), and 24–A Tr. 4–93 (Oct. 10, 2002)." *Carr*, 136 S. Ct. at 638 n.2.

    Carr was consolidated with another case involving a different set of facts but the same legal issues. Justice Scalia's opinion for the Court recited those facts more succinctly. *Id.* at 637–38 ("Less than one month after Sidney Gleason was paroled from his sentence for attempted voluntary manslaughter, he joined a conspiracy to rob an elderly man at knifepoint. Gleason and a companion 'cut up' the elderly man to get $10 to $35 and a box of cigarettes. Fearing that their female co-conspirators would snitch, Gleason and his cousin, Damien Thompson, set out to kill co-conspirator Mikiala Martinez. Gleason shot and killed Martinez's boyfriend, and then Gleason and Thompson drove Martinez to a rural location, where Thompson strangled her for five minutes and then shot her in the chest, Gleason standing by and providing the gun for the final shot.").

2. *Id.* "For the Birchwood murders, the jury convicted each brother of 4 counts of capital murder, 1 count of attempted first-degree murder, 5 counts of aggravated kidnaping, 9 counts of aggravated robbery, 20 counts of rape or attempted rape, 3 counts of aggravated criminal sodomy, 1 count each of aggravated burglary and burglary, 1 count of theft, and 1 count of cruelty to animals. The jury also convicted Reginald of three counts of unlawful possession of a firearm."

3. *Id.* at 642, 646.

4. *Id.* at 646, 648, 651 (Sotomayor, J., dissenting). Here is Scalia's full response to Sotomayor's argument that the Court should have not reviewed the case, allowing the Kansas Supreme Court to "overprotect" criminal defendants:

The Kansas Supreme Court's opinion leaves no room for doubt that it was relying on the Federal Constitution. . . . For this reason, the criticism leveled by the dissent is misdirected. It generally would have been "none of our business" had the Kansas Supreme Court vacated Gleason's and the Carrs' death sentences on state-law grounds. But it decidedly did not. And when the Kansas Supreme Court time and again invalidates death sentences because it says the Federal Constitution *requires* it, "review by this Court, far from *undermining* state autonomy, is the only possible way to *vindicate* it." "When we correct a state court's federal errors, *we return power to the State, and to its people.*" The state courts may experiment all they want with their own constitutions, and often do in the wake of this Court's decisions. But what a state court cannot do is experiment with our Federal Constitution and expect to elude this Court's review so long as victory goes to the criminal defendant. "Turning a blind eye" in such cases "would change the uniform 'law of the land' into a crazy quilt." And it would enable state courts to blame the unpopular death-sentence reprieve of the most horrible criminals upon the Federal Constitution when it is in fact their own doing.

Id. at 641–42.

5. Michelle Malkin, *Winona and the Wichita Massacre,* Town Hall, Nov. 8, 2002, http://townhall.com/columnists/michellemalkin/2002/11/08/winona_and _the_wichita_massacre.

6. David Horowitz, *Black Racism: The Hate Crime That Dare Not Speak Its Name,* FrontPageMag.Com, July 16, 2002, http://www.freerepublic.com/focus/f-news /716979/posts.

7. Amy Renee Leiker, *What Courts Did in the Carr Brothers Case; What's Next,* Wichita Eagle, Oct. 29, 2016, http://www.kansas.com/news/local/crime/article 111386262.html; Amy Renee Leiker, *Ouster Group Disappointed 'Voters Left Bad Justices in Place,'* Wichita Eagle, Nov. 8, 2016, http://www.kansas.com/news/pol itics-government/election/article113467483.html ("The group wanted four of the five justices seeking retention unseated for vacating death sentences given to five men, including Jonathan and Reginald Carr. The brothers committed a string of crimes over a nine-day period in 2000.").

8. *Crawford v. Washington,* 541 U.S. 36 (2004).

9. *Ohio v. Roberts,* 448 U.S. 56, 66 (1980). In particular, a defendant's right to confrontation was satisfied when the court determined that out-of-court material either (1) fit within pre-established hearsay exceptions or (2) was particularly trustworthy.

10. *Davis v. Washington,* 547 U.S. 813 (2006); *Hammon v. Indiana,* 546 U.S. 1213 (2006); Joan Biskupic, *Scalia Replacement Could Move Court Rightward on Criminal Justice,* CNN, Dec. 7, 2016, http://www.cnn.com/2016/12/07/politics/scalia -criminal-justice-trump/index.html.

11. *Michigan v. Bryant,* 562 U.S. 344 (2011); *Ohio v. Clark,* 135 S. Ct. 2173 (2015).

12. *Id.* at 2184 (Scalia, J., concurring in the judgment).

13. *Apprendi v. New Jersey,* 530 U.S. 466 (2000); *Blakely v. Washington,* 542 U.S. 296 (2004); *United States v. Booker,* 543 U.S. 220 (2005); *Oregon v. Ice,* 555 U.S. 160, 178 (2009) (Scalia, J., dissenting) ("The Court's reliance upon a distinction without a difference, and its repeated exhumation of arguments dead and buried by prior cases, seems to me the epitome of the opposite. Today's opinion muddies the waters, and gives cause to doubt whether the Court is willing to stand by *Apprendi*'s interpretation of the Sixth Amendment's jury-trial guarantee.").

14. *Johnson v. U.S.,* 135 S. Ct. 2551, 2557 (2015).

15. *U.S. v. Jones,* 132 S. Ct. 945 (2012); *id.* at 958 n.3 (Alito, J., concurring in the judgment) ("The Court suggests that something like this might have occurred in 1791, but this would have required either a gigantic coach, a very tiny constable, or both—not to mention a constable with incredible fortitude and patience.").

16. *Kyllo v. United States,* 533 U.S. 27 (2001); *Maryland v. King,* 133 S. Ct. 1958, 1980 (2013) (Scalia, J., dissenting):

The Fourth Amendment forbids searching a person for evidence of a crime when there is no basis for believing the person is guilty of the crime or is in possession of incriminating evidence. That prohibition is categorical and without exception; it lies at the very heart of the Fourth Amendment. Whenever this Court has allowed a suspicionless search, it has insisted upon a justifying motive apart from the investigation of crime.

It is obvious that no such noninvestigative motive exists in this case. The Court's assertion that DNA is being taken, not to solve crimes, but to *identify* those in the State's custody, taxes the credulity of the credulous. And the Court's comparison of Maryland's DNA searches to other techniques, such as fingerprinting, can seem apt only to those who know no more than today's opinion has chosen to tell them about how those DNA searches actually work.

17. *Glossip v. Gross*, 135 S. Ct. 2726, 2747 (2016) (Scalia, J., concurring). On the unusual oral concurrence, see Chapter 4, note 40 above.

18. *McCleskey v. Kemp*, 481 U.S. 279, 286 (1987).

19. Justice Scalia's memorandum may be found in the *McCleskey v. Kemp* case file (http://law2.wlu.edu/powellarchives/page.asp?pageid=1350) in the papers of Justice Lewis Powell housed at the Washington and Lee Law Library. The document appears at page 147 in the subfile named "McCleskey v. Kemp—basic file" posted at http://law2.wlu.edu/deptimages/powell%20archives/McCleskeyKempBasic.pdf (last visited Dec. 12, 2016). Years later, Scalia could not recall why he did not write a separate opinion expressing these views. Joan Biskupic, American Original: The Life and Constitution of Supreme Court Justice Antonin Scalia 153 (2009).

20. *Walton v. Arizona*, 497 U.S. 639, 671–72 (Scalia, J., concurring in part and concurring in the judgment), *rev'd on other grounds, Ring v. Arizona*, 536 U.S. 584 (2002).

21. *Stanford v. Kentucky*, 492 U.S. 361 (1989), *rev'd, Roper v. Simmons*, 543 U.S. 551 (2005).

22. *Id.* at 610–11, 622, 627 (Scalia, J., dissenting).

23. *Miller v. Alabama*, 132 S. Ct. 2455 (2012); *Montgomery v. Louisiana*, 136 S. Ct. 718, 744 (2016) (Scalia, J., dissenting). The Court issued *Montgomery* on January 25, 2016, the last date the Court issued opinions before Justice Scalia's death. On the same date, Scalia also wrote a dissent in *F.E.R.C. v. Electric Power Supply Association*, 136 S. Ct. 760 (2016) (Scalia, J., dissenting).

24. *Penry v. Lynaugh*, 492 U.S. 302, 352 (1989) (Scalia, J., concurring in part and dissenting in part).

25. *Adkins v. Virginia*, 536 U.S. 304 (2002).

26. *Id.* at 349 (Scalia, J., dissenting). On the argument that excessive punishment did not violate the Eighth Amendment, see his partial plurality opinion in *Harmelin v. Michigan*, 501 U.S. 957 (1993) and his concurrence in *Ewing v. California*, 538 U.S. 11, 31 (2003) (Scalia, J., concurring in the judgment).

27. *Id.* at 349–52 (Scalia, J., dissenting).

28. *Herrera v. Collins*, 506 U.S. 390, 427–28 (Scalia, J., concurring); *Schlup v. Delo*, 513 U.S. 298, 342 (1995) (Scalia, J., dissenting); *In re Davis*, 557 U.S. 952 (2009)

(Scalia, J., dissenting); *McQuiggin v. Perkins,* 133 S. Ct. 1924, 1937 (2013) (Scalia, J., dissenting).

29. Barry Friedman, *How Did Justice Scalia Shape American Policing?,* The Atlantic, Aug. 20, 2016, http://www.theatlantic.com/politics/archive/2016/08/scalia-and-american-policing/496604. The cases Professor Friedman linked to in the excerpted passage are: *Missouri v. Siebert,* 542 U.S. 600 (2004); *U.S. v. Patane,* 542 U.S. 630 (2004); *Berghuis v. Thompkins,* 560 U.S. 370 (2010); and *Salinas v. Texas,* 133 S. Ct. 2174 (2013).

30. *Hudson v. Michigan,* 546 U.S. 586, 591 (2006); *id.* at 605 (Breyer, J., dissenting); see also *Murray v. U.S.,* 487 U.S. 533, 541 (1988) (Scalia, J.) ("Invoking the exclusionary rule would put the police (and society) not in the *same* position they would have occupied if no violation occurred, but in a *worse* one.").

31. *Hamdi v. Rumsfeld,* 542 U.S. 507, 509 (2004) (O'Connor, J., plurality opinion).

32. *Id.* at 577–78 (Scalia, J., dissenting). Justice Scalia also dissented that day in *Rasul v. Bush,* 542 U.S. 466 (2004), holding that aliens at Guantánamo could bring claims for habeas corpus in federal court.

33. Michael Isikoff, *Supreme Court: Detainees' Rights—Scalia Speaks His Mind,* Newsweek, Apr. 2, 2006, http://www.newsweek.com/supreme-court-detainees-rights-scalia-speaks-his-mind-107921; *see also* Biskupic, *supra* note 19, at 321–23; *Hamdan v. Rumsfeld,* 548 U.S. 557, 655 (2006) (Scalia, J., dissenting).

34. *Id.* at 666–68.

35. *Boumediene v. Bush,* 553 U.S. 723, 798 (2008).

36. *Id.* at 828–29 (Scalia, J., dissenting).

37. *Id.* at 826, 849.

38. Eric Lichtblau, *U.S., Bowing to Court, to Free 'Enemy Combatant,'* N.Y. Times, Sept. 23, 2004, http://www.nytimes.com/2004/09/23/politics/us-bowing-to-court-to-free-enemy-combatant.html.

39. John H. Cushman, Jr., *Appeals Court Overturns Terrorism Conviction of Bin Laden's Driver,* N.Y. Times, Oct. 16, 2012, http://www.nytimes.com/2012/10/17/us/politics/appeals-court-overturns-terrorism-conviction-of-salim-ahmed-hamdan-bin-ladens-driver.html; *Hamdan v. U.S.,* 696 F. 3d 1238 (D.C. Cir. 2012), *overruled on other grounds, Al Bahlul v. U.S.,* 767 F. 3d 1 (D.C. Cir. 2014) (en banc); Andrea J. Prasow, *The Yemenis at Guantanamo,* Slate, Mar. 13, 2014, http://www.slate.com/articles/news_and_politics/jurisprudence/2014/03/salim_hamdan_and_the_yemeni_prisoners_who_can_t_leave_the_prison_at_guant.html.

40. Scott Sayare, *After Guantanamo, Starting Anew, in Quiet Anger,* N.Y. Times, May 25, 2012, http://www.nytimes.com/2012/05/26/world/europe/lakhdar-boumediene-starts-anew-in-france-after-years-at-guantanamo.html.

Chapter 8. The Justice of Contradictions

1. Matt Pearce, *Scalia's Death and Lack of Autopsy Brings Out the Conspiracy Theories,* L.A. Times, Feb. 17, 2016, http://www.latimes.com/nation/la-na-scalia-conspiracy-20160217-story.html.

2. Debra Cassens Weiss, *Scalia Was at Texas Ranch with Member of Exclusive Hunting Society and Former GOP Lawyer,* ABA J., Feb. 25, 2016, http://www.abajournal.com/news/article/scalia_was_at_texas_ranch_with_members_of_secretive_hunting_society_and_a_g; Mark Berman & Jerry Markon, *Why Justice Scalia Was Staying for Free at a Texas Resort,* Wash. Post, Feb. 17, 2016, https://www.washingtonpost.com/news/post-nation/wp/2016/02/17/justice-scalias-death-and-questions-about-who-pays-for-supreme-court-justices-to-visit-remote-resorts/?utm_term=.c641db7c6cf6; Eva Ruth Moravec, Sari Horwitz, & Jerry Markon, *The Death of Antonin Scalia: Chaos, Confusion and Conflicting Reports,* Wash. Post, Feb. 14, 2016, https://www.washingtonpost.com/politics/texas-tv-station-scalia-died-of-a-heart-attack/2016/02/14/938e2170-d332-11e5-9823-02b905009f99_story.html?utm_term=.6304a4f71d48.

3. Amy Brittain and Sari Horwitz, *Justice Scalia Spent His Last Hours with Members of This Secretive Society of Elite Hunters,* Wash. Post, Feb. 24, 2016, https://www.washingtonpost.com/world/national-security/justice-scalia-spent-his-last-hours-with-members-of-this-secretive-society-of-elite-hunters/2016/02/24/1d77af38-db20-11e5-891a-4ed04f4213e8_story.html.

4. Danny Dominguez, Presidio County Sheriff's Office Offense Report 16-066, Feb. 13, 2016, https://www.washingtonpost.com/apps/g/page/politics/presidio-county-sheriffs-office-report-on-justice-antonin-scalias-death/1968/?tid=a_inl; Pearce, *supra* note 1.

5. *Id.*; Texas Code of Criminal Procedure Article 49.08 (West 2016) (permitting a justice of the peace or county judge to conduct an inquest based on information the justice receives from any credible person).

6. Dominguez, *supra* note 4.

7. Adam Liptak, *Antonin Scalia, Justice on the Supreme Court, dies at 79,* N.Y. Times, Feb. 13, 2016, http://www.nytimes.com/2016/02/14/us/antonin-scalia-death.html.

8. David Warren, *A Letter from the Supreme Court's Doctor Says Antonin Scalia Suffered from Coronary Artery Disease, Obesity and Diabetes, Among Other Ailments that Probably Contributed to the Justice's Sudden Death,* Associated Press, Feb. 23, 2016, AP Online, http://www.usnews.com/news/us/articles/2016-02-23/ap-newsbreak-scalia-suffered-from-many-health-problems; Lawrence K. Altman, *Scalia Autopsy Decision Divides Pathologists,* N.Y. Times, Feb. 20, 2016, http://www.nytimes.com/2016/02/21/health/antonin-scalia-autopsy.html.

9. Lindsey Bever, *Scalia's Son: Conspiracy Theories About Father's Death Are a 'Hurtful Distraction,'* Wash. Post, Feb. 18, 2016, https://www.washingtonpost.com/news/post-nation/wp/2016/02/18/scalias-son-conspiracy-theories-about-fathers-death-are-a-hurtful-distraction/?tid=a_inl.

10. Warren, *supra* note 8.

11. *Id.*; Adam Liptak, *Justices Disclose Privately Paid Trips and Gifts,* N.Y. Times, Jun. 22, 2016, http://www.nytimes.com/2016/06/23/us/politics/justices-disclose-privately-paid-trips-and-gifts.html.

12. Jordyn Phelps, *Antonin Scalia's Supreme Court Bench and Chair Draped in Black,* ABC

News, Feb. 16, 2016, http://abcnews.go.com/Politics/antonin-scalia-supreme-court-chair-bench-draped-black/story?id=36969588.

13. *Video and Text: President Obama's Statement on Justice Scalia's Death, The Death of Justice Scalia: Reactions and Analysis*, N.Y. Times, Feb. 13, 2016, http://www.nytimes.com/live/supreme-court-justice-antonin-scalia-dies-at-79/video-president-obamas-statement-on-scalias-death/.

14. *Id.*

15. Burgess Everett & Glenn Thrush, *McConnell Throws Down the Gauntlet: No Scalia Replacement Under Obama*, Politico, Feb. 13, 2016, http://www.politico.com/story/2016/02/mitch-mcconnell-antonin-scalia-supreme-court-nomination-219248; Jonathan Martin, *Republican Candidates Unite Against Obama on Replacing Scalia*, N.Y. Times, Feb. 13, 2016, https://www.nytimes.com/2016/02/14/us/politics/republicans-unite-against-president-obama.html. Senator Grassley initially did not rule out hearings for an Obama nominee, but said he preferred Obama's replacement to name the justice. Mark Landler & Jennifer Steinhauer, *President Raises Stakes in Supreme Court Nominee Battle*, N.Y. Times, Feb. 16, 2016, http://www.nytimes.com/2016/02/17/us/politics/senator-charles-grassley-hearings-supreme-court-nominee.html. But Grassley never scheduled any hearings for President Obama's nominee, Judge Merrick Garland.

16. Michael D. Shear, Julie Hirschfeld, & Gardiner Harris, *Obama Chooses Merrick Garland for Supreme Court*, N.Y. Times, Mar. 16, 2016, http://www.nytimes.com/2016/03/17/us/politics/obama-supreme-court-nominee.html. Indeed, "In 2010, when Garland was under consideration for the Supreme Court vacancy that went to Justice Sonia Sotomayor, Sen. Orrin G. Hatch (R-Utah) told Reuters that he had known Garland for years and that he would be 'a consensus nominee.'" Jerry Markon, *Merrick Garland Has Been Considered for the Supreme Court Before. Is This His Year?*, Wash. Post, Mar. 10, 2016, https://www.washingtonpost.com/world/national-security/merrick-garlands-been-considered-for-the-supreme-court-before-is-this-his-year/2016/03/10/0b141bcc-e6d5-11e5-a6f3-21ccdbc5f74e_story.html.

17. Tony Leys, *Grassley Cruises to Seventh U.S. Senate Term*, Des Moines Register, Nov. 8, 2016, http://www.desmoinesregister.com/story/news/politics/2016/11/08/grassley-cruises-seventh-us-senate-term/93087588/; CNN, Exit Polls, Election 2016, Nov. 23, 2016, http://www.cnn.com/election/results/exit-polls.

18. Donald Scarinci, *Could Hillary Clinton Really Overturn Citizens United?*, Observer, Oct. 6, 2016, http://observer.com/2016/10/could-hillary-clinton-really-overturn-citizens-united/ (quoting Clinton's July 18, 2016, speech stating "Today I'm announcing that in my first 30 days as president I will propose a Constitutional Amendment to overturn Citizens United and give the American people, all of us, the chance to reclaim our democracy. I will also appoint Supreme Court justices who understand that this decision was a disaster for our democracy."); Release, Donald J. Trump Finalizes List of Potential Supreme Court Justice Picks, Sept. 23, 2016, https://www.donaldjtrump.com/press-releases/donald-j.-trump-adds

-to-list-of-potential-supreme-court-justice-picks ("Mr. Trump stated, 'We have a very clear choice in this election. The freedoms we cherish and the constitutional values and principles our country was founded on are in jeopardy. The responsibility is greater than ever to protect and uphold these freedoms and I will appoint justices, who like Justice Scalia, will protect our liberty with the highest regard for the Constitution. This list is definitive and I will choose only from it in picking future Justices of the United States Supreme Court. I would like to thank the Federalist Society, The Heritage Foundation and the many other individuals who helped in composing this list of twenty-one highly respected people who are the kind of scholars that we need to preserve the very core of our country, and make it greater than ever before.'"); Jeremy Kidd, Riddhi Sohan Dasgupta, Ryan Walters & James Phillips, *Searching for Justice Scalia: Measuring the 'Scalia-ness' of the Next Potential Member of the U.S. Supreme Court* (unpublished draft dated Nov. 28, 2016), *draft available at:* https://papers.ssrn.com/sol3/papers.cfm?abstract_id=2874794.

19. Donald J. Trump (@realdonaldtrump), twitter (Nov. 29, 2016 0:55 AM), https://twitter.com/realDonaldTrump/status/803567993036754944; Alex Griswold, Fox & Friends *Did Segment on Flag-Burning Just Before Donald Trump Tweet*, Mediaite, Nov. 29, 2016, http://www.mediaite.com/online/fox-friends-did-segment-on-flag-burning-just-before-donald-trump-tweet/.

20. *Texas v. Johnson*, 491 U.S. 397 (2001); David M. Jackson, *Trump Denounces Flag Burning, Twitter Points Out It Is Constitutional*, USA Today, Nov. 29, 2016, http://www.usatoday.com/story/news/politics/onpolitics/2016/11/29/donald-trump-flag-burning-supreme-court/94593636/. Video of this portion of the CNN interview is posted at: https://www.youtube.com/watch?v=oDF321wWUms&feature=youtu.be.

21. *BMW v. Gore*, 517 U.S. 559, 598–99 (1996) (Scalia, J., dissenting).

22. *U.S. v. Windsor*, 133 S. Ct. 2675, 2698 (2013) (Scalia, J., dissenting); *Shelby County v. Holder*, 133 S. Ct. 2612 (2013).

23. Honorable Neil M. Gorsuch, *Of Lions and Bears, Judges and Legislators, and the Legacy of Justice Scalia*, 66 Case Western Res. L. Rev. 905, 906 (2016); Richard L. Hasen, *Gorsuch Is the New Scalia, Just as Trump Promised*, L.A. Times, Jun. 27, 2017, http://www.latimes.com/opinion/op-ed/la-oe-hasen-gorsuch-scalia-20170627-story.html; Adam Liptak, *Sidebar: Confident and Assertive, Gorsuch Hurries to Make His Mark*, N.Y. Times, Jul. 3, 2017, https://www.nytimes.com/2017/07/03/us/politics/neil-gorsuch-supreme-court.html; *Perry v. Merit Systems Protection Bd.*, 137 S. Ct. 1975, 1990 (Gorsuch, J., dissenting); *Gil v. Whitford*, No. 16-1161, Tr. Oral Arg., at 60 (Oct. 3, 2017).

24. Bill Mears, *'Get Over It': Justice Scalia's Most Memorable Quotes*, FoxNews.Com, Feb. 15, 2016, http://www.foxnews.com/politics/2016/02/15/get-over-it-justice-scalias-most-memorable-quotes.html (quoting 2004 Justice Scalia speech to Philadelphia Bar Association).

INDEX